Feminist Economics and the World Bank

The past decade has witnessed a paradigm shift at the World Bank from a focus on structural adjustment to a focus on poverty reduction. As evidenced by the Bank's 2001 report, *Engendering Development: Through Gender Equality in Rights, Resources, and Voice*, an increased attention to gender issues has been an important part of this process. The premise of the report is that economic growth and development cannot be effectively addressed when gender inequality is not taken into account, because poverty increases gender inequalities and gender inequalities hinder economic development.

This book brings together a range of responses from feminist economists and other social researchers on the issues raised in this report. With contributions from highly esteemed scholars such as Violet Eudine Barriteau, Diane Elson, Gale Summerfield, and Zafiris Tzannatos, this anthology critically examines the relationships between gender, growth, development, and the World Bank. It develops a history of the World Bank's perspectives on gender, empirically evaluates the impacts of the Bank's policies on three different regions of the world, explores the ideological and methodological commitments of the report from a variety of feminist and interdisciplinary social science perspectives, and inquires into future directions for feminist economic research.

The book shows the importance and challenge of taking gender into account in development theory and policy. Its complex and nuanced analyses of the social relations of gender in a global context will be an important resource for policymakers, activists, and scholars.

Edith Kuiper is Researcher at the Department of Economics and Econometrics at the Universiteit van Amsterdam, The Netherlands.

Drucilla K. Barker is Professor of Economics and Women's Studies at Hollins University, Virginia, USA.

Routledge IAFFE Advances in Feminist Economics

IAFFE aims to increase the visibility and range of economic research on gender; facilitate communication among scholars, policy-makers, and activists concerned with women's well-being and empowerment; promote discussions among policy-makers about interventions which serve women's needs; educate economists, policy-makers, and the general public about feminist perspectives on economic issues; foster feminist evaluations of economics as a discipline; expose the gender blindness characteristic of much social science and the ways in which this impoverishes all research, even research that does not explicitly concern women's issues; help expand opportunities for women, especially women from underrepresented groups, within economics; and encourage the inclusion of feminist perspectives in the teaching of economics. The IAFFE book series pursues the aims of the organization by providing a forum in which scholars have space to develop their ideas at length and in detail. The series exemplifies the value of feminist research and the high standard of IAFFE sponsored scholarship.

Feminist Economics and the World Bank

History, theory and policy

Edited by
Edith Kuiper and Drucilla K. Barker

LONDON AND NEW YORK

First published 2006
by Routledge
2 Park Square, Milton Park, Abingdon, Oxon, OX14 4RN

Simultaneously published in the USA and Canada
by Routledge
270 Madison Ave, New York, NY 10016

Routledge is an imprint of the Taylor & Francis Group

© 2006 Selection and editorial matter, Edith Kuiper and Drucilla K. Barker;
individual chapters, the contributors

Typeset in Bembo by
Keystroke, Jacaranda Lodge, Wolverhampton
Printed and bound in Great Britain by
MPG Books Ltd, Bodmin

British Library Cataloguing in Publication Data
A catalogue record for this book is available from the British Library

Library of Congress Cataloging in Publication Data
A catalog record for this book has been requested

ISBN10: 0–415–70064–7   ISBN13: 9–78–0–415–70064–1 (hbk)
ISBN10: 0–415–76381–9   ISBN13: 9–78–0–415–76381–3 (pbk)

Contents

Figures and tables

Figures

Tables

Contributors

Rose-Marie Avin is Professor of Economics at the University of Wisconsin-Eau Claire. She received her Ph.D. in Economics from the University of Maryland-College Park, USA. She teaches courses on the economic development of the Third World and of Latin America, and on women and economic development. Her research interests focus on women in the Third World, especially in Nicaragua. She has written articles on gender issues in Latin America, more specifically on economic restructuring, the empowerment of Nicaraguan women, free-trade zones, the changing economic role of women in Brazil, and the role of international organizations in economic development.

Drucilla K. Barker is Professor of Economics and Women's Studies at Hollins University, Virginia, USA. She received her Ph.D. in Economics from the University of Illinois at Champaign-Urbana and her B.A. in Philosophy from Sonoma State University. A founding member of the International Association for Feminist Economics (IAFFE), she is the co-author (with Susan Feiner) of *Liberating Economics: Feminist Perspectives on the Families, Work and Globalization*, and the co-editor (with Edith Kuiper) of *Toward a Feminist Philosophy of Economics* (also published by Routledge).

Violet Eudine Barriteau is Senior Lecturer and Head of the Centre for Gender and Development Studies, University of the West Indies, Cave Hill, Barbados. She is the author of *The Political Economy of Gender in the Twentieth-Century Caribbean*. Her most recent publications include *Confronting Power Theorizing Gender: Interdisciplinary Perspectives in the Caribbean*, and "Women Entrepreneurs and Economic Marginality: Rethinking Caribbean Women's Economic Relations" in *Gendered Realities: Essays in Caribbean Feminist Thought*. She is the inaugural Dame Nita Barrow Women in Development Fellow, Ontario Institute for Studies in Education, University of Toronto.

Suzanne Bergeron holds a joint appointment in Women's Studies and Social Sciences at the University of Michigan Dearborn, USA, where she is also the director of the Women in Learning and Leadership program. She is the author of *Fragments of Development: Nation, Gender, and the Space of Modernity*, as well as numerous articles on gender, development and the World Bank.

Cheryl Doss is the Director of Graduate Studies for the M.A. Program in International Relations and a Lecturer in Economics at Yale University, USA. She has a Ph.D. in Applied Economics from the University of Minnesota. Her research focuses on gender and intrahousehold issues related to rural households in Africa, especially those in Ghana, Kenya and Ethiopia. In particular, she is interested in the gender implications of technology for agricultural households. Currently, she is working to understand risk management strategies among pastoralist households in East Africa, with a focus on the implications for women, and she is involved with a project looking at women and the distribution of wealth.

Diane Elson teaches courses on gender, development and human rights in the Department of Sociology and Human Rights Centre at the University of Essex. She has previously held posts in the universities of Manchester, Sussex, York and Oxford. In 1998–2000, she served as Special Advisor to the United Nations Development Fund for Women (UNIFEM); and in 2004 she was the vice-president of the International Association for Feminist Economics. She is a member of the UN Taskforce on the Millennium Development Goals. Her recent publications include *Progress of the World's Women 2002*; "International Financial Architecture: A View from the Kitchen", *Femina Politica*, 11(1) 2002; and "Human Rights and Corporate Profits: the UN Global Compact-Part of the Solution of Part of the Problem?" in *Global Tensions*, also published by Routledge.

Edith Kuiper is Researcher at the Department of Economics and Econometrics at the Universiteit van Amsterdam. Her research interests are in the history and philosophy of economics. She is co-editor of *Out of the Margin: Feminist Perspectives on Economics* (Routledge, 1995), author of *The Most Valuable of All Capital: A Gender Reading of Economic Texts* (2001) and she co-edited (with Drucilla K. Barker) *Towards a Feminist Philosophy of Economics* (Routledge, 2003). She is a founder and former President of the Dutch Network of Feminist Economics (FENN) and coordinator of the European Chapter of the International Association for Feminist Economics (IAFFE-Europe).

Carolyn M. Long, now an independent consultant, was previously Vice-President of InterAction, the US coalition of NGOs, where she oversaw the organization's initiatives to strengthen the development operations of US NGOs and to promote appropriate policies and programs for sustainable human development at the World Bank and other public donor agencies. She is the author of *Participation of the Poor in Development Initiatives: Taking Their Rightful Place*, which analyzes progress made in incorporating participation of the poor in projects and policies of large public donor agencies and recipient government agencies over a ten-year period. Focused largely on the World Bank, the book also analyzes strategies used by NGOs aligned with activists inside donor agencies to promote this work. She has worked extensively in sub-Saharan Africa.

Sakuntala Narasimhan is a national award-winning Indian journalist specializing in gender and development. She taught a course on women and development at Virginia Tech, USA, on a Fulbright assignment (1990) and is the author of ten books including *Empowering Women: An Alternative Strategy from Rural India*. She has presented papers at the annual conferences of the International Association for Feminist Economics at Oslo (2001), Barbados (2003) and Oxford (2004) and was commissioned to report on the Fourth World conference on women (Beijing 1995), UNGASS (Beijing +5, New York 2000) and the World Summit at Johannesburg (2002).

Aida Orgocka received her doctoral degree in Human Development and Family Studies from the University of Illinois at Urbana-Champaign. She helped found one of the first women's non-governmental organizations in Albania. Her research interests address gender, health, international migration and development. Her most recent work on Albanian female high-skilled migration will appear in *The New Albanian Diaspora*. She is also publishing her work on Muslim immigrant women in the USA in professional journals such as *Sex Education*.

Laura Parisi is Assistant Professor of Women's Studies at the University of Victoria in Victoria, BC, Canada. Her areas of specialty are gender, feminist theory, international political economy, human rights, and international law and organization. She was a delegate to the UN Beijing +5 women's conference in New York in 2000, and is the author of several publications on women's human rights issues, including her most recent publication "Feminist Praxis and Women's Human Rights" in the *Journal of Human Rights* (2002, vol. 1).

Karin Schoenpflug received her Ph.D. in economics from the University of Vienna and works in the economic policy division of the Austrian Ministry of Finance. She has taught at the Universities of Klagenfurt and Graz in Austria and at the University of Southern Maine in the USA. Her cultural and political commitments include working at Rosa Lila Villa, a GLBTQ center in Vienna, attending and organizing the world's oldest Women's Camp on Femø, Denmark, recently focusing on the lessons from the Northern European women's movement of the 1970s. She is a member of International Association for Feminist Economics and her research interests include exploring utopian visions of feminist economics.

Stephanie Seguino is Associate Professor and Chair of the Department of Economics at the University of Vermont, USA. A central issue her research explores is the welfare effects of globalization. She has also studied the interrelationship between output, growth, and income distribution, exploring how the distribution of income between genders affects macroeconomic outcomes. Her most recent work has explored the effects of economic growth on gender equity in well-being in Latin America and the Caribbean as well as Asia. A second branch of her work explores the determinants of investment and the effect of capital mobility on productivity, wages, and growth. She has also worked on living wage issues. Her worked is published in a wide variety of journals, including the *Journal of Development Studies*, the *Cambridge Journal of Economics*, *World Development*, and the *Journal of Post-Keynesian Economics*. She has also served as consultant to the World Bank, USAID, the United Nations, and UNRISD.

Gale Summerfield is Director of the Women and Gender in Global Perspectives Program and Associate Professor of Human and Community Development at the University of Illinois at Urbana-Champaign. She has written extensively on gender aspects of reforms in post-socialist and developing countries. Her articles appear in journals such as *International Journal of Politics, Culture, and Society, Feminist Economics, World Development*, and *Review of Social Economy*. She is co-editor (with Nahid Aslanbeigui and Steven Pressman) of *Women in the Age of Economic Transformation* (Routledge, 1994), and (with Irene Tinker) of *Woman's Rights to House and Land: China, Laos, Vietnam*. Her current research interests address gender, human security, and transnational migration.

Zafiris Tzannatos is Advisor to the World Bank Institute and at the time of writing the chapter in this volume he was Professor and Chair of the Economics Department at the American University of Beirut, Lebanon. He has previously held senior appointments in UK universities and the World Bank including being Advisor to the Bank's Managing Director for Human Development, Manager for Social Protection in the Middle East and North Africa Region, and Leader of the Child Labor Program. He has advised many governments and international organizations on issues relating to development and social policy and has numerous publications, including 14 books, in the areas of gender equality, child labor and trade unions and more broadly labor economics.

Mariama Williams, Ph.D., is an international economics consultant and an Adjunct Associate at the Center of Concern, Washington, DC. She is also the Research Adviser for the International Gender and Trade Network/ Caribbean Gender and Trade Network and co-research Coordinator, Political Economy of Globalisation (Trade), and Development Alternative with Women for a New Era (DAWN). Williams is also a former member of the board of the Association for Women's Right and Development (AWID) and a Director of the Institute for Law and Economics (ILE-Jamaica). She is also a member of the International Working Group on Engendering Macro-economics and International Trade and a consultant adviser for Gender and Trade to the Commonwealth Secretariat.

Cynthia A. Wood is an economist and Associate Professor of Interdisciplinary Studies at Appalachian State University, whose work has appeared in *Feminist Economics* and *Nepantla: Views from South*. Her research interests include gender and development, Latin American economics, and postcolonial feminist theory.

Brigitte Young is Professor of International and Comparative Political Economy at the Institute of Political Science at the University of Muenster. She also taught at the Institute of Political Science, Free University of Berlin from 1997 to 1999. From 1994 to 1995 she was Research Associate at the Centre for German and European Studies, School of Foreign Service, Georgetown University, Washington, DC, and from 1991 to 1997 she was at Wesleyan University, Connecticut. Her research areas are globalization, financial markets, GATS, international political economy, feminist economics, and multimedia intercultural education. She has published widely in English and German. Her recent publications include: *Gender, Globalization, and Democratization* (co-edited) and *Global Governance* (co-edited). She is presently working on two manuscripts, *Engendering the WTO* (forthcoming) and *Finance, Power and Social Reproduction* (forthcoming).

Acknowledgments

This book is the result of both our enthusiasm about the leap made by the World Bank Gender Office in taking feminist economic interests and research into account in *Engendering Development: Through Gender Equality in Rights, Resources, and Voice*, and our concerns about its limitations. We acknowledge Andrew Mason, of the Gender Office of the World Bank, for his participation in conference sessions on the report. We also thank Zafiris Tzannatos for his support and years of commitment to open discussions on these matters in an international forum of feminist economists.

We thank all those who joined the discussions at the conference of the International Association for Feminist Economics (IAFFE) in Los Angeles. Thanks also to IAFFE for providing us with an international forum and network for these discussions and a place to bring together scholars committed to critical discussions on gender and development.

We also thank Robert Langham, Routledge economics editor, for his continued support and interest in this project.

We thank the organization of the Marie-Jahoda Visiting Professorship for International Women's Studies Chair of the Ruhr-Universität Bochum (Germany) for providing the environment in which to work on the completion of this book. Thanks also to Ilse Lenz and Brigitte Young for their discussions that helped us to further articulate the conception of this book. Thanks also to Hollins University (USA) for their research support.

We acknowledge and thank the Women's Edge Coalition for permission to adapt "The Advocate's Guide to Promoting Gender Equality at the World Bank." The full paper is available at www.womensedge.org. We also acknowledge Routledge for permission to reprint "Adjustment With a Woman's Face: Gender and Macroeconomic Policy at the World Bank," by Cynthia Wood, reprinted from *Struggles for Social Rights in Latin America*, edited by Susan Eckstein and Tim Wickam-Crowley, New York: Routledge, 2003.

1 Feminist economics and the World Bank

An introduction

Drucilla K. Barker and Edith Kuiper

In the past decade the World Bank has made a substantial shift both in theory and policy. Previously economists in Washington determined the boundaries and conditions for World Bank programmes and loans. Now macroeconomic models and top-down approaches are augmented by cooperation with local groups and non-governmental organizations. This has been accompanied by a renewed focus on fighting poverty, a decentralization of authority, and an increased involvement of national governments. An increased attention to gender issues has been an important part of this process.

During the 1980s only scant attention was paid to gender and women's issues in the Bank's publications and policies. This changed in the 1990s as the Bank began to study the effects of women's education on poverty and fertility rates. The 1995 Fourth World Conference on Women in Beijing provided further impetus for the Bank to pursue research on gender and development. At that conference James Wolfensohn, the President of the World Bank, made a commitment to develop a framework for gender and development in cooperation with NGOs and other international organizations working on these issues. In this process the attention paid to the relationship between gender and development broadened from a relatively narrow economic focus to a more interdisciplinary one that included discussions of identity, culture, and North–South relations. This research, which culminated in the 2001 report *Engendering Development: Through Gender Equality in Rights, Resources, and Voice*, calls for including women's economic status as a major economic indicator in the evaluation of World Bank projects (World Bank 2001).

Taking the economic framework of the World Bank as a starting point for analysis, *Engendering Development* makes the case that economic growth and development cannot be effectively addressed when gender inequality is not taken into account. It starts from the premise that poverty increases gender inequalities and that gender inequalities hinder economic development. As James Wolfensohn puts it in his Foreword to the report,

> The World Bank is committed to a world free from poverty. And it is clear that efforts to achieve this must address gender inequalities . . . ignoring gender disparities comes at great cost – to people's well being and to

countries' abilities to grow sustainably, to govern effectively, and thus to reduce poverty.

(Wolfensohn 2001: xi)

Of course, promoting gender equality is a complex undertaking, as the authors of the report, Elizabeth M. King and Andrew D. Mason, acknowledge in their preface. The research informing the report is multidisciplinary and draws on economics, law, demography, sociology, and other disciplines. The report is organized around the principal pathways through which gender inequalities are generated and persist: the role of social institutions, of economic institutions, of household power relations, resources and decision-making, and of economic change and development policy. Acknowledging that addressing persistent gender inequalities requires more than just economic growth, the Report proposes a three-part strategy for promoting gender equality:

- Rights: Reform institutions to establish equal rights and opportunities for women and men.
- Resources: Foster economic development to strengthen incentives for more equal resources and participation.
- Voice: Take active measures to redress persistent disparities in command over resources and political voice (World Bank 2001: 1–2).

Given the importance of the topic, and the sustained level of interest in it, *Engendering Development* can, in many ways, be seen as a major achievement for scholars, policy-makers and activists who have argued for including gender in economic theory and policy. The publication of this report, its explicit claim that gender issues are economic issues, the use made of feminist economic research, and the reception of the report in the World Bank motivated the editors of this volume to organize a set of sessions at the annual meetings of the International Association for Feminist Economics (IAFFE) in 2002 in Los Angeles.

The overwhelming interest in these sessions, attended by many of the authors in this anthology, most of whom have been involved in discussions about women, development, and the Bank for many years, as well as Andrew Mason, one of the authors of the report, motivated this project. It brings together a range of viewpoints from feminist economists and other social researchers on the paradigm shift articulated in *Engendering Development*. The essays in this anthology critically examine the relationships between gender, growth, development, and the World Bank from historical, empirical, and theoretical perspectives, and explore futures directions for research, policy, and activism.

Gender and the World Bank: an institutional history and assessment

The first section of this book sets the stage for a feminist examination and critique of the World Bank's policies on gender and development by providing a historical overview of the Bank's gender policies and an examination of the institutional processes that culminated in the *Engendering Development* report. Zafiris Tzannatos, who has been involved in the research and development of gender policies and strategies at the Bank for many years, provides an insider's perspective. Carolyn Long, a consultant on the civil society organizations in development, connects the report to advocacy efforts carried out by both Northern and Southern women's organizations, and Sakuntala Narasimhan brings a journalist's eye to the issues.

Tzannatos provides a historical overview of the World Bank's genesis, mandate, and approach to development, poverty, and gender. He locates the evolution of the Bank's position on women and gender against the background of the larger changes in the Bank's policies from reconstruction, to structural adjustment, to its current focus on poverty alleviation. His discussion of the evolution of gender issues within the Bank in terms of philosophy, internal organization, and activities allows the reader to better understand the institutional character and culture of the institution.

The Bank's preoccupation with macroeconomic issues and structural adjustment policies meant that thematic issues such as gender equality received scant attention until it began to prepare for the 1995 Beijing conference. Since then the Bank came to endorse the position that gender inequalities hamper growth, called for attention to gender equality in development efforts, and outlined how gender issues were to be identified and incorporated into Bank-supported projects and programs. Tzannatos concludes that although attention to gender issues at the Bank continue, and have become particularly visible since the onset of the new millennium, their impact on development and on women in developing countries and more generally on development is unclear.

From her extensive experience in women's organizations and other international NGOs, Carolyn Long assesses the Bank's attention to the promotion of gender equality in its policies and projects. Her account of the Bank's approach to gender in terms of history, organizational structure, and institutional culture is framed in terms of gender advocacy efforts carried out by women's organizations and other external actors, and complements Tzannatos' insider's account. She includes a discussion of the actions that a number of Northern and Southern women's organizations consider essential in promoting gender equality in Bank-funded initiatives.

Long's account is particularly critical of the lack of real institutional support for gender at the Bank. She considers the Bank's gender strategies and adoption of Country Gender Assessments (CGAs), which analyze the gender dimensions of development across sectors and identify gender-responsive measures that will contribute to poverty reduction, growth, and human well-being, as an important step forward. The problem, however, is the lack of real institutional support, in terms of either budgets or administrative authority. The integration of gender concerns into projects and policies varies by region and depends on the interest, or lack thereof, of the particular Bank employees and countries in promoting gender equality. External pressure from NGOs and women's organizations in both the North and South will be necessary to create the institutional changes necessary to turn the rhetoric of gender equality into real integration of women and women's issues into Bank policies.

This section concludes with a comment by Sakuntala Narasimhan. She asks whether the Bank has learned from its past mistakes and whether the changes now under way will make a positive difference in the ways that development funding affects women. Dam projects on the Narmada river in upper India, a road development project on the slopes of Kilimanjaro in Tanzania, and the building of a coal-fired power plant in Orissa state in India are just three examples that lead her to doubt the learning abilities of the Bank. She concludes that development funding continues to have a negative effect on the well-being of many poor women in the South. Narishimhan agrees with Long that external pressure on the Bank is necessary to effect real reforms, and this in turn requires that the voices of poor, mostly rural, mostly uneducated, women in the South be heeded and the chasm between them and privileged, urban, educated women be closed.

not enough support to foster policies by institutions

Policy evaluations

The second section of the book examines the explicit and implicit policy implications of the report in light of the actual economic conditions in three different regions: Latin America, Africa, and Southeast Asia. As all of these chapters point out, the Bank assumes that economic growth is, for all practical purposes, synonymous with development. In development literature and in development practices, however, the concept has evolved to include a variety of non-economic dimensions including freedom, dignity, capabilities, inclusion, and so forth. Defined in this broader sense, development and gender equity can go hand in hand. In contrast, economic growth alone may not improve the well-being of the vast majority of people in the developing world, nor will it necessarily contribute to gender equity and the empowerment of women.

Rose-Marie Avin's chapter challenges the report's assertion that women's status and gender equality actually improved in parts of Latin America during the structural adjustment period of the 1980s and 1990s. Case studies from Brazil and Nicaragua provide the evidence for her challenge. In the Brazilian case, large numbers of women migrated to Rio de Janeiro and São Paulo to find work. However, due to capital-intensive import-substitution many of these women were not able to find jobs in the manufacturing sector and found work in the informal sector as street vendors, prostitutes, cooks, maids, and nannies. All women were not, of course, affected equally. Segmented labor markets meant that middle-class, Euro-Brazilian women were able to take advantage of educational and occupational opportunities while millions of poor, working-class women were relegated to the low-paying, low-status occupations. Thus the Bank's assertion that economic growth improves the status of women depends on its disregard of the importance of race, ethnicity, and class in determining women's economic status.

→ class determination in Brazil

The Nicaraguan case tells an interesting story. During the period between 1979 and 1990, when the Sandinista government was in power, major policies were introduced that enabled women to participate fully in the political, economic, and social life of the country. For the first time working-class and peasant women had voice. With the defeat of the Sandinistas in 1990, advancements toward gender equity came to a halt. Structural adjustment policies resulted in widespread female unemployment and women's burdens in households also increased. *By who? where they taken over?*

Cheryl Doss explores gender and development in an African context. She begins with the premise that improved agricultural technologies are key to reducing poverty and increasing the standard of living in Africa and notes that the report does not directly address issues of agricultural and technology, nor does it directly address issues of power relations. In order to improve the well-being of women in Africa it is necessary to develop policies and technologies that will improve agricultural productivity, and for such polices and technologies to be efficacious, it is necessary to investigate power and gender relations in households, communities, and countries. Women will only benefit from new technologies if the accompanying policies increase their options and control over their own lives. *Women need own land*

Doss considers three dimensions of the effects of technologies on women farmers. First she considers their effects on women's workloads. Technologies that increase productivity may have a negative effect on well-being if women have to work harder or longer or lose control over the output. Technologies can also impact women's access to resources, land in particular. Since women often acquire land rights through male relatives or village heads, technologies that increase the value of land may actually make it more difficult for them to acquire such rights. Finally, if women lose control over their activities once they become profitable, then their well-being will be harmed. Since women's lives and situations are so varied, it is not possible to tell *a priori* how technologies will affect them. A nuanced sense of power relations in particular contexts is necessary to understand whether technologies will enhance or diminish women's power and hence their well-being, and the report fails to provide this. *Q + Hard to get tech*

Concerns about the effects of economic growth on women's well-being inform the chapter by Stephanie Seguino. She notes that well-being is improved by paid work at living wages and by gender-wage parity. In developing countries, however, the combination of women's segregation in export industries and increased capital mobility constrains their ability to improve their wages and working conditions. Credible threats of firm relocation effectively dampen women's bargaining power relative to that of capital even as the demand for their labor increases. This leads her to question the Bank's assumption that trade and market liberalization are beneficial to women's well-being.

Using the case of the Asian semi-industrialized countries (SIEs), she demonstrates an inverse relationship between economic growth and gender-wage parity. Evidence shows that the countries with the largest gender-wage gaps were the ones that grew the most rapidly during the period between 1975 and

1995. Using a neo-Kaleckian model to further illuminate the relationship between female wages and macroeconomic outcomes in an open economy, she shows that the decline in output and female employment resulting from higher female wages is more likely to occur if capital is footloose, if the price elasticity of exports is high, and if the spending propensities of capitalists and workers are similar. A more optimistic scenario in which higher female wages are consistent with economic growth is possible if firms have an incentive to innovate or if higher wages stimulate productivity. The case of South Korea demonstrates that this is possible, and the precise conditions need to be investigated further.

A comment by Karin Schoenpflug concludes this section. She uses Michel Foucault's discourse analysis to reflect on the arguments made by Avin, Doss, and Seguino and to deconstruct the rhetoric and policies of the World Bank. Four localities are particularly germane to her analysis: the constitution of subjectivity and issues of voice, processes of legitimization and the power of definition, the role of hierarchal dualisms, and the material consequences of practices of inclusion and exclusion. From this framework she concludes that *Engendering Development* is a powerful piece of institutional rhetoric that creates its own logic and legitimizes World Bank policies. These issues are explored further in the next section. what is the WB doing?

Disciplinary paradigms/development paradigms

The third section of this book examines the ideological and methodological commitments of the report from a variety of feminist and interdisciplinary social science perspectives. It explicitly considers the ways in which disciplinary paradigms and boundaries contribute to the sense-making and legitimization of the report. These chapters note that although the Bank has adopted a new, multidisciplinary paradigm that includes attention to problems of poverty and other social issues, the changes are more apparent than real.

We begin this section with Suzanne Bergeron's examination of the Bank's break with a narrow, economistic approach in favor of an approach that is responsive to poverty and inequality. She argues that although economists are encouraged to take a multidisciplinary approach and account for social and cultural factors in their analyses, they do in ways that preserve and strengthen the disciplinary core of economics. Rationality and market efficiency remain privileged concepts, and the critical and the transdisciplinary methods that characterize feminist theorizing remain outside the Bank's framework.

The new approach does account for the significance of market failures and externalities, norms, values, and institutions. It draws attention to the importance of health and education for women. However, the disciplinary boundaries of economics remain intact and intersectionality, a central concept in women's studies, remains absent. Differences among women are obscured by universalistic accounts of women's behavior and experiences. Integration into formal labor markets is seen as the key to women's emancipation from traditional, patriarchal cultures. Women's emancipation is not, however, seen as an end in itself, but rather as instrumental to the goals of economic growth. In contrast, a feminist transdisciplinary methodology would call on social constructivist and post-colonial insights to consider difference and representations and consider how both market and non-market social processes affect women's agency and well-being.

Cynthia Wood agrees with Bergeron that neoclassical economics remains the dominant paradigm at the Bank. She argues that as long as it remains dominant, neither political pressure nor other institutional changes will eliminate gender bias in adjustment policies. Neoclassical economics, with its emphasis on markets, prices, and economic growth, precludes gender analyses and marginalizes any consideration of the effects of structural adjustment on unpaid domestic labor.

The Bank's discussion of gender downplays considerations of structural adjustment and macroeconomics and focuses instead on social issues such as education, population, and health. Wood argues that publication of *Engendering Development* will do little to change this because, in reality, engendering macro-economics entails considering unpaid domestic labor, and the current paradigm precludes doing this in any meaningful way. Moreover, eliminating gender bias in economic theory and policy requires not only that non-market activities be recognized and valued, but that differences in intrahousehold relations be considered.

Intrahousehold relations are the subject of the next essay by Aida Orgocka and Gale Summerfield. Although the fourth chapter in *Engendering Development* analyzes intrahousehold bargaining processes, Orgocka and Summerfield argue that it has limitations. It does not include new interdisciplinary developments, and it is quite selective in the work it does include, stressing econometric studies rather than qualitative approaches. Moreover, the Bank's analysis is focused on adult, heterosexual partners, and considers children mainly as the recipients of the parents' largesse or as investments for the parents' future support. Orgocka and Summerfield, in contrast, argue that understanding parent/child dynamics would contribute to a deeper understanding of the distribution of power and resources in households. And a better understanding of mother/daughter relationships is fundamental to constructing policies that promote gender equity since history is replete with examples of mothers passing down hurtful traditions to their daughters because their economic well-being was dependent on adherence to patriarchal gender norms.

They use their qualitative research on gender and Muslim immigrants in the Midwestern United States to illustrate how factors overlooked in the Bank's discussion enrich our understanding of mother/daughter interactions within the household regarding sex education for young women. Sex education is, of course, a key component of policies concerning health and reproduction. Orgocka and Summerfield's work points to the importance of using qualitative research methods so that policy-makers can better understand different contexts and different expressions of agency in diverse groups of people.

V. Eudine Barriteau provides a contextualized critique of the Bank's report. She argues that it is best understood as a form of gender mainstreaming and explores the major shortcomings of gender mainstreaming in the context of the Commonwealth Caribbean. Gender mainstreaming views gender as arising from differences in male and female bodies and does not include feminist inquiries into ideology, power relations, and conditions of subordination. The report suffers from the same flaw and so its policies will not disrupt gender hierarchies.

Barriteau points out that the report does not differentiate between the Caribbean and rest of Latin America. The experience of the Commonwealth Caribbean, however, provides evidence that women's access to material resources is insufficient for bringing about positive change. Despite the fact that women have equal access to education and are becoming dominant in traditional male occupations, they remain economically disadvantaged relative to men. Men continue to be politically, economically, and socially dominant because the ideological dimensions of gender hierarchies are not fundamentally challenged. Thus, she argues that the Bank needs to revisit its conceptual analysis of gender. For Barriteau, material and ideological relations of gender are relations of power. The former concerning the relative access to resources by women and men, the latter concerning the social meanings of masculinity and femininity. Dismantling gender inequality requires a consideration of both.

This section ends with a comment by Laura Parisi. She concludes that rather than promoting gender equality, the World Bank's approach reifies masculinist neoclassical/liberal ideology. Observing that the term "engendering" can also mean "facilitating" or "enabling," she argues that its use in the title of the report serves to divert attention away from the intersections of gender, race/ethnicity, class, and sexuality in the development dialogue. The report focuses on promoting neoclassical economic development rather than gendering development processes. Like women in development frameworks (WID), the World Bank seeks to include women in existing development projects rather than challenging the notion of development itself.

Explorations: future directions of feminist research

The chapters in this section of the book briefly explore further directions for feminist economic research, activity, cooperation, and dialog on engendering development. It begins with an essay by Drucilla K. Barker, which explores some of the methodological challenges and dilemmas facing feminist scholars and practitioners who engage with large development institutions. She briefly summarizes some of the history of feminist economic engagement with gender, development, and transnational institutions. Throughout this history, feminist policy-makers and academics have endeavoured to start from the perspective of poor women and other marginalized people. The question is, how can they, located as they are in places of privilege such as academe or transnational organizations, discern what this perspective is. This chapter considers some possible answers to this query and concludes with a discussion of disciplinary and institutional power in feminist economics. Feminist economists are both insiders and outsiders in institutions such as the World Bank, a contradictory position that ultimately makes intervention and transformation possible. Some possible transformations and interventions are discussed in the next three chapters.

Mariama Williams argues for feminist intervention in the coherence framework being constructed by the World Bank, the International Monetary Fund (IMF) and World Trade Organization (WTO). The coherence framework coordinates the activities of these institutions in order to ensure consistency and complementarity in international economic policy-making, and it promotes trade liberalization as a tool for achieving economic development and growth. This should be troubling to feminists because the legally binding trade agreements of the WTO are already superseding national macroeconomic policies, regulatory regimes, and social welfare policies. The coherence framework being pursued will speed up and strengthen this process. Williams argues that the far-reaching influence of the policies prescribed by the World Bank, the IMF, and the WTO, backed up by a coherence framework, will not guarantee sustainable development nor will it foster a gender-balanced approach to economic growth. Feminist economists need to analyze and promote awareness of the impact of the coherence framework on social reproduction and social relations.

The chapter by Brigitte Young provides an insight into promises and limitations of integrating gender into a high-level parliamentary report. In response to increasing controversies regarding the political, social, and economic effects of globalization, the German Parliament set up a commission to systematically investigate issues relating to globalization. Its mandate was to study the economic, social, and political impacts of globalization. Gender-mainstreaming was central to this mandate. Young was the only woman on the commission and provides the readers with an insider's view of the processes through which gender was incorporated into a parliamentary report.

Diane Elson's chapter concludes this section. She critiques the treatment of women's rights in *Engendering Development* on both a conceptual and an empirical level and offers an alternative account. The articulation of women's rights in the human rights declarations and treaties of the United Nations, particularly the Convention on the Elimination of All Forms of Discrimination Against Women (CEDAW), informs the conceptual alternative. In this context, women's rights are ends in themselves and subordinate to economic policy. Her empirical alternative focuses on outcomes rather than inputs and brings in new data sources to evaluate the progress. The evidence presented belies the report's rosy picture of progress toward gender equality and suggests instead that there has been regress rather than progress for women's economic and social rights in many countries. Having no interest in rosy pictures, the authors in this anthology present complex and nuanced analyses of the social relations of gender in a global context. We hope these insights will inform policy-making and motivate further research.

References

Wolfensohn, James D. (2001) "Foreword", in *Engendering Development: Through Gender Equality in Rights, Resources, and Voice*, New York: Oxford University Press.

World Bank (2001) *Engendering Development: Through Gender Equality in Rights, Resources, and Voice*, New York: Oxford University Press.

Part I

Gender and the World Bank

An institutional history and assessment

2 The World Bank, development, adjustment and gender equality

Zafiris Tzannatos

Introduction

Though the world is integrating in many respects and location does not matter, capital constraints and gender inequality still matter big time in developing countries which are the focus of operations of the World Bank (from now on, the Bank). And location may also matter for the Bank: being situated between the International Monetary Fund and the White House, the Bank has not infrequently attracted the charge that it is an agent of uncritical liberal policies or an arm of US economic and political interests and more broadly foreign policy (Wade 2000). Thus, the "initial conditions" for an objective or at least a generally acceptable assessment of what the Bank does in the area of gender (or any other area) are not promising: the Bank's resources are limited,[1] critics of mainstream economics are many (though often short of providing a unified alternative), and the efforts by the remaining superpower to influence international outcomes are on the increase especially post–September 11, 2001.

Against this context it is easy to come up with a verdict of failure. This is so because, first, the scale of poverty (hence development) is huge: two billion people live on less than $2/day. Second, any deviation even from the simplistic notion of what unfettered markets can achieve in theory must encounter the difficult issue of what the correct mix of public/private shares should be, when and in what sectors. Third, the charge that the Bank can swing at the wish of any single government needs to take into account the Bank's collective governance structure in which practically all countries, industrialized and developing ones, are represented.[2] Finally, the Bank is a changing institution, and its assessment – friendly or critical – must take into account the time period in which evaluations are undertaken: the recent statement "The Washington Consensus has been dead for years. It's been replaced by all sorts of other consensuses" may have come late but is no less than a revolution in the Bank's history (Wolfensohn 2004).[3]

These methodological, political and philosophical issues have not been resolved in the six decades of the Bank's existence and are beyond the ability of a single chapter to summarize them or come up with definitive conclusions. In less ambitious terms, this chapter focuses on the activities and approach of a living international organization, the Bank, which tries to accomplish its mission of poverty reduction amidst conditions of changing economic realities, improvements in knowledge (including richer economic analyses), political realignments and international flux.

The chapter starts with a review of the Bank's genesis and its changing focus from reconstruction and structural adjustment to poverty reduction and more comprehensive approaches to development. It then focuses on the evolution of gender issues within the Bank in terms of philosophy, internal organization and activities. Given that many criticisms of the Bank evolve around the issue of human rights, the chapter discusses how the Bank's economic mandate positions it versus a rights-based approach. Finally, the chapter summarizes some assessments of the Bank's involvement with gender issues.

The Bank

Genesis and structure

The World Bank was created at the United Nations Monetary and Financial Conference held in Bretton Woods, New Hampshire in 1944, to facilitate the flow of international capital to a war-torn Europe.[4]

Following the successful growth of Europe, the Bank subsequently expanded its operations in developing countries and the official name became "International Bank for Reconstruction and Development" (IBRD).[5] The name "World Bank" came to be used for the International Bank for Reconstruction and Development (IBRD) and the International Development Association (IDA – see below). These two organizations provide low-interest loans, interest-free credit, and grants to developing countries.

The World Bank has now evolved into the World Bank Group (WBG) that consists of five closely associated institutions (the year is when each institution was established):

1   The International Bank for Reconstruction and Development (IBRD) (1945);
2   The International Finance Corporation (IFC) (1956);[6]
3   The International Development Association (IDA) (1960);
4   The International Centre for Settlement of Investment Disputes (ICSID) (1966);
5   The Multilateral Investment Guarantee Agency (MIGA) (1988).

All five specialize in different aspects of development but all focus on the "overarching goal" of the Bank, which is poverty reduction.

The Bank is owned by 184 countries and is run like a cooperative.[7] Member countries are represented by a Board of Governors. The Governors (typically ministers of finance or development) carry ultimate decision-making power in the Bank. They meet annually to decide on key Bank policy issues, admit or suspend country members, decide on changes in the authorized capital stock, determine the distribution of net income, and endorse financial statements and budgets.

Because the Governors meet only once a year, they delegate specific duties to their Executive Directors. The Bank currently has 24 Executive Directors who work onsite and constitute a "resident board" based in its headquarters in Washington, DC. The five largest shareholders (the United States, Japan, Germany, the United Kingdom and France) have one Executive Director each as do some others (such as China, Russia and Saudi Arabia). Other member countries are represented in groups ("multi country constituencies") by the remaining Executive Directors. The Executive Directors and the President of the Bank – who serves as Chairman of the Board – are responsible for the conduct of the Bank's general operations and perform their duties under powers delegated by the Board of Governors.

While the Bank is best known as a financier, one of its most important roles is in the provision of analysis and advice. In this respect the role of the Bank as an "intellectual actor" has been significant. In short, one can think of the Bank today not narrowly as a bank but rather a United Nations' specialized (that is, development) agency. It is a complex institution as (a) its operations cover practically every aspect of development; (b) despite its focus on economics, its cooperative nature implies that its Executive Directors (acting on behalf of the Governors) bring into the Bank's policies and operations the political views of the countries they represent; and (c) political considerations aside, the Bank is often stranded by conflicting guidance provided by economics – the dismal science.[8]

Internal dissatisfaction with the effectiveness of its operations as well as external criticisms coupled with changes in the economic paradigm (from Keynesianism and fixed exchange rates to monetarism and structural adjustment and then adjustment with a human face) have led the Bank to evolve over time and also to introduce internal and external oversight and monitoring mechanisms which range from objective assessments to (what amounts to) policing.

More specifically, the Bank has a number of internal and external monitoring systems which include:

1   The Operations Evaluations Department (OED) which reports directly to member countries on the Bank's performance;[9]
2   An independent inspection panel which responds to concerns of people affected by Bank projects and ensures that safeguard policies are being enforced;
3   An Internal Quality Assurance Group (QAG) which monitors projects during implementation when adjustments can still be made;
4   An Internal Auditing Department which oversees risk management and internal controls in accordance with the Standards for the Professional Practice of Internal Auditing of the Institute of Internal Auditors;
5   A corruption and fraud investigation unit (called the Department of

Institutional Integrity, INT) that investigates allegations of fraud and corruption within the Bank Group or in connection with Bank-financed contracts, and any allegations of unethical behavior by Bank staff;

6   The Ethics Office which reports directly to the Bank's President and is responsible for outreach and communications on ethics matters; and

7   A Quality Assurance and Compliance Unit which gives advice on safeguard issues in projects and ensures the consistent implementation of safeguard policies, such as the policy on indigenous people or the policy on involuntary resettlement.

In addition the Bank undertakes periodic assessments of its overall operations as well as of more general development assistance. For example, in 2002 the Bank undertook a study of the effectiveness of development assistance over the past half-century (World Bank 2002a).[10]

Through its own learning based on the results of these monitoring and evaluation mechanisms, as well as changes in economic realities and thinking, the Bank started moving away from supporting narrow infrastructure projects, and its mission evolved into poverty reduction incorporating more explicitly the gender dimension, as the next sections indicate. But the process has been neither linear nor smooth. The Bank went through a phase in the 1980s when its policies were derived from what came to be known as the "Washington Consensus"[11] while its operations focused on structural adjustment without explicitly incorporating social concerns (in a belief that the benefits of macroeconomic adjustment will quickly "trickle down" to the social sectors).[12] Then, by 2004, the Washington Consensus was declared dead. This long journey is discussed in the next sections.

Changing focus: from reconstruction to adjustment and poverty reduction

Postwar international economic order was very much shaped by the International Monetary Fund (IMF), the General Agreement on Tariffs and Trade (GATT) and the Bank. The creation of the former two organizations was based on rather clear justifications. The monetary disorder of the interwar period had taught policymakers the value of international monetary cooperation. Similarly, there was a need for a multilateral mechanism to induce "closed economy/inward looking" governments to commit themselves to nondiscriminatory trade policies. Thus the debate surrounding the creation of the IMF and GATT was based primarily on *how* they should operate, not over *what* they should do.

In contrast, the writing of the Articles of Association (constitution) of the Bank required a lot of elbow grease: why is there a need for a multilateral institution to lend to governments when capital had been traditionally channeled through private capital markets or loans and grants provided on a bilateral basis? Thus the debate surrounding the creation of the Bank was (and still remains) very much about *what* it should do, not just *how* it should do it. The four add-on institutions to what was originally one World Bank and the switching of focus from reconstruction to development to adjustment and later on to poverty reduction and a more comprehensive approach to development attest to the struggle of an organization that tries to define what it does.

A critical junction in the Bank's history was the appointment as its president of Robert McNamara, formerly US Secretary of Defense during the Vietnam era. During his tenure at the Bank (1968–81), the Bank shifted from an emphasis on infrastructure to agriculture and rural development in an attempt to address people's basic needs, particularly the rural poor. Poverty was adopted "big time" into the Bank's thinking in 1972 backed by the admission that 40 percent of the world's population lived in absolute poverty. During the rest of the decade the Bank's work on poverty was very much linked to human development which culminated with the 1980 *World Development Report*[13] *on Poverty*. During the McNamara era, the Bank promoted the view that directing investment (in basic infrastructure and human resources development) toward the poor through redistribution would contribute to economic growth as well as to poverty reduction. It should be noted that it was during McNamara's era that the Bank first introduced structural and sectoral adjustment lending (in 1979)[14] though the Bank was not then part of the general movement towards supply-side economics that was already taking place in the academic profession since the 1970s.

The adoption of supply-side economics came to be a prominent feature of the Bank in the 1980s. An appropriate instrument (adjustment lending) was already in place when the steady advance of poverty reduction was halted by the global economic crisis of the early 1980s, soon after McNamara left the Bank. In fact adjustment (or policy-based) lending as a broad instrument of aid was widely used by the Bank during the early years after World War II, but thereafter the focus shifted to investment lending. In the years after McNamara left the Bank, which coincided with the Ronald Reagan presidency in the United States, program lending was resurrected and poverty was moved to the back burner (Stern and Ferreira 1997: 549).

Under a new president (A. W. Clausen, 1981–86) the Bank changed its poverty focus and gave less prominence to measures hinging on ideological stances (such as population control). Attention switched mainly on to achieving growth through structural adjustment.

Adjustment, in terms of its theoretical justification or results on the ground, became a thorny issue for the Bank in the 1980s. The charge here is that the Bank directed reforms in a specific direction (the Washington Consensus) through its lending program, policy dialogue, and selective research (Edwards 1997). The developing countries' massive move toward trade liberalization and structural adjustment in the late 1980s and early 1990s has been associated by many analysts with the role of the Bank (and the IMF). In addition, there were "less impressive performances" of the Bank throughout the 1980s associated with the mounting levels of debt in developing countries (where more stringent monitoring by the financial institutions was called for), the reluctance of client countries to adopt the Bank's policies (bypassed through "conditionality"), pessimism that the resumption of growth will be quick (slow "trickle down") and a neglect of environmental issues. Somewhat paradoxically, in the 1980s there was little emphasis on cost-benefit analysis and even that was in decline (Little and Mirrlees 1991) notwithstanding the fact that the Bank's focus was to "get the prices right."

The worse-than-anticipated effects of adjustment policies, if not noticed internally, were noticed by others. For example, UNICEF's *Adjustment with a Human Face* (Cornia *et al.* 1987) and UNDP's *Human Development Report* (1990) called for a richer approach to development than just focusing on structural adjustment programs in a hopeful pursue of economic growth. In fact, during the tenure of the next president (Barber B. Conable, 1986–91), the Bank continued seeing economic growth brought about by conventional policies as a precondition for reducing poverty but also acknowledged that supplementary actions were necessary. This was reflected in the 1990 *World Development Report* as a two-part strategy, namely, to increase the income of the poor through broad-based growth and ensure that the poor had access to basic social services. This *World Development Report* also noted transfers and safety nets as important complements to the basic two-part strategy.[15]

The fiftieth anniversary of the genesis of the Bank (1994) provided an additional impetus for renewing demands for a radical transformation in the Bank's approach and practices. In the meantime (1992) "a damning document came to be written" (Kapur *et al.* 1997). The document was commissioned by yet another president of the Bank (Lewis Preston, 1991–95). The so-called Wapenhans Report (Effective Implementation: Key to Development Impact, 1992) was an in-house assessment of the Bank's entire loan portfolio (World Bank 1992b). The gist of the Wapenhans Report was that a large and increasing number of Bank projects were failing, even when assessed only on narrow economic criteria. The "50 Years is Enough" campaign and the appointment of a new president (James D. Wolfensohn, 1995–2005) resulted in greater attention being given to openness, accountability, debt reduction, participatory approaches, institutions and an end to environmentally destructive lending and structural adjustment.

The experience with adjustment lending and its mixed outcomes during this period lent impetus to the Bank's internal learning process. Several OED and Bank reviews analyzed the economic and social impact of adjustment and fed back the lessons learnt into the design of adjustment operations. Today, internal evaluations no longer shy away from admitting that the performance of adjustment operations has been mixed, especially during the 1980s.[16] They also indicate that heavy reliance on conditionality was ineffective for several reasons: it can be difficult to monitor whether a government has in fact fulfilled the conditions, particularly when external shocks muddy the picture; governments may revert to old practices as soon as the money has been disbursed; and when assessments are subjective, donors may have an incentive to emphasize progress in order to keep programs moving. They finally notice the difficulty in securing country commitment to reform: naturally, governments change over time and do not

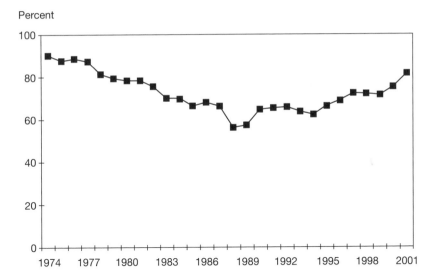

Figure 2.1 Projects rated as achieving satisfactory outcomes, 1974–2001.
Source: World Bank, internal evaluations.

feel obliged to fulfill their predecessors' policies. It is thus not surprising that only 60 percent of adjustment operations achieved (per OED evaluations) satisfactory or better outcomes in the 1980s, a figure that rose to above 80 percent in the 1990s following design improvements and increased country selectivity based on lessons of experience (Figure 2.1).

Similarly, the issue of insufficient attention to the social sectors, which was a particular problem of early adjustment operations, is now given more attention. Though the Bank is still thoroughly committed to the statement that "on balance poor people benefit from adjustment and reform as much as other groups," it does now recognize that "even successful, market-friendly reforms have benefits and costs that are distributed unevenly, especially in the near term, and the design and implementation of adjustment operations need to take this factor into account."

Irrespective of whether the Bank could have done better in the past or can do better today, it is very much a different organization than it was in the 1980s. In the 1980s the Bank's support for education, health, nutrition and other social services accounted for less than 6 percent of its lending but exceeded 18 percent in the 1990s (World Bank 2001a: 5). Today the Bank is the world's largest external funder of education and of the fight against AIDS, while it remains among the most important ones of health programs. Similarly, since 1988, the Bank has become one of the largest international funders of biodiversity projects and its environment strategy covers from poor people in rural areas in developing countries to broader issues of climate change, forests and water resources.

In 1996, the Bank and the International Monetary Fund (IMF) launched the Heavily Indebted Poor Countries (HIPC) Initiative to reduce the external debt of the world's poorest, most indebted countries, thus enabling them to reorient their budgetary priorities toward key social and human development sectors.[17]

The way the Bank is doing business also changed over time with increasing reliance on stakeholder participation and partnerships, both local and international.[18] Unlike in earlier periods when most projects were prepared and supervised from Washington, the Bank has now offices in 70 countries around the world that reach out to and collaborate with nongovernmental organizations (NGOs) in a variety of areas ranging from education to the environment and AIDS. In recent years, more than two-thirds of development projects approved by the Bank involved the active participation of NGOs in their implementation, and most of its country strategies benefited from consultations with civil society. The Bank has also increased its activities in the areas of corruption and conflict-affected economies.[19]

More recently (1999) the Bank introduced the Poverty Reduction Strategy Papers (PRSP) approach which was approved by the Boards of both the IMF and the Bank. This approach is based on poverty reduction strategies prepared by the countries themselves and serve as a framework for development assistance. The underlying goals of the PRSP are to ensure broad-based country ownership of poverty reduction strategies; develop strategies that take a comprehensive, long-term perspective; focus on results that matter for the poor; and build stronger partnerships between low-income countries and the international donor community. An internal Bank review of the PRSP process claimed that there seems to be widespread agreement (among national PRSP teams, donors and civil society organizations) that in low-income countries with active PRSP programs there is an increased emphasis on "pro-poor spending." While these results are encouraging, this is obviously a narrow measure of success. It is important to bear in mind that these budgetary reallocations will translate into improved poverty outcomes only if there are corresponding improvements in budget execution and service delivery.

All this does not mean that the situation is rosy. A more interesting issue relates to whether the much-heralded international debt relief policy in the 1990s had an impact on economic growth. A recent independent study found that international debt relief in the 1990s had only limited efficiency, effectiveness and relevance (Ministry of Foreign Affairs (The Netherlands), 2003). The amounts of debt relief were too small to start with, were given in the wrong modalities and were accompanied by too many new loans. Only in a minority of countries has debt relief led to visible stock or flow effects and in none has the debt burden become sustainable. Debt relief has rarely contributed to economic growth, particularly in the poorest and most highly indebted countries. This may suggest that the inflow of new loans from multilateral institutions to HIPC threatens their long-term debt sustainability. There is an element of *déjà vu* in all this as it resembles the case of structural adjustment: sound framework and intentions but perhaps too good to be true given the inherent conflict of interest when the IFIs (International Financial Institutions) act as both gate-keepers and creditors, a conflict that entails the risk that countries receive aid precisely because they have already a high debt burden.

The Bank and gender equality

The Bank's thinking and activities on gender (or other thematic) areas[20] can be only as good as its overall philosophy and quality of operations. In situations like those outlined in the previous section, when the Bank shifted to broad macroeconomy issues accompanied by an ideological belief that all that is needed is to just get some liberal economic fundamentals right, gender issues were sidestepped.

Indeed, the Bank has been relatively slow in addressing the role of women and broader gender issues in the economic development process. Academic attention on gender issues may be said to have started with Esther Boserup's seminal publication on *Women's Role in Economic Development* (1970). Around that time, gender anti-discrimination policies started being introduced (at least in the majority of OECD economies). The Bank created a position of an Advisor for Women in Development only in 1977 (Table 2.1). It then gradually started paying some attention to gender issues and issued the *Operational Manual Statement 2.20*[21] (OMS 2.20) in 1984 (World Bank 1984). This statement presented an overview of the general objectives and key features of the appraisal of investment projects. Within this broad framework, the statement discussed how to investigate and address the impacts of investment (*not* adjustment) projects on women.[22]

The Bank's regularly published statistical compendium (*World Development Indicators*) included information on some female indicators (such as maternal mortality, education and health) for the first time in 1988 at a time when only one-quarter of Bank reports included references to women in development. Then things starting changing relatively fast, for example, two years later substantial discussion or recommendations on women in development were included in 62 percent of all economic and sector reports (ESW) produced by the Bank. This was partly because of external pressure either directly (for example, the "50 Years Is Enough" Campaign) or indirectly (for example, the publication of critical research on gender, adjustment and macroeconomics). Viewed from heterodox macroeconomics and feminist analyses, the Bank's operations did not score highly (Çagatay *et al.* 1995). A special issue of the journal *World Development*[23] contained papers arguing that, while progress has been made in the inclusion of reproductive work into national income accounting and gender-disaggregated analysis of structural adjustment policies and programs (Benería 1995), there were major shortcomings in the way gender issues were conceptualized (or not) in the macroeconomic approaches and programs of the World Bank (and IMF).

Emphasis on gender issues started increasing relatively fast in the first half of the 1990s – partly in preparation for the Bank's participation in the Beijing

Table 2.1 Evolution of the World Bank's attention to gender and development issues

Year	Event
1977	First Women in Development Advisor is appointed.
1984	Operational Manual Statement 2.20 addresses the impact of Bank assistance on women as part of project appraisal for certain types of projects.
1986	Women in Development (WID) Unit is created.
1990	Operational Directive (OD) on poverty reduction recommends that women's issues be considered in designing poverty reduction programs.
1994	In the Policy Paper *Enhancing Women's Participation in Economic Development* the shift to gender analysis becomes visible.
	Operational Policy (OP) 4.20 is issued establishing the goals of reducing gender disparities and enhancing women's participation in economic development.
1995	The publication *Toward Gender Equality: The Role of Public Policy* explicitly recognizes that Governments can play a significant role in the reduction of gender inequalities.
1996	External Gender Consultative Group is established.
1997	Gender and Development Board is established.
1998	Position of head of the Gender and Development Board is raised from a chief/manager to a director level.
2001	The publication of *Engendering Development: Through Gender Equality in Rights, Resources, and Voice* provides an analytical framework for gender inequalities and derives implications for relevant policies.
	Publication of *Integration of Gender Into the World Bank's Work: A Strategy for Action.*
2003	Operational Policy 4.20 revised.
	Bank Procedure 4.20 statement issued.

Conference (1995).[24] By 1994, the Bank's Board endorsed for the first time a Policy Paper in the area of gender (*Enhancing Women's Participation in Economic Development*), and the Bank issued an Operational Policy statement on the gender dimension of development (*Operational Policy 4.20*). The Bank's policy was to focus operationally on five sectors (agriculture, education, health, financial services and labor) but did not – and still does not – require that all investment programs address gender issues. Structural adjustment programs – representing at least one-third of total Bank commitments – were not included under the Operational Policy.

In 1995 the Bank prepared a report *Toward Gender Equality: The Role of Public Policy* which followed a simple but powerful line.[25] It first observed that gender inequalities persist or, alternatively (though not so bluntly) that "trickle down" takes time. It then discussed how inequalities hamper growth and concluded that public policies can have a significant effect on development. More importantly, the report argued that such policies were not to be restricted only to economic ones but to be extended to other areas (such as the legal framework). The report was part of the preparation for the Bank's participation at the Fourth World Conference on Women held in Beijing in 1995 and was followed by another report (*Advancing Gender Equality: From Concept to Action*) also published in the same year. The latter report provided an overview of the Bank's support to the efforts of member countries to integrate gender equality into the development efforts and outlined how gender issues are identified and incorporated into Bank-supported projects and programs.

In its "Beijing+5" report (World Bank 2000) the Bank noted three main points: disparities persist; they are costly; and rights and institutions are important complements to growth policies. The report recommended establishing legal, economic and social institutions, including equality of rights, promoting growth and undertaking active measures to promote equality in the command of resources and political voice. Though these recommendations were not derived from a human rights perspective, they did nevertheless acknowledge the link between economics and rights – an issue discussed below.

The link between gender equality and poverty reduction was forcefully made in another publication (the *2000/2001 World Development Report, Attacking Poverty*) that argued that gender relations affect all aspects of poverty, including income, opportunity, security and *empowerment* (World Bank 2001b). Examples cited were that girls in poor families may receive lower quality nutrition, less health care and inferior education than their brothers. Likewise, female household members often have less access to and control over the household's productive resources and income than do male family members. Overall, the report questioned at times the relevance of the standard neoclassical economic theory (whereby households are usually regarded as sharing a single utility function and an equitable distribution of resources and well-being) while results of studies based on less conventional paradigms were openly acknowledged.

By far the most important analytical basis for the Bank's involvement in gender issues was included in the report *Engendering Development: Through Gender Equality in Rights, Resources, and Voice* (World Bank 2001c).[26] The subtitle is in itself indicative of the Bank's broadening its approach to the study of gender issues. The report focused on gender inequalities and their economic and social implications in developing and transition economies. It examined the conceptual and empirical links between gender equality, public policy and development outcomes, and made a strong case for applying a gender perspective to the design of development policies. It argued that societies that discriminate by gender pay a high price in terms of their ability to develop and reduce poverty. The report recognized that there is growing evidence that several aspects of gender relations – the gender-based division of labor, disparities between males and females in power and resources, and gender biases in rights and entitlements – act to undermine economic growth and reduce the well-being of men, women, and children. Gender-based divisions of labor and gender inequalities also contribute to poverty.

The report spent some time in identifying (or restating findings from previous research) that the primary channels through which gender systems affect growth are the productivity of labor and the allocative efficiency of the economy (specifically through investments in human capital, especially girls' and women's education[27] and health), investments in physical capital (especially women's access to capital) and the functioning of markets and institutions.[28] The report also emphasized the beneficial effects on improving women's rights, resources and voice (World Bank 2001c: Chapter 2) as well as the role of infrastructure, equal access to productive assets and resources, and quality of governance. As far as the implications for countries are concerned, the report proposed a three-part approach that emphasizes institutional reforms based on a foundation of equal rights for women and men, policies for sustained economic development, and active measures to redress persistent gender disparities.

The Bank's gender strategy

By the start of the millennium, the World Bank was in a position to recognize from its own learning that its effectiveness in helping member countries can increase by paying more attention to gender issues. The time was ripe to come up with a more coherent and holistic gender approach. This materialized with the discussion of the Bank-wide gender mainstreaming strategy at the Board of Directors in 2001 (World Bank 2001d).

The Gender Strategy called for a selective integration of gender issues into the Bank's work based *on the readiness* of countries. It thus adopted a soft-pedal approach[29] towards the clients (developing countries). It proposed

to work with governments and civil society in client countries, and with other donors, to diagnose the gender-related barriers to and opportunities for poverty reduction and sustainable development; and will then identify and support appropriate actions that will reduce these barriers and capitalize on the opportunities.

The Gender Strategy thus envisages that the Bank should play a supportive *vis-à-vis* member countries creating an enabling environment. More specifically, the basic process for the implementation of the Gender Strategy has three steps: preparation of periodic, multi-sectoral Country Gender Assessments (CGAs – see below); development and implementation of relevant policy and operational interventions; and monitoring the implementation and impacts of these policies and interventions. The Bank thus would play an advisory role towards creating an enabling environment and, where governments choose particular gender-responsive actions involving Bank assistance, the Bank would provide additional support for changing the gender patterns that are deemed to be costly to growth, poverty reduction and human well-being.

The process of mainstreaming gender issues within the Bank is to be implemented through four actions: integration of the gender dimension into analytical work; support of the integration of gender issues into Bank operations; alignment of resources with the new Gender Strategy; and development and implementation of systems to monitor and evaluate processes and impacts.[30] The implementation of the Gender Strategy thus involves a potentially wide range of activities that range from analytical work to policy advice and lending.

The Country Gender Assessments

A key component of the Gender Strategy is the Country Gender Assessment (CGA), that is, a study analyzing country-level gender critical areas in which gender-responsive actions are likely to enhance growth and reduce poverty.

A CGA would normally include:

- A profile of: (i) the different socio-economic roles of males and females, including their participation in both the market and household economies; (ii) gender disparities in access to, control over and use of assets and productive resources; (iii) gender disparities in human development indicators; (iv) inequalities between males and females in the ability to participate in development decision-making at the local and national levels; and (v) laws, institutional frameworks, norms and other societal practices that lead (implicitly or explicitly) to gender discrimination and/or gender inequality;
- the country context, including the country's policies, priorities, legal and regulatory framework and institutional arrangements for implementing its gender and development goals; and
- a set of gender-responsive priority policy and operational interventions that are important for poverty reduction and development effectiveness.

The CGA may be a stand-alone document or a section of another report. It may contain original analytical work or may simply refer to such work, produced by the Bank or by other agencies (government, international, academic).

Operational Policy/Bank Procedure on Gender

The developments since the mid-1990s culminated with the issuing of a new version of the existing Operational Policy (OP) as well as the introduction of a Bank Procedure (BP) on Gender and Development (OP/BP 4.20). The foundation for both the OP and the BP was indeed the Gender Strategy, especially the basic process of creating an enabling environment for country-led, country-specific strategies with the Country Gender Assessments as the basic instrument.

OPs are Bank policies that follow from the Bank's Articles of Agreement and the general conditions and polices approved by the Board of Executive Directors. They establish parameters for the conduct of operations and are focused statements of policies. The OP on Gender and Development (OP 4.20) includes a statement of philosophy, clearly linking the OP to the Bank's poverty mandate and emphasizing the need for sustainability. The OP also includes a statement of policy for all Bank assistance, detailing how the Bank will work with its clients, and a commitment to monitoring and evaluation. The new OP finally stresses the need to cross reference other relevant Bank policies, such as those on poverty reduction, investment and adjustment lending, and project supervision.

The objective of Bank Procedures (BPs) is to explain how Bank staff are to carry out the policies set out in the OPs. Hence, BPs spell out the procedures and documentation required to ensure Bank-wide consistency and quality. The BP 4.20 focuses on the procedural steps for the preparation of CGAs and lays out the minimum content of a CGA. The BP also prescribes that consultation with country stakeholders is a central feature of the CGA process. Included in the BP are also steps for integrating the CGA findings into the Bank's assistance program for a country and for monitoring and evaluation.

In conclusion, the Strategy, the Country Gender Assessments, the Operational Policy and the Bank Procedure provide a clear framework and instruments for the Bank to deal with gender issues in the context of development and poverty reduction. The internal arrangements for dealing with gender issues are examined separately below.

Gender and family issues within the World Bank

The internal treatment of gender equality was naturally perceived by the Bank as key to its credibility when discussing gender issues with developing countries in the sense of aligning preaching to practices. In 1992 the Bank commissioned an internal report (the Stern Report[31]) that provided its first action plan for recruiting, retaining, and promoting women at decision-making levels. It had no less than 33 recommendations and introduced numerical targets. For example, the ratio of women in middle level management jobs was to increase to 27 percent by 1997 (a target reached before that date) while the target to increase women in top jobs was to increase from 7 percent to 15 percent (this was met by 1997).

The report also recommended more attention to work-life issues. Many of the ideas of those days have subsequently become reality as AWS (Alternative Work Schedule),[32] part-time work options, telecommuting, and supportive services such as advice on child care, elder care, housing, education.[33]

Additional recommendations related to sexual harassment. Since 1992, the Bank has adopted strong sexual harassment policies and created a network of Anti-Harassment Advisors as well as an integrated Conflict Resolution System; and has provided guidelines on *Working with Respect in the Bank Group* to every staff member. Many of the gender issues are now rightly addressed in the broader context of diversity as many of the strategies for improving women's representation are applicable to other subgroups.

There was a follow-up to the Stern Report in 1998 (World Bank 1998b). The new report reviewed pay, promotion and performance with a view to identifying and redressing remaining gender differences among staff. It was based on econometric analysis and also a qualitative assessment undertaken by external (consulting) firms. The report noted that while differences in pay still exist, there was a marked decline in the unexplained part of salary gender differentials from about 17–25 percent in 1992 down to 6 percent in 1998. It identified that the main source of current differences is not discrimination in promotion but at the recruitment stage (grade assignment at entry and resulting salary offers).

Comparisons and evaluations

The International Finance Corporation (IFC)

Recall, the World Bank refers conventionally to two organizations: IBRD and IDA. The discussion so far referred to these two units but the role of the private arm of the Bank (IFC) is potentially increasing in the era of globalization and the greater role of the private sector. Though the Bank and IFC share the same Board of Directors, their policies are not always identical. For example, IFC does not have an operational policy on gender issues. Still, all IFC projects must comply with applicable environmental, social and disclosure policies designed to ensure that the business areas in which it invests are implemented in an environmentally, socially and financially responsible manner. The IFC's manual on public consultation (World Bank 1998a)[34] explicitly states that consulting women and being gender sensitive are key components of a successful consultation program. In terms of monitoring results, IFC focuses on areas such as job creation for females working in industry and small-to-medium enterprises; access to credit for poor and low-income women; increased access to affordable education for poor and middle-income females; and increased opportunities, advice and financing for female entrepreneurs. Thus, technically, the Bank's Gender Strategy is of limited relevance to the way IFC conducts its business. For example, IFC does not have to conduct the same kind of country-level analytical studies that the Bank (IBRD and IDA) conduct. Still, there may be areas where the Bank and IFC can collaborate with IFC, for example on issues of common interest such as female entrepreneurship or women-owned businesses.

Comparison with other multilateral and bilateral development agencies

The Bank's current approach to gender equality and its Gender Strategy compare favorably to what other multilateral and bilateral organizations do (see Table 2.2).

Table 2.2 Gender policies of multilateral donor agencies

Institution	Gender-related objective
AfDB	Increased support for functional literacy programs; elimination of gender disparity in primary and secondary education; infant and maternal mortality; one of two cross-cutting issues in four areas of focus. The focus is on women.
ADB	Improved status of women and elimination of discrimination is one of five strategic objectives. From 1998, it adopted gender mainstreaming as the key strategy to promote " gender equity," but the focus remains the improvement of the status of women with concurrence and cooperation of men.
EBRD	No gender considerations explicitly indicated.
IDB	Fuller integration of women into all stages of the development process and improvement in their socioeconomic situation through a gendered analysis.
UNDP	Gender equality and advancement of women. Focus on equality of capacities and opportunities to ensure that women and men participate equally in the development process as agents and beneficiaries.
WB	Reduced gender disparity and increased women's participation in economic development as part of overall poverty reduction strategy.

Source: World Bank (OED), 2001a: 7.

In fact, the Bank was the first multilateral donor organization to mandate consideration of impacts on women as part of project appraisal. However, other multilaterals, like the Asian Development Bank (ADB), African Development Bank (AfDB), and Inter-American Development Bank (IDB) have adopted policies and process-related goals focused on increasing economic opportunities and reducing barriers to the economic and social well-being of women. Their approaches are justified, as in the case of the Bank, on the grounds of efficiency, equity and poverty reduction.

Evaluations

The Operations Evaluation Department (OED) undertook two recent assessments in the area of gender equality: *Integrating Gender in World Bank Assistance* (World Bank 2001a) and *The Gender Dimension of Bank Assistance: An Evaluation of Results* (World Bank 2002b). Both noted progress and identified areas of improvement.

The first report examined how the Bank has performed at country level. It noted that, on the positive side, gender issues have been better integrated in the Bank's work since the 1994 policy was introduced. At regional level, some regions (such as Africa and South Asia) achieved better integration in their

Table 2.3 Gender analysis in Bank projects by sector 1988–1999 (%)

Sector group	Investment only % of projects approved with gender analysis	Investment and adjustment % of projects approved with gender analysis
Population, health and nutrition	89	88
Agriculture	56	53
Education	68	66
Water supply and sanitation	34	34
Social protection	73	74
Electric power and energy	7	7
Environment	34	34
Finance	16	12
Industry	14	13
Mining	12	17
Multisector	13	24
Public sector management	11	11
Transportation	7	7
Urban development	30	29
Oil and gas	4	4
Telecommunications	0	0
Weighted average	29	30

Source: World Bank (2001a).

country programs. The report also noted that the Bank's analytical work in these regions is becoming clearly more gender aware. Improvements in the other regions (such as East Europe and Central Asia as well as Latin America and the Caribbean) were either more recent or lacking. In the health and education sectors, two of the five sectors of focus identified in the 1994 strategy paper, the Bank has progressed well. In another sector, agriculture, the Bank has made progress, but there still remains a need for uniform treatment of critical issues such as access to and control over productive assets and services. The report concluded that there remains a long way to go in terms of implementation especially in the so-called hard sectors (see Table 2.3).

The second report examined the results of the Bank's activities during the previous decade. It addressed the extent to which the Bank helped to (a) reduce gender disparities in the education and health sectors; (b) increase the participation of women in economic activities; and (c) influence institutional changes that support the advancement of women. The evaluation was based on 12 countries and, like the 2001 report mentioned above, found satisfactory results in the education and health sector. Though the report acknowledges that causality is difficult to establish, it found weak or mixed results with respect to the other two areas (economic participation and institutional aspects). The report noted that projects tended to have better on-the-ground impacts when gender issues had been analyzed at the country and project levels, and gender-differentiated needs or impacts were recognized in project and program design.

More recently (2003) a monitoring report on the implementation of the Gender Strategy during its first year (World Bank 2003a) noted that five CGAs were prepared (in addition to the 7 CGAs already completed) and another 26 were planned. This (38 CGAs) compares to about 100 countries that are active borrowers of the Bank. While this is encouraging, the report noted that of 39 core diagnostic reports prepared since the Gender Strategy was issued only seven had integrated the gender dimension into their analyses. The situation was better (in terms of increased attention to gender issues) in terms of lending, especially in selected sectors such as education, health and social protection. The report identified as challenges the need to increase the attention to gender issues in analytical and lending activities, ability to work with partners, and the evaluations not just of inputs but of outcomes.

Needs versus rights

The objective of the Bank's gender and development policy is

> to assist member countries to reduce poverty and enhance economic growth, human well-being, and development effectiveness by addressing the gender disparities and inequalities that are barriers to development, and by assisting member countries in formulating and implementing their gender and development goals.

In other words, in the economic context within which the Bank operates it assists member countries to design gender-sensitive policies and programs to ensure that overall development efforts are directed to attain impacts that are equitable and beneficial for both men and women. Still, as an international organization, the Bank may need to go further than this as it cannot ignore key universal declarations (such as, for example, the Universal Declaration of Human Rights, 1948).

In addressing human rights issues the Bank has traditionally exercised caution.[35] In principle, the Bank's Articles of Association prohibit interference in the political affairs of its members. Also, the Bank's clients are sovereign. Finally, the Bank needs to exercise restraint in its use of conditionality. Despite its economic focus, the Bank is increasingly becoming more vocal (though more often through its officers than in official forms) about the links between the economic participation of poor people and equality in dignity and rights (Stern 2003).[36] A series of Bank publications (such as *World Development Report 2000/01*) recognize the importance of fair and inclusive institutions, empowerment, accountability, transparency and participation. The Bank supports the Millennium Declaration and the Monterrey Consensus which endorse respect for human rights as part of a multifaceted response to the development challenge. The Bank would argue that the objectives of sustainable poverty reduction, human well-being and development effectiveness underlie its operational policies, including specifically those aimed at promoting gender equity and protection of vulnerable groups, in particular, indigenous peoples and those subject to involuntary resettlement.

Two issues that need to be taken into account in assessing the Bank's approach to human rights are, first, the Bank has no means to legislate human rights obligations for its members, nor is it nor can be the world's policeman that enforces its members' human rights obligations: the Bank has neither the mandate nor the instruments to do so. Second, rights-based approaches as stated by the United Nations, "with a rights-based approach, effective action for development moves from the optional realm of charity into the mandatory realm of law with identifiable rights, obligations, claim-holders and duty-bearers" (UN 2000) are rather categorical for an organization that seeks to develop effective and efficient policies under *economic* constraints and budget *choices*. The principle of indivisibility of human rights results in the absence of guidance on how to prioritize in a resource-constrained environment which characterizes an economic organization. An unsatisfied need as a violation or abuse of human rights provides little guidance as to how to resolve a policy or resource constraint or to rectify what all may agree is an unsatisfactory situation. The generality and ambiguity of many human rights provisions present difficulties of interpretation and implementation. And many will recognize that enactment of laws alone does not ensure fair and equitable treatment of all citizens.

A more relevant issue here is whether the Bank's contributions are consistent with efforts to promote achievement of human rights. It can be argued that many of the Bank's practices are or can be supportive, albeit indirectly, of practices which are fundamental to human rights. Such practices include, first, the identification of the poor (especially with respect to particular subgroups, such as women and men, children, youth and the elderly, or particular ethnic or regional groups), second, participatory approaches to project design and implementation and third, accountability and transparency of information systems.[37]

The Bank's move (if only in rhetoric terms – as critics would put it) into the area of human rights was preceded by its in-house research. For example, it is now acknowledged that gender equality – not only in health and education, but also in voice and rights – is an important element in development (Goldin *et al.* 2003). Aside from the obvious direct benefits for women, equality in these dimensions is seen having instrumental benefits in terms of growth and poverty reduction. The Bank's cross-country research confirms that low investment in female education has been a barrier to growth in South Asia, Sub-Saharan Africa, and the Middle East and North Africa, compared with East Asia, which has closed the gender gap in education more rapidly.

Since the 1990s, the Bank has increasingly emphasized the importance of establishing the rule of law and of the state playing a role of facilitator and enabler of development. It acknowledges that increasing the efficiency of legal and judicial systems, providing greater access to justice, and reforming the public sector at large to enhance accountability and transparency can significantly contribute to the achievement of human rights. The Bank now supports judicial reform projects that strengthen good government and good governance. Such projects are not justified on the grounds of human rights *per se* but because they can enhance the effectiveness of Bank support as it is the absence of information on people's rights and means to pursue them which often prevents policies and projects from realizing their intended benefits.

Summary and conclusions

For more than half of its history the Bank has addressed women's and gender issues both in development and also in its internal organization and, since the 1990s, it started making accelerating progress in integrating gender issues into its activities. For example, between 1995 and 2000 the Bank lent more than $3.4 billion for girls' education programs, and was also the single largest lender in the world for health, nutrition and population projects, three-quarters of which contained gender-responsive actions. Attention to gender issues in various key Bank documents[38] also increased during the 1990s. Several organizational changes designed to facilitate greater attention to gender and development issues were also institutionalized, including the issuing of an Operational Policy on the gender dimension of development in 1994 and its subsequent revision (2003), the creation of a Gender and Development Board (1997), the adoption of a Gender Strategy in 2001 and the issuing of the Bank Procedure in 2003.

The Bank has been contributing to capacity-building and has been organizing conferences on diverse areas relating to gender issues such as laws and more broadly institutions. These typically cover issues such as gender equality and citizenship, women's relationship to the State, gender-based violence, how laws can provide equality of rights and access, and how institutions can create the enabling environment to enforce rights. The Bank's lending continued to be on a wide range of areas affecting gender equality such as support for artisan enterprise institutes, "women and justice" programs, community empowerment projects, water and sanitation, reducing female genital cutting, and helping poor women and girls obtain identity cards and birth certificates to enable them to "become citizens" (and, thus obtain, for example, microcredit and access to basic services). The Bank is also active in promoting gender equality through nonlending activities, including work on gender and human immunodeficiency virus/acquired immune deficiency syndrome and on emerging issues such as gender and the digital divide. A new initiative on gender and macroeconomic policy is under way that aims to identify effective actions for integrating gender into country level analysis and policy dialogue.

Though the Bank was slow to start with, it moved relatively fast in the 1990s and found itself well positioned in the new millennium. Engendering development is at least being discussed and (to an extent still to be assessed) mainstreamed in the Bank's approach and operations. Internally, there have been significant improvements in the employment conditions and prospects of female staff at all levels as well as their partners and families. And more recently the Bank became fully committed to the attainment of the Millennium Development Goals (World Bank 2003b).[39]

The Bank has now an analytical understanding that authorizes it to get involved with gender issues through economic justifications (instead of human rights ones). It has a clear Gender Strategy and also the operational tools to put theory into practice. As a broad development institution (rather than a specialized one – such as UNIFEM) the Bank would never be able to focus 100 percent on a specific issue. This means that it will always be debatable whether dedicating 30 percent or 60 percent of its activities to gender issues would constitute little or enough attention.[40]

At the broadest level, the Bank's evolution and current state is effectively the result of an organization that has a mission related to a difficult (if not an unsolvable, in some specific time horizon) problem, that is, development and poverty reduction. In short, the Bank does not have a narrow technical mission. Approaches to development and poverty are characterized by analytical uncertainty and easily dominated by ideological or interest-based disagreements about goals, priorities and causation. Although in the 1980s the Bank adopted with little reservation the recipes of supply-side economics, this was not the case before and surely things are different today. Less easy to agree is whether the change has been substantial and whether progress has been too little too late.

Some or many may argue that the 1980s were a lost decade for the Bank. Its belief that markets in *developing* countries would respond *fast and efficiently* to structural adjustment did not materialize. The collapse of the planned economies did not help either as it lead towards the belief that since one economic system was proven wrong, its theoretical alternative (that of unfettered markets) must be right. Whether it was due to the "50 Years Is Enough" campaign or the Bank's new president in 1995 or the financial crises of the late-1990s, the Bank today is a different institution than it was during the post-McNamara era till sometime in the 1990s. Different does not necessarily mean better and the point here is that, by focusing on the aggregate macroeconomic picture, women and development got the short stick from the Bank in the 1980s and this continued for sometime into the 1990s.

The more recent treatment of gender issues at the Bank does not, however, support the view that the Bank is now gender blind. This can improve further somewhat paradoxically because of the hegemonic tendencies of some of the Bank's stakeholders (Wade 2001). For example, the US Executive Director at the Bank in the 1990s did push hard for augmenting the Bank's gender agenda.

The first year's implementation report of the Gender Strategy concluded

> despite the progress to date in gender mainstreaming, the Bank's effectiveness can be improved by paying more systematic and widespread attention to gender issues in the context of our poverty reduction mandate. The opportunities for improving the development impact of the Bank's work through gender mainstreaming include making Bank interventions more responsive to country gender conditions and commitments, making these

interventions more strategic, and improving the alignment of Bank policies, processes, and resources to support such interventions.

In conclusion, if the economist's answer is "the glass is twice as big as it ought to be," then perhaps the Bank is too small to address all developmental issues. But despite past failures (partly due to reasons of biased ideology or hegemonic interferences), the Bank seems to have come a long way on gender issues. Again from an economist's perspective "on the other hand, the Bank has some way to go."

Acknowledgments

The author would like to thank Drucilla Barker, Edith Kuiper, Karen Mason, Susan Razzaz and Haneen Sayed for useful comments on an earlier draft. Remaining omissions and errors are of the author.

Notes

1   The Bank provides approximately $20 billion/year in development assistance against another $40–50 billion provided by other multilaterals and bilaterals. This total of $60–70 billion of official aid is only a fraction of private flows which can be more than five times the amount transferred through official aid in a typical year.
2   The Bank has 184 members.
3   Jim Wolfensohn was then the Bank's president. In July 2005 he was succeeded by Paul Wolfowitz, former US deputy defense secretary in the George Bush administration.
4   The Bank and the International Monetary Fund (established at the same time) constitute the Bretton Woods institutions and can be viewed as the crowning achievement of the English economist John Maynard Keynes. Another, lesser known protagonist was the American Harry Dexter White who later became a victim of Senator Joseph McCarthy's anti-communist campaign.
5   Though the initial emphasis of the Bank was on Europe, countries in other regions were also getting significant support, for example, Japan and India. By 1960 the Bank had lent $1.4 billion to eight Asian member countries out of 13 total members. The early years reflected the Bank's worldwide emphasis on infrastructure projects.
6   IFC is the private arm of the Bank and cofinances private undertakings and provides services to the private sector in developing countries.
7   To become a member of the Bank a country must first join the International Monetary Fund (IMF). Membership in IDA, IFC and MIGA are conditional on membership in IBRD.
8   It is a little known fact that the Bank made a loan equivalent to $40 million to Italy to build an atomic power plant in 1959. There were no protests at the time.
9   OED is the evaluation unit at the Bank, independent of management and reports directly to the Board of Executive Directors. It evaluates outcomes by considering (a) the relevance of the intervention's objectives in relation to country needs and institutional priorities; (b) the efficacy of the intervention – that is, the extent to which the developmental objectives have been or are expected to be achieved; (c) the efficiency of the intervention – that is, the extent to which the objectives have been or are expected to be achieved, using the minimum resources. In addition, the benchmark for a satisfactory investment project is an economic rate of return of

at least 10 percent. Additional consideration is given to sustainability of benefits over time and the institutional development impact on the ability of a country to make more efficient, equitable and sustainable use of its human, financial and natural resources.

10 The study noted the progress overall during this period which included global gains of life expectancy at birth in developing countries by 20 years, the drop in adult illiteracy by nearly half (from 47 percent to 25 percent), and the decline of the number of people living in abject poverty (defined as living on less than $1 a day) after rising through most of the nineteenth and twentieth centuries. The study noted, however, that development assistance has not been always fully effective and the development process has been uneven. For example, Africa as a region saw no increase in its overall per capita income between 1965 and 1999, AIDS reversed gains in social indicators, and many of the transition economies of Eastern Europe and Central Asia experienced sharp rises in poverty in the 1990s.

11 This refers to a package of policy prescriptions attributed to the World Bank and IMF and includes fiscal discipline, reorientation of public expenditures, tax reforms, interest rates liberalization, competitive exchange rates, trade liberalization, openness to foreign direct investment, privatization, deregulation and securing property rights.

12 "Trickle down" (or Trickle Down Economics – TDE) refers to the belief that once free market policies are introduced at the macro level, there will be significant and quick beneficial effects on the whole economy (especially in terms of employment creation and improvements in the social sectors).

13 *World Development Reports* are annual and constitute the flagship publication of the Bank. They vary in the subjects they cover (for example, poverty, the role of the state, labor or infrastructure).

14 McNamara left the Bank in 1981 having maintained the position that the Bank should remain independent of the US Government.

15 Subsequent *World Development Reports* started presenting a more balanced view on the appropriate role for the state in human development, infrastructure and began undertaking some excursions into the areas of political economy.

16 They go on to identify the fact that this is more the result of insufficient country ownership and insufficient attention to social dimensions.

17 As of 2003, 26 countries are receiving debt relief projected to amount to US$40 billion over time. With other forms of debt relief, the HIPC Initiative will cut by two-thirds the external debt in these countries, lowering their indebtedness to levels well below the average for developing countries overall.

18 Examples of such partnerships are: with the World Wildlife Fund to protect forests; with the Food and Agriculture Organization (FAO) and the United Nations Development Programme (UNDP) to sponsor the renowned Consultative Group on International Agricultural Research; with the Consultative Group to Assist the Poorest (CGAP) which aims to improve the capacity of microfinance institutions to deliver financial services to the poorest people; with UNICEF and ILO in the area of child labor; with WHO, UNAIDS and the Global Fund for AIDS, Tuberculosis and Malaria (GFATM); or with partnerships which are formed around specific initiatives such as the one to fight river blindness which has successfully prevented more than 600,000 cases of blindness, has opened 25 million hectares to cultivation, and annually treats more than 22 million people for the disease.

19 The Bank has launched (since 1996) more than 600 anticorruption programs and governance initiatives in nearly 100 client countries and currently works in 40 conflict-affected countries supporting international efforts to assist war-torn populations, resume development and prevent relapse into violence.

20 The Bank defines "gender" as a "theme," not a sector. A theme is cross-sectoral and applies to all sectors, and this is obviously the right way of approaching the issues concerned.

21 The Bank subsequently started a process of converting Operational Manual Statements to Operational Policy and Bank Procedures statements. This process resulted in richer language on the economic, financial, social and institutional analysis of investment projects.

22 However, OMS 2.20 was never clear in its intent as (a) some argued that gender analysis is required in projects where it is generally acknowledged that women are a particularly important group of project participants or beneficiaries and (b) others have argued that an analysis is required in all projects to determine when women are important participants or beneficiaries. Still, in the mid-1990s (and till the onset of the new millennium) the Bank's gender and development policy was embodied in the aforesaid document plus a policy paper, *Enhancing Women's Participation in Economic Development* (World Bank 1994a) and Operational Policy 4.20 (The Gender Dimension of Development).

23 *World Development*, Vol. 23, No. 11, November (1995).

24 It would be wrong, though, to assume that the Bank was idle on gender analysis before the mid-1990s. For example, Elson (1995) rightly criticized the Bank for applying gender-blind structural adjustment programs in the 1980s but did not fail to note the significant analytical work the Bank or researchers sponsored by the Bank were carrying out in key areas for gender and development (such as agriculture: see Collier (1990, 1994) or Moock (1976)) or the "pioneering study by Tzannatos (1992) [that] demonstrated that if gender discrimination patterns of occupation and pay were eliminated, total output, as well as women's income, could increase significantly)" (Elson 1995: 1857).

25 Some of the theoretical underpinnings of the report can be found in Tzannatos (1999).

26 This research report was supported in part by the governments of Norway and the Netherlands.

27 It should be recognized that though education does not guarantee rights or power, it is a critical condition for empowering women.

28 Greater gender equality and a less rigid or extreme gender-based division of labor is expected to promote growth by raising the total level of productive capital in the society, and specifically by increasing *female* productive capital – capital that has important pro-growth effects.

29 There is a lively debate whether policies (including legislation) should reinforce/ legitimize existing trends or lead to new directions.

30 The report went further to specify accountabilities, funding, staffing, tools, capacity-building and partnerships for the successful implementation of the strategy.

31 Named after Ernie Stern, a Managing Director at the Bank.

32 Flexibility over weekly working hours.

33 Since 2002, the Bank has extended conventional family benefits to same sex partners. Ironically, despite its mission to support the poor in developing countries, the equal treatment of same sex partners for benefit purposes has the practical implication that the additional benefits the Bank will have to pay will most likely accrue almost exclusively to US nationals as foreigners have to be heterosexual spouses to get a visa from the US authorities.

34 See also http://www.ifc.org/enviro/Publications/Practice/practice.htm.

35 The Bank does not use the human rights record of its client countries to determine its assistance to them, although the quality of policies and institutions is used to determine the level of IDA assistance the poorest countries receive.

36 Nicholas Stern was the Chief Economist of the World Bank from 2000 to 2003.

37 For example, in the area of core labor standards where many Bank members have signed declarations and research can show that there can be positive economic effects (Aidt and Tzannatos 2002), the Bank encourages the promotion of good practice associated with human rights such as freedom of association.

38 Such as the Country Assistance Strategies (CASs) which outline the Bank's program in member countries.
39 This document reiterates the strong linkages between gender equality and all the MDGs and argues that working for gender equality offers a compelling, win-win approach for policy-makers and planners towards attaining and implementing the goals in areas such as poverty, education, health, nutrition and the environment. It also provides examples of how gender equality can be integrated into MDG policies and interventions. It concludes with a call to integrate gender into MDG policies and interventions especially in the areas of poverty, education, health and nutrition, and the environment.
40 Of course, if gender is defined not as a sector but as a (cross-cutting) theme, then nothing less than 100 percent can be satisfactory, and the issue then becomes one of both substance and measurement.

References

Aidt, T. and Z. Tzannatos (2002) *Unions and Collective Bargaining: Economic Effects in a Global Environment*, Washington, DC: World Bank.

Benería, L. (1995) "Toward a Greater Integration of Gender in Economics," *World Development*, 23(11): 1839–50.

Boserup, E. (1970) *Women's Role in Economic Development*, London: Gower.

Çagatay, N., D. Elson and C. Grown (1995) "Introduction" (to special issue on Gender, Adjustment and Macroeconomics), *World Development* 23(11): 1827–38.

Collier, P. (1990) "The Impact of Adjustment on Women," in *World Bank Analysis Plan for Understanding the Social Dimensions of Adjustment*, World Bank, SDA Unit, Africa Region.

—— (1994) "Gender Aspects of Labor Allocation During Structural Adjustment – A Theoretical Framework and the Africa Experience," in S. Horton, R. Kanbur and D. Mazumdar (eds), *Labor Markets in an Era of Adjustment*, Vol. 1, Washington, DC: World Bank.

Cornia, G., R. Jolly and F. Stewart (eds) (1987) *Adjustment with a Human Face*, Oxford and New York: Clarendon Press.

Edwards, S. (1997) "Trade Liberalization Reforms and the World Bank," *American Economic Review*, 87(2), Papers and Proceedings of the Hundred and Fourth Annual Meeting of the American Economic Association, May: 43–8.

Elson, D. (1995) "Gender Awareness in Modelling Structural Adjustment," *World Development*, 23(11): 1851–68.

Goldin, I., H.R. Rogers and Nicholas Stern (2003) *The Role and Effectiveness of Development Assistance Lessons from World Bank Experience*, Washington, DC: The World Bank (A Research Paper from the Development Economics Vice Presidency of the World Bank).

Kapur, D., J. Lewis and R. Webb (eds) (1997) *The World Bank: Its First Half Century*, Washington, DC: Brookings Institution Press.

Little, I.M.D. and J.A. Mirrless (1991) "Project Appraisal and Planning Twenty Years On," in *Proceedings of the World Bank Annual Conference on Development Economics*, Washington, DC: World Bank: 351–82.

Ministry of Foreign Affairs (Netherlands) (2003) *Results of International Debt Relief 1990–1999*, Policy and Operations Evaluation Department, May.

Moock, P. (1976) "The Efficiency of Women as Farm Managers: Kenya," *American Journal of Agricultural Economics*, 58: 831–5.

Stern, N. and F. Ferreira (1997) "The World Bank as an Intellectual Actor," in D. Kapur, J. Lewis and R. Webb (eds), *The World Bank: Its First Half Century*, Washington, DC: Brookings Institution Press: 523–609.

Stern, Nicholas (2003) "Development and Human Rights," Address to Panel at the LSE Workshop, Washington, DC, March 5.

Tzannatos, Z. (1992), "Potential Gains from the Elimination of Labor Market Differentials," in *Women's Employment and Pay In Latin America, Part I: Overview and Methodology*, Regional Studies Program Report No. 10, Washington, DC: World Bank.

—— (1999) "Women and Labor Market Changes in the Global Economy: Growth Helps, Inequalities Hurt and Public Policy Matters," *World Development*, 27(3): 551–69.

UN (2000) *The United Nations System and Human Rights: Guidelines and Information for the Resident Coordinator System*, New York: United Nations Administrative Committee on Coordination (ACC), March.

UNDP (1990) *Human Development Report*, New York.

Wade, R. (2000) "US Hegemony and the World Bank: Stiglitz's Firing and Kanbur's Resignation," mimeo.

—— (2001) "The US Role in the Malaise at the World Bank: Get Up Gulliver!" paper presented at a panel on International Institutions and North/South Conflict, American Political Science Association Annual Meetings, San Francisco, August 28–30.

Wolfensohn, J.D. (2004) Address at the Shanghai Conference on Scaling Up Poverty Reduction. Shangai: People's Republic of China, May 26.

World Bank (1980) *World Development Report on Poverty*, New York: Oxford University Press.

—— (1984) *Operational Manual Statement 2.20*, Washington, DC: World Bank.

—— (1990) *World Development Report on Poverty*, New York: Oxford University Press.

—— (1992a) *The Stern Report (Excellence Through Equality: An Increased Role for Women in the World Bank. A Report of the Advisory Group on Higher-Level Women's Issues*, April, Washington, DC: World Bank.

—— (1992b) *The Wapentians Report* (Effective Implementation: Key to Development Impact), Washington, DC: World Bank.

—— (1994a) *Enhancing Women's Participation in Economic Development: A World Bank Policy Paper*, Washington, DC: World Bank.

—— (1994b) *Operational Policy 4.20*, Washington, DC: World Bank.

—— (1995a) *Toward Gender Equality: The Role of Public Policy*, Washington, DC: World Bank.

—— (1995b) *Advancing Gender Equality: From Concept to Action*, Washington, DC: World Bank.

—— (1998a) *Doing Better Business Through Effective Public Consultation and Disclosure: A Good Practice Manual*, Washington, DC: International Finance Corporation.

—— (1998b) *Assessing Bias in Pay and Grade at the World Bank*, Development Research Group, Washington, DC: World Bank.

—— (2000) *Advancing Gender Equality: World Bank Action Since Beijing*, Washington, DC: World Bank.

—— (2001a) *Integrating Gender in World Bank's Assistance*. Operations Evaluation Department, Washington, DC: World Bank.

—— (2001b) *2000/2001 World Development Report: Attacking Poverty*, New York: Oxford University Press.

—— (2001c) *Engendering Development: Through Equality in Rights, Resources, and Voice*, Washington, DC: World Bank.

—— (2001d) *Integrating Gender into the World Bank's Work: A Strategy for Action*, Washington, DC: World Bank.

—— (2002a) *The Role and Effectiveness of Development Assistance: Lessons from World Bank Experience*, Washington, DC: World Bank (OED).

—— (2002b) *The Gender Dimension of Bank Assistance: An Evaluation of Results*, Washington DC: The World Bank (OED).

—— (2003a) *Implementation of the Gender Mainstreaming Strategy: First Annual Monitoring Report*, Washington, DC: World Bank.

—— (2003b) *Gender Equality and the Millennium Development Goals*, Washington, DC: World Bank.

—— (2003c) *Operational Policy 4.20* (revised), Washington, DC: World Bank.

—— (2003d) *Bank Procedure 4.20*, Washington, DC: World Bank.

3 An assessment of efforts to promote gender equality at the World Bank

Carolyn M. Long

Introduction

During the past 25 years, donor agencies and other development organizations have worked to promote gender equality in their programs with varying degrees of commitment and success. As time has gone by, research and actual experience have shown that gender equality is *essential* to development effectiveness. In order for countries to grow and prosper, all human resources must be maximized. If left unaddressed, gender disparities undermine otherwise well-conceived policies and programs.

One of the most important public donor agencies is the World Bank. Its record thus far in promoting and institutionalizing gender equality in its policy and operational initiatives has been quite unsatisfactory. However, by the Bank's own admission, the Fourth World Conference on Women held in Beijing in 1995, and, in particular, NGO advocacy efforts which were launched there, motivated the Bank to increase its efforts to promote gender equality within its initiatives (World Bank 2000: 2). Since 2001, the World Bank has taken three important steps to increase its commitment to gender equality. These are:

1   Public release in 2001 of a critical evaluation of the Bank's efforts to promote gender equality during the previous four years. The evaluation was carried out by the Operations Evaluation Department (OED), an internal but autonomous part of the Bank.
2   Publication of a major policy research report which documents the pervasiveness of gender discrimination and defines a three-part strategy to promote gender equality. *Engendering Development: Through Gender Equality in Rights, Resources, and Voice* (2001a) proposes a strategy to reform institutions to establish equal rights and opportunities for women and men; to foster economic development to strengthen incentives for more equal resources and participation; and to take active measures to redress persistent disparities in command over resources and political voice.
3   Adoption by Bank management and endorsement by its board of Executive Directors of a new gender mainstreaming strategy, a central component of which is a Country Gender Assessment (CGA) to be prepared for all active

borrowing countries. The results of these assessments will be used in dialogue with borrower governments to identify priority gender-responsive policies and interventions in high-impact sectors important for poverty reduction and economic growth.

Whether these steps will result in significant progress by the Bank in promoting gender equality remains to be seen. To fully understand these recent steps, it is important to place them within the historical context of the Bank's efforts to incorporate a focus on gender equality in its operations. This chapter provides a brief history of steps taken by the Bank to promote attention to gender equality in policies and projects, an assessment of how well the organization has done in these activities thus far, current thinking at the organization and a description of advocacy efforts carried out by women's organizations and other external actors. The chapter also includes views of a number of Southern and Northern women's organizations on gender advocacy at the Bank and what actions they think are essential in order to promote gender equality in Bank-funded initiatives.

Where gender staff is situated in the World Bank

In 1997, the most recent reorganization of the Bank created a matrix organization. As of November, 2003, there were four managing directors, six regions and six networks, each headed by a vice president. These networks are Poverty Reduction and Economic Management (PREM), Environmentally and Socially Sustainable Development (ESSD), Human Development (HD), Financial Sector (FSI), Operations Policy and Country Services (OPCS), and Private Sector Development and Infrastructure (PSI). The role of the networks is to provide corporate and human resources functions, knowledge management, quality control and technical assistance to the regions.

The PREM network houses the Gender and Development Unit (also called the "anchor") which has 14 staff members. The PREM network has a Gender and Development Board (a "sector" board) chaired by the Unit's director. Members of the board currently include representatives from each region as well as several sectors and networks across the Bank. Examples of sectors and networks represented in the Gender and Development Board include the World Bank Institute, the legal department, transport, human development, social development and human resources.

The sector board functions as a board of directors for the gender anchor, and as such, determines the overall approach to be taken to promote gender concerns (subject to approval by management and the Executive Directors (EDs)). Unlike most sector boards which are made up of managers with budgets, the Gender Sector Board's members are primarily gender specialists who are not managers and, in most instances, have no budgets.

Each region has a gender coordinator. The effectiveness of these specialists varies considerably, depending on their particular approaches to their task and their ability to influence their regions or to raise money from donor trust funds.

Philosophical approach to gender issues at the World Bank

First and foremost, gender issues at the World Bank are analyzed *within* the organization's prevailing paradigm of economic reform and globalization. Although in recent years, social inclusion, empowerment and good governance have come to be seen by the Bank as essential elements of development, the core of the paradigm continues to be economic reform and globalization. Bank staff members striving to promote gender equality do not question whether this emphasis, itself, contributes to the continuing marginalization and impoverishment of women in their societies.

Within the Bank's economic paradigm, gender equality is promoted primarily through an "economic efficiency" argument, i.e. that attention to gender concerns is important so as to develop better projects and policies in order to achieve economic growth and reduce poverty. A different philosophical approach – which feminists around the world espouse – is that women have the right to equality, and they should be assisted in standing up for their rights *vis-à-vis* their husbands and families, communities, local government and the state. This second argument is not voiced by many in the Bank because it implies that women's rights are human rights. The Articles of Agreement that established the Bank specify that the organization is not to engage in politics. Therefore, historically, the Bank has not taken stands on human rights issues but, under pressure from civil society groups and UN organizations, it is beginning to consider a human rights approach. The Bank's recently completed policy research report (World Bank 2001a) should help advance the debate in the direction of gender equality as a woman's right. For now, gender specialists in both the anchor and the regions still primarily use the efficiency argument and see their task being to win the "hearts and minds" of Bank staff regarding the importance of gender concerns.

Many, perhaps even most, staffers interpret the Bank's gender policy as representing a Women in Development (WID) rather than a gender-analysis approach. A WID strategy involves efforts to incorporate or include women and their concerns in development initiatives. A gender-analysis development approach (GAD) examines both women's and men's roles to determine how they contribute to development, the constraints each faces in striving to be productive members of society, and appropriate interventions to enable each to achieve a higher level of well-being. At the Bank, the WID approach remained dominant. This may explain partly why girls' education is an area where the Bank has vastly increased its investments over the past several years. Clearly, the Bank increased its investments as a response to research evidence showing the great benefits of closing the gender gap in school. But as a staff person noted, "The Bank seems to have done very well in girls' education because it didn't threaten anyone."

Bank staffers may also be more comfortable with a WID approach in terms of their interactions with borrower governments since the Bank maintains that it cannot impose actions on governments. However, as signatories to the 1995

Beijing Platform for Action from the Fourth World Conference on Women, governments have already espoused gender equality. By promoting attention to concerns of gender equality, Bank staff would simply be encouraging governments to implement these commitments.

Brief history of promotion of gender equality at the World Bank

In 1977, the Bank appointed a Women in Development Advisor and in 1986, established a WID Unit. According to a 1996 joint analysis of Bank efforts toward gender equality done by the International Center for Research on Women and the Overseas Development Council, "Serious momentum in the Bank began in the mid-1980s." However, the report also states

> The Bank has done significantly more on behalf of women as mothers than as workers . . . There is in the Bank an intellectual consensus surrounding the importance of investing in women in the social sectors that does not exist with regard to women's roles in economic development.
>
> (Buvinic *et al.* 1996: 2)

In 1994, four years after the Bank adopted poverty reduction as its overall mission, the Bank's board endorsed the first gender policy paper from which the Operational Policy statement on the gender dimension of development (Operational Policy 4.20) was derived. The Bank's policy was focused operationally on five sectors (agriculture, education, health, financial services and labor) and did not – and still does not – require that all investment and structural adjustment programs address gender issues. It is important to note that structural adjustment programs – representing at least one-third of total Bank commitments – were not included under Operational Policy 4.20.

After the arrival of James Wolfensohn as Bank president in 1995, and his statements of support for gender integration into Bank work – including his attendance at the Fourth World Conference on Women in 1995 – the Bank began to increase its emphasis on the promotion of gender equality. Persuaded by the importance of girls' education for advances in family health and well-being, the Bank has lent approximately US$5.3 billion for girls' education since the Beijing conference (Mason 2002). In the areas of health, population and nutrition, the Bank is now the largest provider of external funds for such programs in low and middle-income countries. Since Beijing, two-thirds of these loans have included gender-related goals. In terms of the future, a report prepared by the Bank in early 2000 for the Beijing Plus Five meeting reinforces the Bank's overall commitment to gender equality, at least rhetorically, when it says

> Recently the Bank has renewed its focus on poverty reduction as its primary mission and adopted a broad definition of poverty that includes empowerment, opportunity, and security as well as income as necessary to the fight

to end poverty. These changes have set the stage for the Bank to sharpen its focus on gender equality.

(World Bank 2000: vi)

Assessment of progress on gender equality at the World Bank through 2000

Mainstreaming a focus on gender issues

According to the *Evaluation of the Gender Dimensions of World Bank Assistance's Phase I Report* (World Bank 2001b), prepared by the OED and reviewed by the Bank's Executive Directors in October, 2001, three basic steps are necessary to successfully mainstream a focus on gender issues in any institution. These include clear instructions to staff, measures to institutionalize and operationalize the policy, and monitoring and evaluating the policy and its implementation (World Bank 2001b: 29).

Measured against these criteria, the Bank still has a great deal to do to systematically integrate gender concerns into its initiatives. In the OED evaluation, the following reasons are given for such limited progress:

- The 1994 gender policy is seen as poorly understood and open to wide interpretation by Bank staff, even among staff who work on gender issues;
- There have been no clear plans set in place to implement the gender mainstreaming strategy;
- There are no effective systems in place to institutionalize the policy;
- Resources for gender mainstreaming have been inadequate;
- No time-bound benchmarks were set to measure the degree of mainstreaming nor has implementation of the strategy been rigorously monitored;
- There aren't incentives for staff to integrate gender issues, nor are there mechanisms in place to determine accountability;
- The Bank hasn't built the necessary capacity among its staff to mainstream gender issues (World Bank 2001b: 5).

These very same issues were noted in OED's evaluation of gender dimensions of Bank assistance done in 1997, an indication of little, if any progress on mainstreaming in recent years![2]

The Bank's gender policy

As an operational policy, the gender policy is required to be followed by staff. However, because the 1994 policy was vague, it was open to wide interpretation, and could be safely ignored by staff without consequence. The gender policy could be contrasted with "safeguard" policies, a group of ten individual polices which cover such issues as environmental assessment and protection, involuntary resettlement, indigenous peoples and dam safety. Bank Procedures (which specify procedures and documentation required for Bank-wide consistency and quality) and Good Practices (statements containing advice and guidance on policy implementation based on experience) are both prepared for safeguard policies but were not for the 1994 gender policy. The absence of these further undermined the policy's effectiveness since the Bank Procedures provide the framework and detailed requirements of a policy which then can be monitored for compliance.

Historically, even in cases where staff has genuinely wanted to pay attention to gender equality in projects and policy formulation, such efforts have been *dependent* on approvals by country directors or project task team leaders for funding. Since the reorganization in 1996, country directors have controlled the budgets for their country programs. It has been only when these directors agreed to specific requests that gender-related activities have been funded. This has been a major impediment to gender mainstreaming. Beyond one's own interest, there have been no incentives for including gender-related activities or sanctions for not doing so. Indeed, trust funds provided by donors (e.g. the Norwegians and the Dutch) have financed at least a portion of gender-related work done by the Bank over many years.

Gender issues in Bank-funded projects

Given the Bank's limited monitoring of its own work to incorporate gender issues into its initiatives, it's difficult to give an accurate portrayal of the extent of mainstreaming. The data that exists indicates the following.

The Bank's published reports include these results:

- From 1965 to 1985: less than 10 percent of Bank-funded projects included specific gender-related actions.
- From 1988 to 1994: the percentage increased to 30 percent, with the strongest efforts made in improvements to women's health and education, and to increase their options in agriculture.
- As of 2000: the percentage of projects including some consideration of gender issues in their design had almost doubled since 1995, climbing to more than 40 percent of all Bank projects.
- The percentage of projects that finance gender-related activities or support policy changes designed to reduce gender inequalities averaged 26 percent in 1995–99 (World Bank 2001b: 9).

Although these statistics show a slow, steady progression, internal Bank evaluations reveal a somewhat different story. The most recent evaluation by OED, completed in late 2000, indicates:

- Between 1988 and 1999, only 38 percent of the Bank's investment projects have any meaningful reference to gender issues;
- Less than 28 percent of these projects included gender action plans or components;

- At least 60 percent of all projects didn't explicitly consider gender issues in a meaningful way during preparation;
- Less than 15 percent of projects used gender disaggregated data in preparation (World Bank 2001b: 17).

Women's participation in policy formulation

Starting in 1997, NGOs around the world began an effort to promote participation of civil society organizations in the formulation of the Bank's Country Assistance Strategy (CAS) in borrower countries. As part of this larger effort, Southern women's organizations began to be invited to meetings held by the Bank. The OED evaluation found that all CASs reviewed which were prepared after 1997 were rated satisfactory as regards gender awareness. However, the evaluation states "even in CASs with good gender analysis, the link with recommendations is weak" (World Bank 2001b: 24).

NGOs have done extensive work to promote systematic and genuine participation of civil society in formulation of the CAS, and the Bank has developed guidelines for staff members to promote such involvement. Nevertheless, NGOs are still not involved systematically in the formulation of the CAS. The more common experience is that NGOs are consulted, and their views may or may not be taken into consideration when the CAS is finalized. Bank systems and procedures that ensure that real participation happens should be enforced more strongly and need to guarantee that women's organizations are always included.

The Poverty Reduction Strategy process, launched in 1999 by the World Bank and the International Monetary Fund (IMF), requires governments to carry out a participatory process with civil society and other stakeholders involved in its formulation. However, according to available reports, gender concerns have been largely overlooked in the first 33 interim Poverty Reduction Strategy Papers (PRSPs) and while certain gender issues were addressed for the first time in some of the first nine final PRSPs completed in November, 2001, they were not treated in the depth necessary (World Bank 2002). One exception is Rwanda whose PRSP does mainstream gender issues with very few exceptions and treats gender concerns in some depth (Zuckerman 2002: 10).

The promotion of gender equality in Bank project and policy initiatives has been largely dependent on individual initiative by gender specialists working in the Bank's regional offices and in the gender "anchor." Therefore, success in integration of gender concerns into projects and policy formulation varies considerably by region, depending on the particular gender specialist, the regional vice president, the regional chief economist and the individual country directors and their willingness, or lack thereof, to promote gender equality.

The Latin America and Caribbean region is considered by many to have been successful in its approach to gender mainstreaming in recent years, largely due to the efforts of the regional gender specialist there until 2002.[3] She defined her work as providing services to task managers based on an efficiency model. She believed that the majority of task team leaders were willing to incorporate gender concerns in their projects if they were given the proper help. She raised money from donor trust funds to underwrite her work and had good results in having gender issues addressed in project formulation and design. She also identified implementation constraints with clients. Because very little technical assistance is provided to borrowers during the implementation phase of projects, she piloted a technical assistance (TA) facility in Ecuador with a gender specialist available to coordinate assistance to projects in several countries. The coordinator identified providers of TA (either consultants or NGOs) in the countries them-selves. When the TA facility was first set up, the regional gender specialist sent an e-mail to 11 Bank task team leaders to ascertain their interest in using it. Nine responded positively within a week (Correia 2001).

According to some Bank staff members, successful work in gender main-streaming is also being done in other regions. However, in Europe and Central Asia, the gender coordinator post remained vacant for well over a year before being filled in 2002, and task team leaders in Africa express little interest in promoting gender equality.

Current thinking and action on promotion of gender equality at the World Bank

Specific work being carried out in the Bank at present is encouraging. The policy research report noted on page 40, this volume, which was completed in 2001, makes the case as to why gender equality must be viewed as an integral part of development initiatives that aim to reduce poverty and encourage economic growth. Other research done earlier by the Bank within the context of the Special Program of Assistance to Africa shows the linkages between gender inequality, growth and poverty and concludes that reducing gender-based asset inequality increases growth, efficiency and welfare (Blackden and Bhanu 1998: 2).

Undoubtedly the most important decision taken in recent years regarding gender equality was the Bank Board's endorsement on September 18, 2001 of a new gender mainstreaming strategy. Under development for much of the previous year, the new strategy has as its centerpiece a Country Gender Assessment (CGA) to be completed in all active borrowing countries. The CGAs are based on analysis and inclusive consultations at the country level and identify gender-responsive policy and operational interventions important for poverty reduction, economic growth and sustainable development.

The Bank's Gender and Development Board developed the new strategy which was written by a team headed by the Director of Gender and Development. Consultations held during the strategy's development in the six regions where the Bank works included civil society groups and government officials, and informal discussions were held with bilateral and multilateral donors. The External Gender Consultative Group (see page 49, this volume) commented on several drafts.

The gender mainstreaming strategy is being made operational through a basic three-step process:

1   Prepare, for each country in which the Bank has an active lending program, a periodic Country Gender Assessment analyzing the gender dimensions of development across sectors and identifying the gender-responsive actions that are important for poverty reduction, economic growth, human well-being and development effectiveness, and use it to inform the Bank's country assistance program;

2   Develop and implement, as part of the Country Assistance Program, priority policy and operational interventions (if any) that respond to the CGA; and

3   Monitor the implementation and results of these policy and operational interventions (World Bank 2002: 18).

Expectations are that, based on the diagnosis carried out through the CGA, a gender dimension will be integrated into relevant analytical work and lending instruments. For example, this would include analytical work in high-priority sectors and social impact analysis associated with adjustment lending, including Poverty Reduction Support Credits, among others.

An important part of the strategy has been the revision of the Bank's gender policy, *Operational Policy 4.20* (see page 43, this volume). In March, 2003, the Bank's board approved the new "Gender and Development" Operational Policy (OP 4.20).

In terms of accountability, regional vice presidents are expected to submit annual gender mainstreaming plans and to prepare year-end reports outlining fulfillment of these plans. In October, 2002 the Gender and Development anchor completed preparation of a new monitoring and evaluation system to track and evaluate implementation of the strategy in Bank work.

The new gender mainstreaming strategy, with its emphasis on Country Gender Assessments, represents a new level of seriousness in how the Bank is to examine gender status and gender disparities in specific countries. Whether the assessments will result in any significant increase in incorporation of gender-responsive actions into policy and operational interventions remains to be seen. The strategy states that while the process should be led by the specific countries, the Bank will play a supportive and proactive role.

The mainstreaming strategy has been adopted at a time when traditional pressures on staff remain, i.e. to formulate, prepare and bring loan proposals to the EDs for approval and to get money disbursed to borrowers. While personnel evaluations have been changed somewhat in the recent past to encourage team-work and a client orientation, staff are still rewarded primarily for getting loans approved. There are no specific incentives offered to encourage Bank staff to embrace this strategy other than the research evidence stated earlier in this report. As noted, accountability for implementation of the strategy is to be through the annual plans and reports of the regional vice presidencies. However, adherence in the past to accountability mechanisms for gender, participation and other social issues has been quite unsatisfactory. There is even some difficulty achieving compliance with the safeguard policies which are considered absolutely mandatory. Therefore, successful mainstreaming will depend in large measure on the ability of gender advocates within the Bank to persuade their colleagues to embrace this plan and on the commitment of the country directors and regional vice presidents to ensure implementation. External monitoring of the strategy's implementation by gender advocates is essential, both at headquarters and in borrower countries.

As regards the board of the Bank, some progress has been made regarding attention to gender. At the present time, those countries whose Executive Directors are most attentive to gender concerns are the Netherlands, the Nordic countries, Germany, the United Kingdom, France and Canada. While in the past, there was a definite split between North and South regarding support for gender equality, the situation among the Southern EDs is becoming more encouraging, with support having been expressed by at least a few of the EDs from borrower countries.

Bank mechanisms for expanded consultation on gender issues

Since the 1995 Fourth World Conference on Women in Beijing, the Bank has created two important mechanisms to increase consultation with gender specialists and women's organizations around the world.

External Gender Consultative Group

In 1996, President Wolfensohn created the External Gender Consultative Group, composed of 14 gender specialists from around the world. Its purpose is to assist the World Bank in the design and implementation of its gender policies, and to help strengthen dialogue on gender-related issues between the Bank, its partners and interested sectors of civil society. The members of the EGCG were chosen by the Bank based on their expertise, experience and geographical representation.

The EGCG has succeeded in raising important issues for consideration by the Bank such as the need to approach gender from a rights perspective rather than simply for efficiency, and to address the harmful effects of structural adjustment and globalization on women. They also provided important input to the policy research report and to the gender mainstreaming strategy. However, the group is a set of individuals who do not represent their organizations in their capacity as members of the EGCG. The group has no formal advocacy program, extremely limited funds, and a once-a-year encounter with the Bank at headquarters. Therefore, their influence is limited.

In 2000, the Bank reduced the EGCG membership from 14 to 9 people, most likely as a cost-saving measure. The EGCG is an important reference group for the Gender and Development anchor and provides a sounding board for internal gender advocates as they consider how to increase attention to gender at the Bank. However, some gender-focused Bank staffers perceive the orientation of the Bank towards the EGCG as a sort of "firefighting" exercise, i.e. Bank management listens to the EGCG in order to keep a positive public relations profile on the topic but the group does not significantly affect Bank behavior toward gender issues.

Consultative Council on Gender for the Middle East and North Africa

This group was created by the Bank in January, 1999 largely as a result of the commitment and dynamism of the MENA gender coordinator to enable it to consult with members of civil society in countries of the region.

NGO advocacy efforts on gender equality at the World Bank

Shortly before she left the Bank in 2001, Jan Piercy, the former US Executive Director, said "Having an external constituency on gender is indispensable" (Piercy 2001). She noted how struck she had been by how priorities of the Bank shift depending on advocacy by external groups. In the months preceding the adoption of the new gender mainstreaming strategy, comments expressed by several Bank staff regarding the status of gender promotion in the Bank revealed the current dearth of external advocacy as well as the work needed to be done inside the Bank. "Gender is nowhere here," said one high-placed female manager who doesn't work on gender at the Bank but who did in another development organization. "Gender is not even on the radar screen," said another Bank staffer familiar with social development issues in the Bank. "No one cares about gender here," said another.

Evidence shows that advocacy by women's organizations around the world has helped to promote the gender advances that have occurred so far in the Bank. While some advocacy work had been carried out subsequent to the imposition of structural adjustment policies in the early 1980s and in the decade following the establishment of the Bank's WID Unit in 1986, efforts began to intensify at the 1995 Fourth World Conference on Women where Bank President James Wolfensohn made a speech indicating the Bank's commitment to promote gender equality. He was the first Bank president to attend any of the United Nations conferences on women.

Women's eyes on the Bank

At the Beijing conference, representatives of women's organizations presented Wolfensohn with a letter signed by over 800 people urging the Bank to take the following four steps:

- To increase the participation of grassroots women in the Bank's projects and economic policy making;
- To institutionalize a gender perspective in all Bank policies and programs;

- To increase Bank investments in women's health services, education, agriculture, land ownership, employment and financial services;
- To increase the number and diversity of women in senior management positions within the Bank (Williams 1997: 33).

This action launched the Women's Eyes on the Bank Campaign (WEOB) which took root in the US and Latin America and the Caribbean (LAC). Following the Beijing conference, 8 to 12 organizations based mainly in Washington created the campaign's US chapter. The only other region where an active campaign ensued was in Latin America and the Caribbean which has continued to have a group of women involved in advocacy in 10 countries (Frade Rubio 2000: 1). In 1997, the US campaign produced an excellent assessment of the Bank's work in the four areas noted above.

Three or four individuals in Washington-based NGOs became the backbone of the US campaign, with most working on WEOB in addition to their regular professional responsibilities. When they left their respective NGO jobs in 1999, work on the WEOB essentially stopped.

Women's EDGE

In 2000, Oxfam America asked Women's EDGE to consider taking up advocacy on gender equality at the Bank after the US coordinator of the Women's Eyes on the Bank Campaign left Oxfam for a job elsewhere. Through support provided by Oxfam America, Women's EDGE researched this topic and began a dialogue with Southern gender activists about advocacy topics of importance to them. The results of that work were published in April, 2002, in a report entitled "The advocate's guide to promoting gender equality at the World Bank." The focus of the Women's EDGE coalition is women and macro-economic issues, and it works to ensure that complex international trade agreements do not harm people living in developing countries. Its constituency includes more than 65 member organizations and more than 7000 individuals on campuses and other key places around the country. The coalition's diverse membership – from the Christian Children's Fund to the Feminist Majority – have come together around a common mission to inject women's economic, social and political rights into US interactions with developing and transitional countries. The organization defines and targets US action broadly; EDGE advocates for women's rights in global trade, official development assistance and US participation in multilateral organizations. It has established relationships with Southern women's organizations interested in and active on macro-economic issues. Unfortunately, due to a lack of funding, it has been unable to continue its work to promote gender equality at the World Bank.

Gender Action

Gender Action is a nonprofit organization established in 2002 to ensure multi-lateral organizations promote gender equality and women's rights in all their investments worldwide. Gender Action's strategies include partnering with Southern civil society groups to convince their governments to mainstream gender concerns into MDB investments in their countries; persuading donor governments to hold the MDBs accountable on gender issues; monitoring and reporting on multilateral progress in mainstreaming gender issues; and conduct-ing gender advocacy directly on the multilaterals. During its initial months, Gender Action has concentrated on engendering PRSPs because of the critical role PRSPs play in country eligibility for multilateral investments and in national planning and budgeting. Gender Action has undertaken PRSP fieldwork collaboratively with Southern partners and direct advocacy with bilateral agencies and other nonprofits. Gender Action has actively participated in the Coalition for World Bank Reform's advocacy campaign by engendering proposed US World Bank (IDA-13) funding replenishment legislation and conditions. Gender Action also contributed to the Coalition report, "Responsible Reform of the World Bank."

Integrating gender into PRSPs

The advent of the Poverty Reduction Strategy process has meant that women's organizations have begun to be involved in these efforts although, as noted on page 46, participation by women's groups and attention to gender issues have been inadequate thus far. According to a Bank staffer, the Bank, itself, is precluded from helping civil society groups become involved in the PRSP process.

The UN Development Fund for Women (UNIFEM) analyzed the treatment of gender concerns in the PRSP as part of a comprehensive review of this process undertaken by the Bank and IMF in late 2001. UNIFEM's comments were drawn from assessments done by NGOs, consultants and national women's machineries in particular countries, and noted these six points:

- One of the key areas where there is a singular lack of gender dimension in the PRSPs is that of data collection to inform poverty diagnoses, policy development and monitoring and evaluation.
- Gender is not addressed as a cross-cutting issue; instead it is often limited to a few specific sectors such as health and education where gender issues are traditionally addressed.
- Gender is rarely addressed in relation to macro-economic and structural policies. These are assumed to be gender-neutral when in fact they are not.
- PRSPs emphasize the market economy at the expense of the household economy, which is mostly female-dominated, based on unpaid labor and has direct contributions to the market economy, especially during business cycle downturns.

- Participation of civil society in the development of PRSPs is often limited, without institutionalized mechanisms that can ensure the views of all groups are actually reflected in the various stages of a PRSP.
- One important omission in PRSPs has been the very limited discussion on violence against women (World Bank 2001d: 1).

Other research undertaken has uncovered additional reasons why gender concerns have not been included in PRSPs thus far:

- Although some participatory processes undertaken to ensure civil society input into preparation of PRSPs have considered gender concerns, the final reports or workshops obscured gender differences by aggregating previously sex-disaggregated data.
- Participants in PRSP writing teams most often are staff from government finance and economics ministries and external consultants, many of whom are insensitive to gender issues.
- Many PRSP stakeholders lack gender-mainstreaming skills; they see the process of engendering the PRSP as mysterious; and they find gender discussions largely conceptual rather than practical.
- The PRSP sourcebook, prepared by the World Bank, is seen as impractical to use. The gender chapter, while very useful in terms of diagnostic and monitoring indicators and tools, does not deal with gender advocacy and gives little attention to the need for gender analysis of macro-economic issues including the national budget which is central to the PRSP (Zuckerman 2002: 10).

Views of Southern NGO gender specialists regarding gender advocacy at the World Bank

The most influential voices regarding gender issues at the World Bank must be those of Southern women themselves. However, historically, women in borrower countries have not been given the opportunity to participate adequately or appropriately in Bank policy and project formulation, design, implementation and evaluation. The recent positive steps taken by the World Bank *may* represent an opportunity to redress this situation.

Although at present there is no way to systematically catalogue or analyze advocacy by women's organizations at the national level, Southern women's groups have been promoting gender concerns to the Bank for many years. Southern women's groups have long been among those civil society organizations working to convince the Bank to end or significantly alter structural adjustment policies imposed on their countries. The LAC-WEOB campaign has been the most active World Bank-focused effort in a Southern region in recent years. Southern women have also been in the forefront of groups urging an end to user fees in health, water and education which governments have imposed as conditions of certain World Bank lending. ISAAF International in India and the Tanzania Gender Networking Program are two of many women's organizations advocating these changes. In many instances, women's groups have been included in the consultative processes with civil society conducted for the formulation of the CAS in borrower countries.

Interviews in recent years with women from Asia, Africa, Eastern Europe, and Latin America and the Caribbean reveal the following issues as those they perceive as most urgent regarding the promotion of gender at the Bank:

- The Bank's promotion of gender equality *within* the prevailing paradigm of economic reform and globalization;
- The technical compartmentalization of gender efforts rather than viewing them within the political context of structural inequalities and patriarchy;
- The Bank's focus on economic efficiency rather than empowerment and rights;
- The emphasis on women as mothers, not as workers;
- The role of the US in maintaining the current World Bank approach to economic reform and globalization.

Southern gender specialists think advocacy should start by questioning the assumptions and values that form the basis of the Bank's policies, as well as its system for delivering loans to Southern countries. This includes economic conditionality and the process of negotiation of macro-economic policies. In the view of Southern gender specialists, the PRSP is an example of a Bank-led initiative to continue imposition of liberal economic reforms, with official claims for poverty reduction goals and broad-based public participation, coupled with conditionality likely to conflict with national development imperatives and long-term poverty reduction. The negotiation process is conducted for the most part without the full knowledge and participation of affected citizens, including women.

Many Southern gender specialists think that the Bank is promoting gender-mainstreaming while it supports macro-economic policies that further the interests of transnational corporations in search of new markets and new sources of cheap labor, thus reinforcing the exclusion of disadvantaged social groups, especially women. Southern women also think that these policies have led to the removal and/or de-legitimization of public policy instruments for the implementation of social development policies and affirmative action policies, including the Beijing Platform for Action.

Conclusion

As detailed in these pages, during the past 25 years the record of the World Bank in promoting gender equality in its policy and operational initiatives has been quite unsatisfactory. However, the recent steps taken by the Bank which have been described in this chapter are encouraging. Gender activists and feminist economists around the world need to seize this opportunity to monitor the implementation of the new gender-mainstreaming strategy, both at the country level and globally, to analyze gender impacts of Bank-funded initiatives and to promote as vigorously as possible gender equality and equitable access to resources and power. *[handwritten: WB only is effective w/ women's group policies interactions.]*

Notes

1 This chapter is adapted from "The advocate's guide to promoting gender equality at the World Bank," published by the Women's EDGE Coalition in April, 2003. The full paper is available at www.womensedge.org
2 Although the current director of the Bank's Gender and Development Unit indicated in July, 2002 that the 1994 gender policy paper was not a mainstreaming strategy, "mainstreaming strategy" was the term used in the OED evaluation cited in this paper.
3 For another view on this matter see Chapter 5 by Avin and Chapter 12 by Barriteau in this book.

Acronyms and abbreviations

CAS	Country Assistance Strategy
CGA	Country Gender Assessment
ED	Executive Director
EGCG	External Gender Consultative Group
IBRD	International Bank for Reconstruction and Development
ICSID	International Centre for Settlement of Investment Disputes
IDA	International Development Association
IFC	International Finance Corporation
IMF	International Monetary Fund
LAC	Latin America and the Caribbean
LAC-WEOB	Latin America and the Caribbean Women's Eyes on the Bank
MENA	Middle East and North Africa
MIGA	Multilateral Investment Guarantee Agency
NGO	Non-governmental organization
OED	Operations Evaluation Department
PREM	Poverty Reduction and Economic Management Network
PRS	Poverty Reduction Strategy
PRSP	Poverty Reduction Strategy Paper
TA	Technical assistance
UNIFEM	United Nations Development Fund for Women
WEOB	Women's Eyes on the Bank
WID	Women in Development

References

Blackden, Mark and Chitra Bhanu (1998) *1998 Poverty Status Report, Special Partnership with Africa*, Washington, DC: World Bank.
Buvinic, Mayra, Catherine Gwin and Lisa M. Bates (1996) *Investing in Women: Progress and Prospects for the World Bank*, Washington, DC: Overseas Development Council.
Correia, Maria, interview, January 24, 2001.

Frade Rubio, Laura (ed.) (2000) *Equity, Participation and Consistency? The World Bank at the Beijing + 5*, Women's Eyes on the World Bank Campaign, Latin American Region, Mexico: Alcadeco, AC.

Long, Carolyn M. (2003) "The advocate's guide to promoting gender equality at the World Bank," published by Women's EDGE Coalition. Online. Available http://www.womensedge.org

Mason, Karen, notes to author, July 18, 2002.

Piercy, Jan, interview, January 25, 2001.

Williams, Lydia (ed.) (1997) *Gender Equity and the World Bank Group: A Post-Beijing Assessment*, Women's Eyes on the World Bank – US in collaboration with Women's Eyes on the World Bank – Latin America, 50 Years is Enough, and US Network for Global Economic Justice, Washington, DC.

World Bank (2000) *Advancing Gender Equality. World Bank Action Since Beijing*, Washington, DC: World Bank.

—— (2001a) *Engendering Development: Through Equality in Rights, Resources, and Voice*. Washington, DC: The World Bank.

—— (2001b) *Evaluation of the Gender Dimensions of World Bank Assistance*, Operations Evaluation Department, Fourth Draft, Washington, DC: World Bank.

—— (2001c) "Development Topics: Participation, Participation in the Poverty Reduction Strategy Formulation, External Reviews," Online. Available http://www.worldbank.org

—— (2001d) "United Nations Development Fund for Women (UNIFEM) Contribution to the World Bank and IMF PRSP Review," Online. Available http://www.worldbank.org

—— (2002) *Integrating Gender into the World Bank's Work: A Strategy for Action*, Washington, DC: World Bank.

Zuckerman, Elaine (2002) *A Primer on Poverty Reduction Strategy Papers and Gender*, Washington, DC: Gender Action.

4 Rhetoric and realities

A comment

Sakuntala Narasimhan

[handwritten: Women worse off]

The two preceding chapters, by Zafiris Tzannatos and Carolyn M. Long respectively, seem to be broadly in agreement over the assessment that the priorities of the first four decades of the Bank's operations were not merely gender-blind but actually caused the feminization of poverty (increasing the percentage of women among those living below the poverty line), leaving women worse off and further marginalized. Both chapters also concede that in recent years (and specifically, after the Beijing conference of women in 1995) the organization has declared its commitment to a more gender-sensitive perspective, and that a number of initiatives, ranging from policy guidelines to setting up gender consultative groups, have been taken.

Where once the Structural Adjustment Policies (SAPs) urged and imposed by the Bank on developing countries desirous of borrowing from the Bank eroded the quality of life for women, while exports rose to pay for debt-servicing, the new policies and initiatives were meant (at least, on paper) to ensure that gender equity did not get pushed off the radar in future funding operations.

But have these initiatives been matched by performance? Long's assessment is that the "corrective measures" that the Bank has undertaken are worth taking note of, but are "not enough." In other words, the scorecard is a C minus or thereabouts, from a feminist point of view. Not satisfactory. Tzannatos likewise, concludes that the Bank has a long way to go in terms of ensuring that gender equity is not compromised by its funding policies.

In reflecting on the thrust of the arguments in the two previous chapters, I find myself raising two basic questions:

- Has the Bank really learnt from past mistakes, or is there still a gap between rhetoric (about becoming gender sensitive) and the reality of the organization's current policies and patterns of functioning? and
- Do the changes initiated within the Bank, as policy shifts and evaluation mechanisms, promise (at least in the long run) to make an abiding difference to the way developmental funding in the borrowing countries affects women?

The first question is best answered in terms of a few examples from around the world. After committing a whopping $450 million for the massive Sardar Sarovar Project on the Narmada river in upper India, the Bank parted ways with the

Indian government in the wake of widespread protests by activists. The project displaced tens of thousands of people, inundated hundreds of villages, and caused massive dispossession among poor tribals. The Narmada project in fact became the world's "test case" of the Bank's willingness and ability to adhere to its own environmental and social guidelines (Mehta 1993). Nonetheless, a decade later, the Bank is reported to have resumed lending for big dams in India despite years of trenchant criticism of its lending policies. In the lush green north-eastern states alone (which have a large population of tribals), dams and river diversion projects are being planned that will cause "ecological disasters," as activists put it. That does not quite look like "learning from past mistakes." Forced migration and displacement put a disproportionately greater burden on females than on males.

As recently as in February 2004, activists from Tanzania drew international attention to the fact that the World Bank was about to fund a major road project around the slopes of Kilimanjaro. "This will spell disaster for the people and pose a serious threat to a world heritage site," the activists point out. This case too, flies in the face of the claims that the Bank makes, of having become "more ecology and environment conscious in its assessment of projects."

In Uganda, a curious resurgence of the practice known as "*mikayi*" has been noted in recent research studies. *Mikayi* also refers to the eldest wife (who traditionally enjoyed seniority and privileges among wives in an African polygamous marriage). Young girls enrolled at the university (even in "modern" courses like gender studies and information technology), it was found, become the *mikayi* of male classmates and provide housekeeping services (cooking, cleaning) in return for money that will go towards paying college fees. Thanks to the structural adjustment policies dictated by the Bank, state allocations for education got cut, and girls who found there was no money forthcoming for their education have ended up reviving, as a coping strategy, a practice that seems anomalous and socially regressive in the context of gender equity. These girls actually end up defaulting on their educational goals because housekeeping chores leave them no time for studying or attending classes. Many even end up victims of violence inflicted by their boy friends (Abuya 2002). This links up with the main argument, because it is the World Bank's policies (of cutting down on social sector expenditure) that drive girls to adopt strategies that could help overcome the reduction in educational funds available. It is a classic example of the feminization of poverty caused by structural adjustment policies.

A more recent report of June 2003 describes how young women trade unsafe sex for survival in Lesotho, because SAP has contributed to rising shortages of food. The World Food Program says increasing prostitution has become a problem in at least six southern African countries (Itano 2003). Similar examples of women's immiseration can be found across the continents, from Thailand to Kenya and Jamaica to Brazil. Despite professions of greater gender sensitivity, the Bank continues to let "economic profitability" dictate its lending and funding decisions in developing countries across the world.

If that is one aspect of "past mistakes," the other is that the damage inflicted, particularly on women's lives, through blinkered policies thrust upon developing economies in the earlier years, cannot be undone – thousands of indigent women in Asian countries (India, Bangladesh, Vietnam) who are caught in exploitative industrial units (garment exports, floriculture and food processing, for instance) find themselves in a no-win situation, with their traditional communities and support systems destroyed and no alternatives to turn to. The People's Charter for Health drawn up by the People's Health Movement (a global coalition of health activists and medical personnel) took note in May 2004 of the "disastrous effects on women's health, of the policies dictated by the World Bank."[1] Thanks to the emphasis on privatization of medical services, maternal mortality and morbidity has actually risen in some regions, as several studies have shown.

Gender and environmental concerns go hand in hand with overlapping agendas, because whatever degrades the environment puts a greater burden on women, especially in the lower economic strata (having to walk further to fetch water for the family's needs, fodder for the cattle and firewood for cooking, more time spent on caring for infants developing respiratory ailments caused by pollution). Regardless, the Bank has, even after 1992 (when the international convention on climate change and environment, also known as the Kyoto Protocol, was signed), financed projects that were actually climate-changing to the tune of $2–3 billion per year, which is 20–30 times the Bank's financing of climate-friendly activities, in terms of renewable energy options. The new coal-fired power plant at Talchar in Orissa state in eastern India (described as "the pride of the Bank") has resulted in the river water becoming coated with thick ash deposits, so women of the region are reduced to digging in the sand with their hands to scoop up water for the family's daily needs. The plant uses millions of gallons of water for its cooling towers, robbing the villages of a once clean and abundant water supply (Wysham and Valette 1997). That, again, is neither "gender-sensitive" nor "learning from experience."

In Bangladesh, the Bank's advice urging a greater focus on export promotion (for earning foreign exchange to pay for debt-servicing) led to rice fields getting converted to shrimp farms. Where once the rice crop fed the farmer and his family, the shrimp cultivated instead of paddy got sent overseas as export. The salination of rice lands caused by the ponds built to raise shrimps in also led to what activists describe as an "ecological disaster" (Ahmad 1992). Agricultural production has fallen by 30 percent, and to the 25 million people who are suffering hunger, the increase in export earnings is hardly a measure of "development" or cause for rejoicing.

This brings me to the second question about the developmental paradigm that the Bank is sworn to, and promotes in the borrowing countries. As Long points out, the original brief was, purely and strictly, economic – increasing money incomes and returns from investments, without reference to dimensions of "equity" or "rights" (in terms of women's right to having their voices heard during processes of decision-making, for example), because these were considered "political" dimensions (to be strictly avoided). In recent years, however, the Bank's policy is supposed to have shifted towards a rights-and-resource

entitlements approach, taking into consideration (at least in theory) the effect
of policy decisions on gender equity. Nonetheless, the basic definition of development remains unchanged – the indices are power generation, highways built,
infrastructure base per capita, foreign exchange earnings. If a project promises
high returns for investment (through power generation that will bring in profits,
for instance) it is still OK under the Bank's criteria. (The benchmark for a
satisfactory investment project is an economic rate of return of at least 10 percent,
as Tzannatos observes in a note.) If it is found that this will create gender
imbalances and social problems, the approach is to "examine" how these effects
could be mitigated rather than questioning the basic definition of "development"
and "progress" itself. As the Bangladeshi activist Nilufar Ahmad asks, what kind
of progress is it, if shrimp exports bring in extra foreign exchange earnings, when
at the same time 25 million people are pushed into starvation because of the
damage to rice fields? The global consensus today, as Tzannatos points out, is
that economics alone is quite inadequate as a matrix for development planning,
and that a multi-disciplinary (economic-social-cultural-human rights) approach
is necessary. In this, the Bank has fallen far short of its avowed, "updated"
intentions that are supposed to be based on "lessons learnt from the past."

The Meltzer Commission report[2] described the Bank's record as "miserable";
Walden Bello has called for the "decommissioning and neutering of the Bank";
and even former senior Bank officials like Nicholas Stern have attacked the
Bank's policy of pampering the rich and penalizing the poor. Whether any
of this has altered the perspectives of the Bank is a moot point. Judging from
the comments from Long and Tzannatos, the answer seems to be, "no" or at
best, "not much."

As part of its "new" and "more sensitive" agenda, the Bank has also mentioned
"a greater participatory role for civic society" – and yet, how many displaced
tribal hordes, or women impoverished by Structural Adjustment Programs, have
access to inspection panels or evaluation units of the Bank? In a way the Bank
is able to conveniently avoid responsibility in this area since it puts the onus on
the country representatives. Tzannatos points out, however, that the country
representatives are themselves either the finance minister or similar high-ranking
official (who might not necessarily be sensitive to issues of gender equity).
Moreover, those authorized to voice opinions at the Bank's deliberations are
not all democratically equal in effect – the top donor countries (US, Japan, UK,
Germany, France – none of them belonging to the category of "developing
countries") have one executive director each, while 176 developing countries
out of the total membership of 184 nations have to make do with just 16 executive directors representing them. Country representation is one thing, having
its voice heard and heeded is another. He who pays the piper, calls the tune
– and it comes as no surprise that global criticism of the Bank's functioning
includes the charge that the Bank's decisions prioritize US multinational
companies' needs (in terms of market access or profits) rather than the needs of
the beneficiary country (or for that matter, the women's component of the
populations therein).

The organizational descriptions provided in the earlier portions of the foregoing chapters reveal other details that strengthen the image of the Bank – even after its recent policy "fine-tuning" exercises – as "insensitive" even to the basic concept of poverty. When the Bank evaluates a proposal or development project, it gets consultants to assess the feasibility and profitability dimensions before the project is sanctioned. These consultants, as the Bangladeshi activist Nilufar Ahmad points out, are invariably from the West (American firms, mostly – one of the conditions the Bank imposes is that foreign consultants have to be engaged) who fly in, and give their expert opinion (regardless of their familiarity with the ground realities of the socio-cultural matrices in the country). Long's chapter takes note of the fact that, in terms of positive measures, the Bank has recently "decentralized" its working and "moved staff to the field." Out of a total of 10,000 employees, over 3,000 are reported to be based in borrower countries. That's a half-filled glass (less than, in fact – 30 percent is still way short of "equity"). Imposing assessments from outside and not heeding local voices on priority needs causes wasteful (and at times even harmful) expenditure.

Criticism of the Bank's policies have included the viewpoint that the Bank's funding has been like pouring water into a leaking tub, because part of the problem in developing countries has been poor implementation – for instance, in power generation, reducing transmission losses and plugging wastage would be a better and far more effective strategy than funding new dam projects that displace communities and cause social unrest. Dam projects

Even after the introduction of "gender-sensitive mechanisms" for fine-tuning project evaluations, as Long's chapter points out, there is neither an incentive for prioritizing a strong gender component, nor accountability (or penalties for ignoring women's needs). The organizational initiatives, in other words, have served as no more than cosmetic moves. "The [External Gender Consultative] group has no formal advocacy program, extremely limited funds, and a once-a-year encounter with the Bank at headquarters. Therefore, their influence is limited." Also, "some gender-focused Bank staffers perceive the orientation of the Bank towards the EGCG as a sort of 'firefighting' exercise, i.e. Bank management listens to the EGCG in order to keep a positive public relations profile on the topic but the group does not significantly affect Bank behavior toward gender issues" (Long, this volume, page 49). More eloquently, the Bank has "reduced the EGCG membership from 14 to 9 . . . most likely as a cost-saving measure" (Long, page 49). Cost-saving does not, presumably, get in the way while flying out, at enormous expense, foreign consultants into developing regions where the average citizen earns in a whole year a fraction of what the consultants spend in a day (and women earn even less). Mindsets, rather than minor adjustments to perspectives and priorities, are the problem. Shifting the perspective and emphasis towards "poverty reduction" makes little sense in the face of insensitivity to, and poor understanding of, the nature and ramifications of poverty. Even where Bank-funded projects have raised incomes, they have resulted in widening the chasm between the haves and the have-nots, with the rich becoming richer and the poor becoming further impoverished (despite

Distribution of income & consolt.

the Bank's mission statement of 2003 claiming that it fights poverty with "passion"). Globally, money incomes rose at the rate of 2.5 per cent annually, while the number of people in poverty increased by 100 million, during the decade of the 1990s (Stiglitz 2002).

A stark example of the Bank's insensitivity to the human dimension of development is its disregard of the recommendations of the World Commission on Dams set up by the Bank itself. Two more indicators of the lack of political will to mainstream gender in the Bank's operations are the woefully inadequate use of gender-disaggregated data (less than 15 percent, by the Bank's own admission of 2001, as Long points out) and the failure to fill posts of gender coordinator lying vacant for "well over a year" (Long, page 47).

The assessment given by Long contains the crucial observation: "Evidence shows that advocacy by women's organizations around the world has helped to promote the gender advances that have occurred so far in the Bank" (Long, page 50). Women's groups, in other words, need to become not only vocal but also network globally, knitting the developed and developing regions together, in order to articulate cross-cutting gender concerns and make a dent in the Bank's operations for promoting gender equity. More importantly, the voices of women from the grassroots in the developing countries need to be heeded because they are the ones who are hit hardest by the inequitable and inappropriate policies of the Bank.

Notes

1   Comment from the People's Health Movement (PHM) in a media report on the WHO director general's speech, May 18, 2004.
2   Walden Bello, executive director of Focus on Global South, in the March issue of *Focus on Trade* (2001a). The Meltzer Committee report argued that the Bank is "irrelevant to the question of solving poverty and should be radically reduced in terms of scale and functions." See also Bello (2001b).

References

Abuya, Pamela (2002) "The Institution of Mikayi: Gains or Challenge?", paper presented at the Eighth Women's Worlds 2002 International Conference, at Kampala, Uganda, July 2002.

Ahmad, Nilufar (1992) "Battling the World Bank: an interview with Nilufar Ahmad," *Multinational Monitor*, October 10, 1992. Available online at http://www.multi nationalmonitor.org/hyper/issues/1992/10/mm1092_09.html (Accessed September 16, 2005).

Bello, Walden (2001a) "The Global Conjecture," *Focus on Trade*, 60, March.

—— (2001b) "Genoa and the multiple crises of globalization," *Focus on Trade*, 64, July.

Itano, Nicole (2003) "Women trade unsafe sex for survival in Lesotho," *Women's eNews*, June 1, 2003. Available online at http://www.womensenews.org/article.cfm/dyn/aid/1350/context/archive (Accessed September 16, 2005).

Mehta, Pradeep (1993) "Fury over a River," *Multinational Monitor*, December.

Stiglitz, Joseph (2002) *Globalization and its Discontents*, London: Penguin Books.

Wysham, Daphne and Vallette, Jim (1997) "Changing the Earth's Climate for Business – the World Bank and the Greenhouse Effect," *Multinational Monitor*, October.

Part II

Policy evaluations

Daisy X

5 *Engendering Development*

A critique

Rose-Marie Avin

[handwritten: Latin America (Nicaragua) + ≈ Brazil]

Introduction

The World Bank Policy Research Report entitled *Engendering Development: Through Gender Equality in Rights, Resources, and Voice* explores the connections between economic development, existing institutions, and gender inequality in the Third World. The Report also discusses in great detail the role of public policy in promoting gender equality in the world.

Given that the Report emphasizes the role of economic development as a key element in improving gender equality in the Third World, this chapter addresses four concerns dealing with the concept of economic development *[handwritten: objective]* and its connections to gender equality. First, the Report does not explain clearly the objectives of economic development and does not make explicit the distinction between economic growth and economic development, sometimes using the two terms interchangeably (World Bank 2001: 1,182). Second, the *[handwritten: society → race]* Report fails to take into consideration the issues of class, race, and ethnicity, a very important omission in the case of Latin American countries where huge income disparities exist. The dynamic process of economic development and its impact on gender equality will play out differently for working-class, middle-class and upper-class women. It is important to acknowledge differences among women in terms of race and ethnicity. Third, I disagree with the Report's conclusion that "on balance the evidence suggests that females' absolute status and gender equality improved, not deteriorated" (ibid.: 215) during the structural adjustment period of the 1980s and 1990s in Latin America.

My contention is that the neoliberal economic model that resulted from *[handwritten: SAPs]* Structural Adjustment Policies (SAPs) has worsened the economic conditions of the majority of women in Latin America. Women have less access to resources and are still bearing the economic, emotional, and physical costs of structural adjustment. Fourth, the Report needs to acknowledge that Third World women, and especially women's organizations, have been and are agents of change in transforming their own lives and societies. Not only should women become the beneficiaries of economic development but also the agents of economic development. All four concerns will be discussed in the context of Latin America, more specifically in the realities of Brazil and Nicaragua.

[handwritten: No access to resources]

Economic development, growth, and gender equality

Why is it important to start the Report with a definition of economic development? Throughout the Report, the authors use the terms "economic growth" and "economic development" interchangeably, which makes it difficult to follow their argument considering that the two terms convey different meanings. It is quite possible that the authors believe that economic growth leads automatically to economic development, a link that has been widely rejected in the development literature. In this case, the authors should reconceptualize their meaning of economic development to include the new scholarship that is widely accepted in the development literature. Incorporating the new meaning of economic development in the analysis is important for three reasons:

1   To present the multidimensional aspect of the concept;
2   To develop a more coherent argument establishing effectively the interconnections between the different dimensions of the development process and the various ways they contribute to gender equality;
3   To help policymakers at the World Bank develop more effective policies to deal with problems in the Third World.

Since World War II, the meaning of development has moved away from the narrower view associated with economic growth, income growth, industrialization, and modernization and toward a broader definition that includes both economic and non-economic dimensions. According to Michael Todaro, there are three "core values of development" (Todaro 2000: 16): sustenance – the ability to meet basic needs; self-esteem – the ability to develop a sense of self-worth and self-respect; and freedom from servitude – the ability to choose and be emancipated from alienating social, material, and political conditions. This definition involves major social, political, and economic changes that can radically alter institutions in Third World societies.

Todaro's definition is also consistent with Amartya Sen's definition of development as "a process of expanding the real freedoms that people enjoy" (Sen 1999: 3). According to Sen, there are five distinct types of freedom: political, economic facilities, social opportunities, transparency guarantees, and protective security. All five elements of Sen's definition are interrelated and are the objectives of development. Based on this definition, a successful development strategy can lead to the improvement of the well-being of all individuals in society. In addition, Sen argues that "freedoms are not only the primary ends of development, they are also among its principal means" (ibid.: 10). His meaning of development is also an agent-oriented view where individuals can shape their own destiny. Sen's definition is important because it captures well the process of social, economic, and political transformation that needs to happen in order to achieve an economic development that promotes gender equality. Sen's analytical framework will be analyzed again at the end of this paper to explain the process of gender empowerment that has been happening in Latin America.

(margin note: attitudes matter)

The definitions of economic development given above make it obvious that economic development is a multidimensional process that can contribute to the empowerment of women and reduce gender inequality. The same argument can not be made for economic growth in the way that the World Bank Report implies. Empirical studies have shown that economic growth alone may not improve the well-being of the vast majority of people in the Third World. "Growth of GNP or of individual incomes can, of course, be very important as 'means' to expanding the freedoms enjoyed by the members of the society" (ibid.: 3). Some empirical studies (Adelman 1975), however, have shown that the poorest members of society may become worse off with economic growth. An extensive empirical study of 43 developing countries by Irma Adelman showed that the primary impact of economic growth has been to decrease both the absolute and the relative incomes of the poor. So, there is no trickle down with economic growth as this Report seems to imply. According to Adelman, "the poorest segments of the population typically benefit from economic growth only when the government plays an important role and when widespread efforts are made to improve the human resource base" (ibid.: 302–3). During the 1960s, many developing countries such as Brazil and Mexico that experienced high rates of economic growth realized that the growth did not bring significant benefits to the poor (Todaro 2000: 152). In Latin America, standards of living of the poor either stagnated or declined in real terms (ibid.: 152). At the same time, gender inequality did not seem to diminish for the vast majority of poor, working-class women.

Considering the wealth of evidence, it is imperative that policymakers at the World Bank reconceptualize the meaning of economic development to show more effectively the relationship between economic development and gender equality and, more importantly, develop more successful policies. The case of Brazil discussed below shows that economic growth is necessary but not sufficient to improve the lives of the vast majority of people and to improve gender equality.

Economic transformation and women in Brazil: 1950–2000

What has been the impact of economic growth on the lives of women in Brazil? Did it lead to an improvement in gender equality as stipulated by the World Bank Report? According to Silvia Berger, women in South America "experienced considerable changes in their economic status as a result of deep transformations in the region's societies" (Berger 1999: 246). The region's emphasis on industrial growth after the 1930s, urbanization, and social movements have all contributed to the transformation of women's lives. The emphasis on industrialization combined with the existence of a highly unequal land distribution in the rural areas led to rapid migration into the major cities of South America, with women forming the largest component of the migrant population (ibid.: 247).

Economic growth and gender equality

Brazilian women migrated to the urban areas in large numbers, with the vast majority going to Rio de Janeiro and São Paulo. As a consequence, the percentage of women working in agriculture fell from 31 percent in 1950 to 15.3 percent in 1980 (Inter-American Development Bank 1987: 104–5). At the same time, their share of services increased from 43.6 percent to 65.7 percent during the same period (ibid.: 104–5). Their labor force participation rate in the formal sector also increased from 16.8 percent in 1960 to 26.6 percent in 1985 (Arriagada 1995: 334) to 30.3 percent in 1990 (Delgado *et al.* 2000: 112). These official data do not capture the full contribution of women to the economy. They tend to underestimate women's participation in the labor market because their work in the household is not measured and also because many women work in the informal sector.

The emphasis on import-substitution industrialization (ISI) based on capital-intensive manufacturing absorbed only a fraction of the labor force. Consequently, the vast majority of female migrants were not able to find jobs in the growing manufacturing sector. Some women found jobs in the textile and garment industries. However, the vast majority of jobs for women were in the services sector. Many women were able to find jobs as shop clerks, secretaries, teachers, and nurses as a result of expanding state services in public education, health, and social security (Berger 1999: 246–57). A few well-educated women found positions in academia and law.

For the women with little education who migrated from the rural areas, it was not easy to find a job in the formal sector. They ended up in what is known as the informal economy, which comprises the self-employed and small-scale family-owned enterprises. They engaged in an array of activities that include street vending and prostitution. Others found jobs as domestic servants. During the 1980s, it was estimated that one-third of the employed women in Brazil were in domestic service, acting as nannies, cooks, and maids (Library of Nations 1987: 65). According to Todaro, workers in the informal sector do not have job security, decent working conditions, or old-age pensions. Most live in *"favelas"* (shanty towns) and lack access to public services such as transportation, and educational and health services (Todaro 2000: 297).

Empirical studies also show substantial segmentation of the labor market by gender, that is women in the labor market are concentrated in a few low-level occupations. In 1980, the vast majority of the personal service workers were women (92.4 percent), and of the maids and washerwomen (92.4 percent) (Arriagada 1995: 33).

In spite of the gains realized by educated Brazilian women in terms of better access to professional jobs, income received by women is lower than income received by men at all levels of education and for all professions. In 1985, women received 52.8 percent of the average male income in São Paulo. Empirical studies have shown that the higher the level of education, the larger the income gap is. Furthermore, male income is always higher for the same occupations. One interesting fact is that, in Latin America, the female working population has higher levels of education than the female population that does not participate in the labor market, and also more education than both the working and non-working male population (ibid.: 335).

In Brazil, there does not seem to exist differences in educational attainment between men and women but there are differences between women at different class levels. In 1998, the female adult literacy rate as a percentage of the male rate was 100 percent (*Human Development Report* 2000: 256). In 1997, the ratio of the female primary age group enrollment as a percentage of the male rate was 94 percent (ibid.: 256). In 1997, the ratio of the female secondary age group enrollment as a percentage of the male ratio was 103 percent. During the period 1994–7, the percentage of female tertiary students as a percentage of males was 116 percent (ibid.: 256). However, huge inequalities based on race and class remain in the educational system.

According to the Brazilian Ministry of Education, "although 44 percent of all Brazilians are blacks and mestizos, they constitute about 70 percent of all poor and indigent" (Ministry of Education 2000: 4). Furthermore, while the illiteracy rate is 9 percent among Caucasians, it is 22 percent among Afro-Brazilians. As for schooling, the Caucasian population has an average schooling rate of 6.2 years compared to 4.2 years for blacks and mestizos (ibid.: 4). Also, it was estimated that 93 percent of domestic workers are women of color (Castro 1995: 28).

Significant demographic changes also took place during the time of rapid economic transformation. Brazil experienced decreases in the mortality rate, increases in life expectancy, and a fall in fertility rates. The fertility rate declined from 5.6 children in 1965 to 3.9 in 1980 and to 2.3 in 1997 (*World Development Report 1999/2000*, 2000). During the period 1990–8, 77 percent of Brazilian women had access to contraception (ibid.: 242). This signifies that women have more control over their lives, and are able to increase their participation in the labor market because of fewer responsibilities at home.

It is obvious that modernization and industrialization in Brazil had different effects on the roles of women of various races and social classes. On the one hand, economic growth and the expansion of higher education created new jobs and educational opportunities for Euro-Brazilian, middle-class women (Alvarez 1990: 9). Gender discrimination continues, however, in the labor market in terms of occupational segregation and earning gaps. Not only does there exist a large income gap between men and women in Brazil, it seems that the higher the educational level, the higher the income gap is. On the other hand, millions of poor and working-class women were pushed into low-paying, low-status jobs in the most exploitative sectors of the economy. As Brazil underwent many economic crises during the late 1970s as a result of the oil crisis, hundreds of thousands of poor, working-class women sought solutions to their families' economic problems by participating in the community self-help organizations and grassroots social movements that sprang up throughout Brazil in the 1960s and 1970s (ibid.). At the same time, the rapid entry of Euro-Brazilian, middle-class women into academia and other professions started a debate about women's equality among Brazilian intellectuals. What role did the women's movement play in the improvement of women's status in Brazil?

Social movements

The Brazilian women's movement played a key role in the promotion of gender equality in Brazil. According to Sonia Alvarez:

> In the 1970s and 1980s Brazilians witnessed the emergence and development of what is arguably the largest, most diverse, most radical, and most successful women's movement in contemporary Latin America. By the mid-1980s, tens of thousands of women had been politicized by the women's movement and core items of the feminist agenda had made their way into the platforms and programs of all major political parties and into the public policies of the New Brazilian Republic.
>
> (Alvarez 1994: 3)

According to the Feminist Center for Studies and Advisory Services (CFEMEA), the decade of the 1970s represented a milestone for the women's movement in Brazil. That time period saw the rise of feminist ideology and of women's groups struggling for the democratization of Brazilian social and political relations. At the same time, the International Women's Year was celebrated in 1975 around the globe. The Decade of Women was also launched and, in Brazil, hundreds of women's groups emerged in the periphery of major cities. Over 400 self-professed feminist organizations were formed during the 1970s and 1980s (CFEMEA 1999: 10).

At the end of the 1970s and during the 1980s, the women's movement broadened and diversified, extending itself into political parties, unions, and community associations. As a consequence, changes were made in the Federal Constitution and in public policies in order to fight the oppression of women in Brazilian society. The Constitution guaranteed the right to family planning, to protection against family violence, and to childcare and pre-school centers. Furthermore, common-law marriage was recognized as a family nucleus and discrimination against children born out of wedlock was prohibited. At the same time, many institutions and programs were created to facilitate women's equality before the law: Women's Rights Councils, special police stations for victims of domestic violence, specific integral health programs, and programs for the prevention of and the care for women victims of sexual and domestic violence (ibid.).

During the 1990s, the women's movement took on a broader scope and a large number of Non-Governmental Organizations (NGOs) arose. This led to a diversity of projects and strategies and new structural and mobilization forms were created. For example, the following organizations were created: the Concerted Action of Brazilian Women (AMB), the National Feminist Network on Health and Reproductive Rights (RedeSaude), networks of rural and urban women workers, women researchers, religious women, Black women, lesbians, and others. Campaigns were launched, such as the For Women's Life campaign to maintain the right to abortion as codified in the Brazilian Penal Code when a pregnant woman's life is at risk or when the pregnancy results from rape (ibid.).

It can be concluded that gender equality improved in Brazil for a small percentage of women as the state sector expanded during the period of the 1970s known as the "Economic Miracle," a period in which many Euro-Brazilian and middle-class women gained access to education and economic opportunities. Furthermore, women's participation in the democratization process during the 1980s created a political space that translated into increased rights as women and as citizens of Brazil. Brazil's economic achievements, however, did not improve the lives of the vast majority of Brazilians, including Brazilian women. For Brazilian women who are poor and working-class, the socioeconomic reality was different. As they poured out of the rural areas, they ended up struggling for economic survival in the informal sector of Brazil's major cities. Women of color, in particular, seem to be at the bottom of the economic ladder.

The results discussed above refute the contention of the World Bank Report that economic growth automatically leads to economic development and to improvements in gender equality. By equating economic development with economic growth and by ignoring the role of class, race, and ethnicity in society the Report failed to correctly identify the various mechanisms through which economic development can lead to increased gender equality.

In the next section, I will discuss how Nicaraguan women made major strides toward gender equality during the 1980s but lost ground as a result of the structural adjustment policies of the 1990s advocated by the World Bank. This case again shows the need for policymakers at the World Bank to redefine economic development.

Empowerment and women in Nicaragua: 1980–2000

In this section, I discuss why I reject the World Bank Policy Research Report's conclusion that "on balance the evidence suggests that females' absolute status and gender equality improved, not deteriorated" (World Bank 2001: 215) during the structural adjustment period in Latin America. My contention is that the neoliberal economic model that resulted from structural adjustment has worsened the economic conditions of the vast majority of women in Nicaragua.

Nicaraguan women made far-reaching gains during the socialist Sandinista government that was in power from 1979 to 1990. A society with extreme concentration of income, wealth and political power was dismantled and replaced by a more egalitarian society. Galvanized by their participation in the revolutionary struggle that overthrew the dictator Anastasio Somoza, women demanded that their agenda make its way into the programs and public policies of the new socialist Sandinista government. For the first time in Nicaraguan society, women had a government that was somewhat sympathetic to their concerns.

During the 1980s, conditions were created that had the potential to radically alter the private and public lives of Nicaraguan women. Major policies were instituted to remove legal, social, and economic obstacles that prevented women from participating as equal citizens in society. In fact, Nicaragua put into effect many of the same policies advocated in the World Bank Report in its three-part strategy to promote gender equality. According to the Report, countries should: 1) reform institutions to establish equal rights and opportunities for women and men; 2) foster economic development to strengthen incentives for more equal resources and participation; 3) take active measures to redress persistent disparities in command over resources and political voice (ibid.: 15–26).

Many laws were instituted to improve women's productive and earning capacity, and to change sex roles in society. In 1981, the Law of Cooperatives was established, which gave women the right to own land. Other laws required that women be provided with maternity leave and receive equal pay for equal work. Furthermore, there were large investments in education. In 1975, one-third of University students were women. By 1985, the number was 56.3 percent, partly due to the existence of the war that began in 1981 between the Sandinista army and a group of Contra Revolutionaries (Contras, for short), created and sponsored by the United States government. Still, in 1992, two years after the war ended, women constituted 51.7 percent of all university students (Hutauruk 1998). There were also increased expenditures on health care, nutrition, and greater access to credit and job training. In addition, women obtained the right to divorce and to have custody of their children. Moreover, a number of institutions were created to increase women's awareness of the new laws and to help in their implementation. In 1979, a women's legal office (Oficina Legal de la Mujer) was created to deal with sex discrimination, non-payment of child support, domestic violence, and other legal problems affecting women (Chamorro 1989; Avin 1993; Chinchilla 1995; Babb 2001).

Women also played a significant role in the political arena. Their political participation was massive, although it varied among women according to their social status. While many poor women entered the political arena at the grassroots level by joining popular organizations, middle- and upper-class women achieved high positions such as ministers or regional party coordinators. One woman, Dora Maria Tellez, became Minister of Health while six other women were vice ministers. In the National Assembly, 18.5 percent were women (Hutauruk 1998). Furthermore, many women occupied high-level positions in various government ministries (ibid.).

An incredible phenomenon took place in Nicaraguan society during the 1980s: working class and peasant women increased their rights, their access to resources, and for the first time had a voice in their community. They were working at the grassroots levels, in both the rural and urban sectors, to increase the level of feminist consciousness among women and in society at large. These women, strong and powerful leaders at the community, national, and international level, were able to articulate the problems of women in Nicaragua and use creative strategies to alleviate them and thus empower women in the process.

Did good
until 1990?
√ ♀'s rights

At the same time, a number of women's centers providing health services, family planning services, consciousness-raising and sexuality workshops were formed throughout the country.

The electoral defeat of the Sandinistas in 1990 brought all the advancements toward gender equality to a stop. The socialist government was replaced by a coalition government, headed by a woman, Violeta Barrios de Chamorro. Programs of economic stabilization and structural adjustment were put into effect to deal with the debt crisis, hyperinflation, and economic stagnation. With the economic restructuring, gone were the subsidies for utilities, public transport, education, health care, and nutritional programs. Gone were the training programs, free lunch meals, paid pregnancy leaves, and childcare programs.

In 1991, the economy deteriorated and women struggled to make ends meet. The small degree of control they had gained over their lives during the 1980s seemed to have evaporated overnight. This is not surprising, considering that women were bearing a disproportionate share of the costs of the structural adjustment policies put into effect by the Chamorro government (Chamorro 1989; Avin 1993; Chinchilla 1995; Babb 2001). Women were the first ones to be laid off, especially in the state sector where they constituted the majority of state workers. Consequently, many joined the informal economy, becoming street vendors, domestic workers, and prostitutes. Furthermore, it is reported that many small industries "had been particularly hard hit and that women, 54 percent of its membership, were the most affected" (Babb 2001: 166). In addition, most female workers in the garment and food industries lost their jobs because of privatization and lower tariffs on imported goods (ibid.).

Women's burden also increased in the households. As primary caretakers, women spent more time caring for children and other members of the household since public health services have not only declined but are also charging fees for visits and medication. Lower incomes and higher prices have meant that many women were unable to provide for their families. Hence, women were spending more time in the labor force and more time on meeting the basic needs of their families (Chamorro 1989; Avin 1993; Chinchilla 1995; Babb 2001).

The inherent gender bias in Nicaraguan society, the restructuring in agriculture and in industry toward large-scale production, the demise of small-scale agriculture and industry, the flood of cheap imports, the collapse of the informal economy where more than 75 percent of women were employed, the elimination of all subsidies have all meant that Nicaraguan women have become more oppressed economically. Currently, 58.8 percent of working-age women are unemployed and underemployed, and of those who are employed 75.5 percent work in the informal sector – the employer of last resort (Agurto Vilchez and Gido Cajina 2001). How are Nicaraguan women surviving today in the new free market economy that emphasizes the manufacturing of export goods in industrial parks?

↑ dev't → ↓ ♀ employment

Growth of Free Trade Zones (FTZs)

In Nicaragua, factories operating under Free Trade Zone (FTZ) policies increased considerably during the period 1991–2001. In 1976, Nicaragua had one industrial park, "Las Mercedes," with 11 factories producing mostly clothes for the United States market (Comision Nacional of Zonas Francas 2001: 12). However, between 1979 and 1980, those factories closed their doors and moved their operations elsewhere in Central America. In 1991, with funds received from the World Bank and the Inter-American Development Bank, new industrial parks were created and the foreign investors came back (ibid.). The sector exploded.

Today, the FTZ system consists of 12 industrial parks. The number of firms increased from 8 in 1992 to 45 in 2001 (ibid.: 13). The sector has also been the most dynamic in terms of job creation: the number of jobs increased from 1003 in 1992 to 38,792 in 2001 (ibid.: 17). At the same time, the value of exports grew from 2.9 million to 230 million dollars during the same period (ibid.: 18). While the sector contributed 7.5 percent to total exports in 1994, its contribution reached 32 percent in 2000 (ibid.). Of the 45 firms operating in the FTZs, 14 are from Taiwan and 13 from the United States (ibid.: 13). In terms of goods produced, the vast majority of firms (73 percent) are engaged in the production of clothes, while 16 percent are in tobacco (ibid.). The firms produce mainly for the United States market.

What has been the impact of such growth on women in Nicaragua? There is no doubt that the FTZs sector is an important source of employment for poor Nicaraguan women. It is estimated that 70 percent of the workers are women, with about 50 percent being heads of households. For Nicaraguan women, having a job in the FTZs means not having to sell food and trinkets on the streets and also not having to leave the country to become maids in Costa Rica. The reality is that there are no jobs in other sectors in Nicaragua (Interview with Sonia Agurto Vilchez, 17 January 2002).

While the FTZs have been a major source of employment for women, they have not created jobs that can bring women out of poverty and contribute to their empowerment. On the contrary, management in these factories pays low wages, provides difficult working conditions and no health care, and tries to suppress the women's labor rights. According to Sonia Agurto of FIDEG, a well-known research institution in Nicaragua, the average monthly salary in the FTZs is 850 cordobas (about US$65) higher than the minimum wage of 400 cordobas (US$29). However, the basic market basket for a family of five cost 2550 cordobas (US$185). It takes three persons working in a FTZ to buy the basic market basket. To make ends meet, many women work extremely long hours (ibid.).

Working conditions are also difficult. There have been reported cases of physical mistreatment, as was illustrated by the revolt at Chentex during the mid-1990s. At Chentex, workers rose up because of poor working conditions and the fact that they were not treated with respect by management. They were treated like "cattle" as one former worker said. As for the suppression of labor rights, the various efforts of Nicaraguan workers trying to form unions have been well recorded in the press. According to Gladis Manzanares, former general secretary of one of the labor unions in the FTZs, one of the major problems is the difficulty of forming labor unions. Workers suspected of forming labor unions get fired and that can be a devastating blow for a female head of household. Furthermore, many women do not know the law and their rights (Interview with Gladyz Manzanares, 17 January 2002).

It is obvious that this neoliberal development model of FTZs has not led to the transformation of women's lives through economic empowerment, but rather reinforces the conditions of marginalization of women in Nicaraguan society. Job segregation from the outset gives women unskilled production jobs that are the poorest paid. Lacking access to on-the-job training, women are not moving up the job ladder and are not acquiring economic, social, and political power. One organization working to empower women is the "Maria Elena Cuadra" (MEC), a women's organization working to improve the human rights of women, especially of women in the FTZs. This organization provides scholarships for nontraditional jobs, has a small credit program for unemployed women, teaches women about their labor rights, and provides training for negotiation techniques. According to Sandra Ramos, the head of MEC, women need to have a consciousness-raising that will empower them to take action in the future, but it takes time. The goal of MEC, then, is to create a space for reflection for the women of the FTZs so that they can achieve personal empowerment (Interview with Sandra Ramos, 17 January 2002).

It can be concluded that structural adjustment and neoliberal policies have not improved gender equality in Nicaragua as stipulated in the World Bank Policy Research Report. On the contrary, the vast majority of women in Nicaragua have lost significant economic grounds during the 1990s as discussed above while at the same time fighting to empower themselves. The following section discusses how women in Latin America have contributed to their own empowerment.

Women's movements and women's agency

In this section, I discuss the need for policymakers at the World Bank to recognize that Third World women have been agents of change in transforming their own lives and societies. As the examples of Brazil and Nicaragua illustrate, women have made a significant contribution to their own empowerment. This implies that policymakers need to make women agents of change in their societies, an idea developed by Amartya Sen in his book *Development as Freedom*. According to Sen, "any practical attempt at enhancing the well-being of women cannot but draw on the agency of women themselves in bringing about such a change" (Sen 2000: 190). Therefore policymakers need to focus not only on the well-being aspect but also on the agency aspect of economic development. Women need to become active agents of change in the transformation of their societies, as women in Brazil and Nicaragua seem to do.

In spite of their economic losses during the 1990s, the women's movement in Nicaragua emerged in 1992 with greater creativity, dynamism, visibility, and diversity than before (Chinchilla 1995: 243). Various sectors of the women's movement broke with the National Organization of Nicaraguan Women, named the Luisa Amanda Espinosa Association of Nicaraguan Women (AMNLAE), after the first female member of the Sandinista army killed in 1970 during the revolutionary struggle. These break-away groups believe that AMNLAE, closely tied to the Sandinista party, had been more responsive to the party's needs than to women's needs. They argue that focus on women's socioeconomic problems and resistance to male domination must be at the center of their work and not the survival of a political party that had become less and less responsive to women's needs. With the formation of new women's centers, groups, and institutes, the women's movement has become more diverse and dynamic. Currently, there are about 150 social-change groups, centers, institutes, organizations, including a radio station (Montenegro 1997: 375).

At the First National Women's Meeting in January 1992, women decided to set their own agendas and to collectivize their survival problems in order to meet the needs of Nicaraguan women. The meeting was organized according to specific themes relevant to women's lives: the economy, violence, and sexuality. At that meeting, national networks were formed to deal with each of them: the Network of Women Against Domestic Violence, the Network of Women for Reproductive Rights, the Network of Women for Health (ibid.: 382). The National Coalition of Women in Politics is an organization formed in 1995 by women politicians from across the political spectrum dedicated to find common solutions to the increasing socioeconomic marginalization of Nicaraguan women. By forming these social-change groups, women in the movement have tried to become less polarized by working on issues and problems common to the vast majority of women in Nicaragua: domestic violence, economic insecurity, and serious problems in reproductive health.

After the defeat of the Sandinista party in 1990, the women's movement became autonomous and has tried to become a political force to be reckoned with. Given that the vast majority of women in Nicaragua are poor, and given that these women are at the base of the women's movement, issues and problems affecting these marginalized women have been at the center of the movement's campaigns to change the reality of women. Their campaign against domestic violence has been particularly successful: there are now various laws protecting women against domestic violence and two women police stations in Managua. The movement has grown in maturity and diversity to become the most dynamic and creative women's movement in Central America.

Conclusion

The World Bank Policy Research Report emphasizes the role of economic growth/development as a key element in improving gender equality in the Third World. In this chapter, I argue the need for the authors to reconceptualize the concept of economic development and to incorporate the issues of class, race, and ethnicity in their analysis in order to develop a more coherent argument and effective policies. I also suggest that the three-part strategy proposed by the Report is inconsistent with the neoliberal agenda of international lending organizations, including the World Bank. I argue that the new development model of free market policies has made it difficult for the three-part strategy to be put into effect in Latin America, especially Nicaragua. The neoliberal policies of the 1990s have not led to greater economic growth and gender equality. In fact, the emphasis on Free Trade Zones in Nicaragua limits women's economic opportunities, reduce their sense of empowerment gained during the 1980s, and exposes them to widespread economic exploitation by multinational corporations.

References

Adelman, Irma (1975) "Development Economics: A Reassessment of Goals," *American Economic Review*, 65(2): 302–9.

Agurto Vilchez, Sonia and Alejandra Guido Cajina (2001) *Mujeres: Pilares Fundamentales de la Economía Nicaragüense*, Nicaragua: Fundacion Internacional Para el Desafio Economico Global (FIDEG).

Alvarez, Sonia E. (1994) "The (trans)formation of feminism(s) and gender politics in democratizing Brazil," in J.S. Jaquette (ed.) *The Women's Movement in Latin America*, second edition, Boulder, CO, San Francisco, CA, and Oxford: Westview Press: 13–63.

—— (1990) *Movements in Engendering Democracy in Brazil: Women's Transition Politics*, Princeton, NJ: Princeton University Press.

—— (1988) *Democratizando o Brasil*, Rio de Janeiro: Paz e Terra.

Arriagada, I. (1995) "Unequal Participation by Women in the Work Force," in James L. Dietz (ed.), *Latin America's Economic Development: Confronting Crisis*, second edition, Boulder, CO: Lynne Rienner Publishers, Inc.: 333–49.

Avin, Rose-Marie (1993) "The Status of Women in Changing Economies: The Case of Nicaragua," paper presented at the annual meeting of the Midwest Economics Association in Indianapolis, Indiana, April 1–3, unpublished.

Babb, Florence E. (2001) *After Revolution: Mapping Gender and Cultural Politics in Neoliberal Nicaragua*, Austin, TX: University of Texas Press.

Berger, Silvia (1999) "Economic History, South America," in Janice Peterson and Margaret Lewis (eds), *The Elgar Companion to Feminist Economics*, Cheltenham, UK and Northampton, MA: Edward Elgar: 246–57.

Castro, Mary Garcia (November 1995) "Mulher negra, resistencia e cidadania; e o lugar da mulata?", *Presenca da Mulher*: 26–33.

CFEMEA (Feminist Center for Studies and Advisory Services) (1999) *Women's Rights and the Legislative in Brazil*, Brasilia, DF.

Chamorro, Amalia (1989) "La Mujer: Logros y Limites en 10 Anos de Revolucion," *Cuadernos de Sociología* (January–February): 117–43.

Chinchilla, Norma S. (1995) "Revolutionary Popular Feminism in Nicaragua: Ideologies, Political Transitions, and the Struggle for Autonomy," *Women in the Latin American Development Process*, Philadelphia, PA: Temple University Press: 242–70.

Comision Nacional de Zonas Francas (2001) *Memoria 1997–2001*, Managua, Nicaragua.

Delgado, Didice G., Paola Cappellin and Vera Soares (eds) (2000) *Mulher e Trabalho: Experiencias de Acao Afirmativa*, São Paulo: Boitempo Editorial.

Human Development Report 2000 (2000) New York, Oxford: Oxford University Press.

Hutauruk, Deborah (1998) "Women in Nicaragua: You've Come a Long Way," *Nica News*, 19 (December).

Inter-American Development Bank (1987) *Economic and Social Progress in Latin America 1987*.

Library of Nations (1987) *Brazil*, Alexandria, VA: Time-Life Books, Inc.

Ministry of Education (2000) *Education in Brazil: 1995–2000*.

Montenegro, Sofia (1997) "Un Movimiento de Mujeres en Auge," in *Movimiento de Mujeres en Centroamerica*, Managua, Nicaragua: Programa Regional La Corriente.

Sen, Amarya (1999), *Development as Freedom*, New York: Anchor Books.

Todaro, Michael P. (2000) *Economic Development*, seventh edition, New York: Addison-Wesley.

World Bank (2001) *Engendering Development: Through Gender Equality in Rights, Resources, and Voice*, New York: Oxford University Press.

World Bank Development Report 1999/2000 (2000), New York: Oxford University Press.

6 Engendering agricultural technology for Africa's farmers

Promises and pitfalls

Cheryl Doss

Improved agricultural technologies are key to reducing poverty and increasing the standard of living in Africa. The logic behind this statement is straight-forward. A majority of Africans live in rural areas and in many countries, as many as 70 percent of people earn their primary income from agriculture. Moreover, African farmers are among the poorest people in the world. One reason for the continuing poverty is that crop yields in sub-Saharan Africa are extremely low. For maize, one of the staple crops, yields in Africa are only 60 percent of those in Latin America and the Caribbean. Similarly, cassava yields are only 75 percent those in Asia and only 40 percent of those in India. Productivity increases in the rest of the world have meant that world prices for these crops have fallen over the past four decades. But these productivity gains have not been matched in Africa. As a result, African farmers face falling world prices but have not had a comparable reduction in the costs of production.

Improved technologies are needed in Africa to increase productivity, reduce poverty, and reduce the pressure for unsustainable land use. In particular, tech-nologies are needed to improve the lives of women farmers in Africa, who work long hours in difficult conditions for low levels of output. A wide variety of agricultural technologies have been introduced to improve agricultural produc-tivity. Some of them have been successful in benefiting women farmers, while others have not. The failures have generated a sense among many that improved agricultural technologies do not benefit women.

The literature critical of improved technologies,[1] as well as that critical of policies to promote economic growth, often seems to suggest that women would be better off without improved technologies and economic growth. Yet clearly this cannot be the case. Instead, we should conclude that technologies to improve agricultural productivity are a necessary, but not sufficient, condition for African women farmers to improve their welfare. Similarly, economic growth is neces-sary but certainly not sufficient for improving women's welfare, especially in the poorer countries. Thus, we need ask how we can develop agricultural tech-nologies, and more broadly, policies for economic growth, that benefit a broad spectrum of society, including women, and are sustainable.

The World Bank Policy Research Report, *Engendering Development* (World Bank 2001), draws some general lessons on how to ensure that women benefit from development. Other chapters in this book provide a detailed critique of this research report. Many of these chapters emphasize the macroeconomic environment and discuss how the World Bank has not incorporated gender issues into its macroeconomic policies. In this chapter, I focus much more on micro-economic issues. I examine the extent to which the lessons derived from the report can be applied to policies to improve the well-being of African women farmers and discuss additional factors that are not considered or emphasized in the report. Although macro policies affect agriculture, this chapter will not spend much time looking at macro issues. Among the other works that have considered the effects of macro policies, especially structural adjustment programs, on women farmers in Africa are Gladwin (1991) and Mehra (1991).

The World Bank report does not directly address the issues of agriculture and agricultural technology. In addition, it does not directly address the issues of power relations within households, communities, and countries. These power relations affect how roles and responsibilities are renegotiated when new opportunities, such as new technologies or new market opportunities, are created. Instead, the report emphasizes the importance of economic growth and discusses some of the conditions necessary for women to benefit economically from economic growth. It is critical to take this report an additional step further and ask how we can develop agricultural technologies and policies that will improve the agricultural productivity and well-being of women farmers in Africa.

One way in which it is critical to move beyond the lessons in the report is to explicitly recognize the power relationships within households, communities, and countries. Many of the reasons that African women farmers have not benefited from new technologies – even when the technologies were specifically designed to benefit them – is that the women did not have the power to negotiate the details to their advantage.

This concern also means that it is difficult to generalize about policies that will benefit all women farmers in Africa. There are many differences among these women farmers. Some of these differences can be described by statistical variables – wealth, income, education levels, and status within the household (as household head or spouse). Other economic variables also may be important. Women's access to markets varies considerably: Those in peri-urban areas may have access to urban markets while for others, limited infrastructure and high transportation costs mean that it is difficult to market their products. Ethnicity and kinship networks shape women's power within their households and communities. National government policies, both economic and non-economic, will affect their abilities to take advantage of new opportunities. Many women still work on subsistence farms, but in some areas, especially in Southern Africa, women work as wage laborers in the commercial agricultural sector. This issue, namely which women benefit and which women lose, is ignored in the World Bank report, but must be taken into consideration.

Women's roles in agriculture production in Africa

It is widely quoted that women in Africa produce 70–80 percent of the food and provide more than 60 percent of the agricultural labor force.[2] Formal labor force statistics indicate that 42 percent of the economically active population in agriculture is female (UN 2003), but these estimates certainly underestimate women's role, since women in farm households are often registered as housewives rather than farmers.

Many studies have attempted to quantify women's contributions to agriculture. Bryson (1981) categorized farming systems as "male predominance," "female predominance" and "equal participation" and found that 52 percent of a random sample of sub-Saharan African societies were "female predominance" systems, compared with only 34 percent worldwide. Only 19 percent of those in sub-Saharan Africa were "male predominance" systems. Saito (1994) found that women work more hours than men in agriculture in Burkina Faso, Kenya, Zambia, and Nigeria. Kumar (1991) found similar results for maize-growing households in Zambia, claiming that the average number of hours spent cropping is higher for women than men. As men increasingly become involved in wage labor, both in rural areas and by migrating to cities, women frequently take over many of the agricultural tasks. Thus, women's contributions are not static and they do vary across locations within Africa, but clearly any consideration of gender issues in development in Africa must consider women farmers.

An extensive literature emerged in the 1980s critiquing the lack of attention to women in agriculture (e.g. Staudt 1987; Cloud 1985; Poats *et al.* 1988). Unfortunately, when this literature was translated into policy circles, it was often simplified to suggest that what was needed was a kind of sensitivity training for policy-makers and researchers. If only policy-makers and senior scientists understood that their clients were women, then technologies to benefit women farmers would be developed, agricultural productivity by women farmers would increase, and poverty would be reduced. Policy failures were usually attributed to policy-makers – and specifically to their lack of knowledge or commitment concerning the problems of women farmers. In hindsight, this view was quaintly naïve. Many policy-makers did in fact need sensitivity training (and some still do) and it is an important step to realize that women are key actors in agricultural production. But good intentions, even if they are genuine, are not enough.

Research institutions, including the international scientific institutions and the World Bank, have been fairly responsive to the idea that women are farmers in Africa. Pushed by grassroots development workers and feminist researchers, they have tried to target technologies and policies toward women. Yet the ways in which they typically do so are not sufficient to ensure that women will benefit from these innovations. Typically, when looking at gender issues in the agricultural sector, women farmers have been marginalized. In an effort to be responsive to the needs of women, these organizations have tried to prioritize "women's crops" and "women's tasks." Both of these approaches compartmentalize women's contributions in agriculture and thus limit the understanding of women's work and women's needs.

For example, many rural Africans can tell you which crops are grown by men and which are grown by women in their area. One crop that is considered a "man's crop" in Ghana is yams. While visiting agricultural households in Ghana, I spoke with the head of a local government office for women and development. She spoke at length to me about the distinctions between men's and women's crops, emphasizing that yams were a man's crop. She then invited me to her yam farm without any sense of irony. This example emphasizes the difference between accepted cultural norms and actual practices. It is rare that these two completely overlap. Both may be important when considering how the rights and responsibilities from new technologies are allocated.

A generalization is often made that men grow cash crops and women grow subsistence crops. Yet the patterns do not hold very tightly under close scrutiny. Using data from the Ghana Living Standards Survey – a nationally representative household survey – I find that there are no major crops grown exclusively, or even primarily, by women or by men (Doss 2002). For example, cocoa is one of the main cash crops in Ghana, yet 23 percent of the farmers growing cocoa on their plots are women. In addition, of the women holding land in Ghana, 12 percent grow cocoa. The comparable number for men is 18 percent. The cropping patterns are gendered – some crops are more likely to be grown by men and others are more likely to be grown by women but there are many exceptions to the rule.[3]

Many staple crops, including those thought of traditionally as men's crops, are grown by women, especially women in female-headed households. Thus, programs that target these crops may have important implications for women. The generalizations have some truth, but the reality of who grows which crops and who performs which tasks is quite complex and varies considerably. Simply accepting the generalizations will mean that much of women's contributions are ignored.

Women provide much of the labor for food production in Africa. Yet the nature of women's contributions varies tremendously, even within countries. In particular, there are large differences in the extent to which women make the decisions and the extent to which women control the output. Women may own and control their own plots of land and the output from these plots. Women may work on household plots, where they have some rights to the output, especially for the output destined for household consumption. Women may also provide labor on men's plots and may or not be directly compensated. Individual women may do more than one of these – they may own their own plots and also work on the household and their husband's plot. This makes it difficult to disentangle women's contributions from overall household production. Yet, understanding women's roles within particular contexts is important in order to understand how they will be affected by changes in technologies.

Discussions of men's and women's tasks usually note that clearing fields and plowing are men's tasks while weeding and post-harvest processing are women's tasks. These distinctions may be clearly defined culturally, yet they may not reflect actual practices. Consider the parallels in the USA, where many might claim that childcare and cooking are women's responsibilities while maintenance of the lawn and car are men's responsibilities. These distinctions suggest the cultural norms, but there are many exceptions within any community. Again, this simplification may ignore many of the contributions that women make and many of the responsibilities that they face.

While there is extensive variation in the gendered patterns of agricultural production across Africa, one of the things that is true throughout the continent is that these patterns are changing. As new economic opportunities develop and as new technologies are available, the traditional patterns change. For example, as men migrate to the cities or take up wage employment in rural areas, women increasingly take over the traditionally male activities of clearing and plowing.

It is less common for men to take over women's tasks. Yet when the returns to a traditionally woman's activity are increasing, either due to new technologies or new market opportunities, we may see men taking over women's activities. Men may become involved in producing crops culturally defined as women's crops when they become profitable. Around Techiman in Ghana, women traditionally have grown tomatoes. When the market forces expanded the demand for tomatoes, the profitability of growing tomatoes increased and men have recently become involved in their production. Similar issues have been documented in Nigeria, where men began to grow crops that were traditionally women's crops, once the market developed (Ezumah and Domenico 1995; Burfisher and Horenstein 1993).

Targeting agricultural innovations towards women based on the tasks that women do or the crops that they grow assumes the environment is static. It does not take into consideration how these activities will change after the new technology is introduced. In particular, it does not address any of the underlying ways in which power relations within households and communities will affect who gains and who loses from the new technologies. The outcomes from new technologies are often contested as is discussed in detail below.

Improving agricultural technologies

Although agricultural production in Africa increased by an average of 3.2 percent per year during the period from 1981 to 2000, much of that growth was due to increases in the area planted, which grew at an average rate of 2.8 percent per year. Yields only increased by 0.36 percent per year, much lower than the average yield increases of 1.8 percent for all developing countries. Modern varieties actually generated growth in production of 0.47 percent but an accompanying decline in other inputs accounted for a 1 percent annual decline in yields (Evenson and Gollin 2003). Thus, new agricultural technologies have had less of an impact in Africa than elsewhere.

Many of the new technologies developed for African farmers have been targeted at smallholder farmers, and hence at women (although that is not always explicitly recognized).

Improved seeds, especially maize and wheat seed, designed especially for smallholders are being developed through the International Agricultural Research Centers (CGIAR), working in conjunction with National Agricultural Research Centers. These seeds have been developed to overcome some of the problems that smallholder farmers face, including low yields, susceptibility to drought, and susceptibility to weed and pest infestations. A recent series of studies compiled in East Africa by the International Center for the Improvement of Wheat and Maize (CIMMYT) in collaboration with National Agricultural Research Systems indicate that the adoption levels of improved seeds are fairly high in some parts of East Africa. Many farmers, however, are recycling seed rather than purchasing new seed, thereby gaining some, but not all, of the potential benefits.[4]

One of the other problems facing agricultural productivity of farmers in Africa is soil fertility. In much of East Africa, the proportion of farmers using either organic or chemical fertilizer is relatively small. Although extension services promote the use of chemical fertilizer, farmers complain that it is expensive and often unavailable at the right time or in the right formulations. Given the current infrastructure and prices in many rural areas, it may not be profitable for farmers to use these technologies. Other technologies to improve soil fertility include management practices. These often require additional labor as an input, rather than purchased fertilizer.

Many changes are taking place for agricultural households in Africa. Farmers – both male and female – respond to new economic opportunities and to new technologies when it makes sense for them to do so. Yet some households and some individuals are better placed to adopt the new technologies and to benefit from them; women are less likely to be among these farmers.

Women's use of improved agricultural technologies

If one group of farmers, such as women farmers or farmers in female-headed households, does not have access to a new technology, then it is unlikely to be of much benefit to them. They might benefit indirectly, if increased agricultural productivity increased nonagricultural opportunities for them or lowered the prices for the foods that they purchase. These indirect effects are likely to be small without significant increases in productivity. The indirect effects may be overshadowed by the direct effects of providing technology to only some in that the disparities between groups will widen over time, as those using the new technologies will increase their power and ability to gain continued access to these resources and technologies.

Kumar (1987) noted that there were three problems with failure to incorporate women's roles when developing new technologies and designing projects. First, she notes the loss of adaptive efficiency from not taking women's operational knowledge into consideration. Second, women's bargaining power within the household may decrease and their workload may increase. Finally, not taking women's roles into account results in lower adoption rates of the new technology by women. The first and third of these are efficiency arguments – making the claim that, in the short run, by not including women some of the potential benefits of new technologies are not captured. The second one provides one way to look at some of these broader issues about how technologies may affect women's well-being. But the real challenge is to know, *a priori*, about the power relations within households and communities so that we can sense whether women will be able to take advantage of any of the benefits.

Generally we find that fewer female farmers than male farmers use improved varieties of seeds and fertilizer. In the twenty-one recent CIMMYT studies[5] that estimated the probability of adoption of improved varieties of wheat and maize, only three included gender as an explanatory variable. In the fourteen studies that included an estimation of the probability of adopting fertilizer, gender was included in only two of them. The measure included in all of these cases was the gender of the household head, not the gender of the farmer. In all of these studies, female-headed households were less likely to use the improved technologies than male-headed households.

In a detailed study examining the adoption of maize technologies in Ghana, we found that only 39 percent of female farmers planted improved varieties of maize in the 1997 cropping year, while 59 percent of male farmers did so (Doss and Morris 2001). Only 16 percent of female farmers used fertilizer while 23 percent of male farmers did so. We were interested in whether these differences could be explained by differential access to the resources needed for farming or whether men and women appeared to making different decisions about technologies, given a particular situation. Once we controlled for access to the key complementary inputs, especially land and extension services, the gender of the farmer was no longer statistically significant in explaining the adoption decision. This result suggests that it is not the gender of the farmer *per se* that affects adoption decisions, but rather that gender is important because it affects farmers' ability to gain access to the necessary inputs.

Further investigation indicated that women in female-headed households were less likely to adopt improved maize seeds, even after for controlling for other inputs, than male or female farmers in male-headed households. Thus, both male and female farmers in male-headed households were making similar decisions, based on their resources, but female-headed households were less likely to adopt new technologies in the same situation. This may be because male household heads have greater access to resources than do female household heads in ways that we could not account for in our empirical analysis.

Many studies looking at the adoption of technology now include a gender variable. Yet, much of the time, it is simply a variable indicating the gender of the household head. In some instances, this may be appropriate, if the household head is the one making the agricultural decisions. In other instances, however, we may want information about the wife who is doing the farming. Examining only the gender of the household head leaves out of the analysis all of the women farmers living in male-headed households. This may be a significant omission. Work on gender patterns of cropping in Ghana (Doss 2002) finds that the patterns differ depending on how you define a "female farmer." Three definitions were used. The gender of the farmer may be defined as the gender of the head of household, the holder of the land, or the one who has the right to keep the proceeds. One important result is that women in female-headed households are more likely to be growing staple crops than women in male-headed households. Thus, the definitions matter.

Household decision-making

Discussions of the costs and benefits of new technologies to men and women implicitly assume that the costs and benefits facing men and women are different. If we think of the household as a single entity, making decisions about how best to allocate the workload and the outputs, then we would expect that the costs and benefits would be shared – and that anyone who faced the increasing costs would receive a proportionate share of the benefits. Yet this doesn't seem to be necessarily the case. Many factors determine who faces the costs and who reaps the benefits of new opportunities. The household bargaining literature suggests women's outside options affect how these costs and benefits are distributed among household members.

For example, recent work in Ghana indicates that when women own a greater share of household assets, household expenditure patterns differ (Doss 1997). A greater share of the household budget is spent on food and less on recreation and on alcohol and tobacco when women own more of the household assets. One interpretation of this is that women with more assets have a greater influence on household spending patterns. Others have found similar effects – when women own more of the assets, they have more power to determine outcomes (e.g. Quisumbing and Maluccio 2003).

Intrahousehold analyses help us to understand when new agricultural technologies will benefit women and when they will make their situations worse off. An extensive literature is developing whereby econometric tools are used to demonstrate the importance of bargaining power. This literature is extensively discussed in the World Bank report in their chapter on intrahousehold issues. The challenge with this empirical literature has been to find measures of bargaining power that are quantifiable. The measures that have been used, such as ownership of land, not only are measures of bargaining power but are also outcomes of individual power within their household and community. The studies are limited both by the availability of data and by the difficulty in conceptualizing and quantifying measures of power. Further limitations of these studies are discussed in Chapter 11 of this volume by Orgocka and Summerfield.

Much of the empirical intrahousehold literature has assumed that households make cooperative decisions and that the outcomes are efficient, often using a measure of Pareto efficiency which assumes that no one individual can be made better off without making another individual worse off. The efficiency is often tested in the literature using consumption decisions as outcome measures. It is important to realize that, given the levels of bargaining power for each household member, an outcome that is inherently inequitable may be efficient. The one area of the empirical literature where noncooperative or inefficient outcomes have been clearly identified is in agricultural production. In the following examples, the introduction of new opportunities resulted in household roles and responsibilities being contested and renegotiated. These examples demonstrate the importance of considering the dynamic impacts of new opportunities.

In The Gambia, rice was traditionally grown on women's plots. A project to increase women's agricultural productivity introduced centralized pump irrigation. The net effect of this project was to shift control of rice production from women to men. Irrigated rice was grown under the authority of the male compound head and was no longer under women's control (von Braun and Webb 1989).

If the technologies require inputs from men, such as labor or cash, then women may have to give up some of the benefits in order to gain access to these inputs. If the technologies don't increase women's outside options, women may not gain the benefits from the new technologies. If women can't obtain the other inputs unless they live within a male-headed household, their outside options will not increase.

One finding that has implications for agricultural technology is that because individuals within households may be making independent decisions, the results may not always be efficient. For example, in Burkina Faso, one study found that by shifting inputs, especially fertilizer, from plots controlled by men to plots planted with the same crops but controlled by women, total level of household production would have increased (Udry 1996). Similarly, in Cameroon, labor was not allocated efficiently across men's rice fields and women's sorghum fields – by reallocating labor across the fields, the total production would have increased (Jones 1993).

A final example looks at decision-making within pastoral households about where to locate the household and the impact of location on women's milk-marketing opportunities (McPeak and Doss 2003). Men traditionally make the decisions about where to locate the pastoralist households among the Gabra of northern Kenya. These decisions have an impact on the ability of women to take advantage of new opportunities to sell milk in local markets. Empirical results suggest that men may make decisions about location specifically to limit women's ability to market milk. This may be to limit women's access to independently controlled income. In this case, a new market opportunity, rather than a new technology, challenges traditional roles and is contested within the household.

These analyses do not sufficiently provide us with an understanding of why a household might reach an inefficient outcome – an outcome where the same resources could have been used to obtain a higher level of production. One explanation that can be inferred from these is that men do not want to give up the power that they hold, even if in the short run there might be gains from doing so. Giving women increased access to resources (whether increased output on their plots or cash from milk sales) may have the effect of shifting the power dynamics within the households. These potential shifts in power are hotly contested, even when there is the possibility for increased production for the household as a whole.

This approach provides us with a starting point for understanding why technologies may have differential impacts on men and women. Yet, it is not sufficient. Simply looking at outside options is only one way of conceptualizing bargaining power. The power relations within households may be more complex. Sen notes the importance of considering perceptions, well-being, and agency (1990), rather than just some of the measure of bargaining power and individualist outcomes. Folbre (2001), among others, critiques the models for their individualistic approach.

Impacts of agricultural technologies on women

Technologies will have a variety of effects. Any given technology may have both positive and negative effects. For example, some improved varieties of seeds have greater yields but they may also require greater inputs, especially in terms of labor. New technologies may reduce the risk that a farmer faces (for example, irrigation technology may ensure an adequate water supply) or they may increase risks, making farmers more vulnerable to changes in weather or market conditions. Even technologies that are designed to benefit women will have both costs and benefits for women associated with them. Thus, we need to explore the circumstances under which technologies benefit women farmers. Individual farmers may come to different conclusions as to whether the costs of a given technology outweigh the benefits. It will matter who bears the costs and who receives the benefits. When technologies increase women's outside options, they are more likely to have a positive effect on women's well-being.

There are three key dimensions along which technologies affect farmers. The effects can vary along the three dimensions, which may make it difficult to predict the net overall effect. These three dimensions provide a useful framework for looking at the potential effects of new technologies and asking how we can develop technologies that benefit African women farmers.

The first dimension is how new technologies affect women's workload. Women are already contributing much of the labor for agriculture, in addition to their household work of preparing meals, fetching water, childcare, laundry, and cleaning. Technologies that reduce women's workload – and especially technologies that reduce the drudgery of some tasks, such as weeding, fetching water or firewood, or pounding grain – will have a positive impact on women. Even technologies that increase the productivity of women's work may have negative impacts on a woman's well-being if they also require her to work longer or harder, or if she does not control the output.

One of the challenges to developing agricultural technologies is that simply looking at the roles and responsibilities of women before the introduction of new technologies does not necessarily tell us how these will be allocated following the introduction of the technologies. These roles and responsibilities respond to economic incentives. An interesting example was described in *The Economist* (2001). Women are usually responsible for collecting water in Africa. However, in South Africa a new technology, the Hippo Roller, has recently been introduced and is gaining wide acceptance. The simple technology involves a plastic barrel that can roll along with a handle that fits into it. Women are able to transport significantly more water per trip using this technology. Young men have apparently decided that this technology is "cool" and have begun collecting water themselves (*The Economist* 2001). It remains to be seen whether young men will continue to collect water after the novelty has worn off! Yet this somewhat trivial example indicates that the gender allocation of these tasks is not static.

Reallocations are more frequently in the other direction. When opportunities for increased productivity open up for men as a result of a technological innovation, such as irrigation or improved seeds, women's labor may be required in men's activities. If the innovations don't increase women's outside options, women may not be able to take advantage of the benefits. Women may be required to contribute additional labor without receiving compensatory benefits.

The second dimension is how new technologies affect access to resources, especially land. Women farmers in Africa obtain access to land in a variety of ways. In some areas women have traditionally held their own rights to land. In other areas, they obtain rights to land through a male relative or through the village head. Many places are moving toward formal systems of titling land that create the possibility for formal land markets (see Lastarria-Cornhiel (1997) for a discussion of the effects of land-titling on women in Africa). With formal land markets, land can be bought and sold. Land may become more valuable as increasing market opportunities become available. Farmers in peri-urban areas are increasingly growing crops for sale in urban areas and sometimes even for export. Increasing productivity also makes the land more valuable.

This suggests that policies to increase agricultural productivity may have an unintended effect of increasing the value of land and, thus, making it more difficult for women to maintain control over land. It is important to consider the ways in which women have access to land in order to understand the potential impacts of new technologies. Women will benefit more from technologies that increase agricultural productivity when they have secure access to the land and when the ownership of land is part of their outside option.

Similarly, as other resources become more valuable, women may have a harder time obtaining access to them. For example, as male wages increase, it will be harder for women to get men to work on their fields. As more farmers are eager for extension services to learn about a newly available technology, it will be harder for farmers who are poorer and less powerful, including women farmers, to gain access to the information. Extension agents are often more likely to go to farmers who are more likely and more able to adopt the recommended technologies. Thus, it is important to have procedures in place at the time that technologies are developed to ensure that they are disseminated to the target audience.

AGRICULTURAL tech is
very variable
→ tech. priorities

[handwritten margin note: Tech can ↑ or ↓ power]

The final dimension is how new technologies affect women's control over their labor and output. Technologies that are designed to benefit women may have unexpected effects if they result in women losing control over activities once they become profitable. When women's labor is required for production of crops controlled by men, they may lose, even if the total output produced by the household increases. While women may have control over outputs when they are for household consumption, they may lose control over the outputs when they are destined for sale in the market.

It is hard to predict *a priori* how new technologies will affect women's workload, access to resources, and control over their labor and output. Certainly having women involved at all stages of the design and implementation of new technologies will help. They will have a more nuanced sense of their power within the household and communities and may have some idea of how these roles and responsibilities will be renegotiated. They may also have some sense of whether the new technologies will enhance or diminish their power.

Engendering Development and agricultural technologies

In the World Bank report, *Engendering Development*, the authors lay out a three-part strategy:

1   Reform institutions to establish equal rights and opportunities for women and men.
2   Foster economic development to strengthen incentives for more equal resources and participation.
3   Take active measures to redress persistent disparities in command over resources and political voice.

These are fairly general strategies, not specifically related to women farmers. In fact, agriculture and women farmers are rarely mentioned in the report. Although agricultural extension services are listed in the index, agriculture is not. Agriculture is discussed in the context of women owning plots of agricultural land. It would not be clear from reading the report that a large proportion of the women in Africa live in rural areas and engage in agriculture.

Yet, these general strategies are useful ways of thinking about how to ensure that African women farmers benefit from the processes of growth and development. In order to increase agricultural productivity and have women share the benefits of this increased production, women must have control over the land that they farm and their own labor. Otherwise, increasing agricultural productivity will result in the further loss of their control over their labor and land. Related to this, the institutions in the rural sector must be available to women. Women must have access to credit and extension services.

Yet, several key things are missing from the report. In some cases, it is because these points are not clearly made in the extensive literature that they reviewed. In other cases, it was simply not emphasized in the report.

[handwritten margin note: WB doesn't present ♀ role in agric.]

In examining the welfare effects of different policies, whether they are new technologies or new markets, it is important to look at both the absolute effects of the policies and on the relative effects across groups, such as between men and women or between urban and rural people. Both are important. They are often used interchangeably, without specifying which matters. The absolute effects clearly are important. But the relative ones matter as well. Much of the intrahousehold literature which examines the effects of bargaining power on household decisions is concerned with the relative bargaining power of men and women in the household. Changing this balance will affect the outcomes. Although quantitative studies have typically been static, we would expect these effects to magnify in the long run.

With all of the focus on gender in the report, women are not differentiated. Although it may be important to keep the focus broadly on gender, it is key to note that from any given policy, there may be some women who benefit and some who lose. Most of the issues of class and ethnicity are ignored. Yet, it is important to always ask which women gain and which lose from any situation. It is rarely the case that all women are similarly affected by a policy.

This particularly comes out in the section of *Engendering Development* where the authors discuss household work. They accurately note that women spend much of their time in unpaid work within the household and on the farm. They suggest that, "where available, hired labor can substitute for family labor on farms or in care activities, thus easing the workload of household members" (World Bank 2001: 186). While it may be true that labor markets may ease some of the inefficiencies within households, it is likely that the person being hired to do this work will be another woman. Developing labor markets for household work simply transfers it to another group of women. Many different factors will affect whether this is to the benefit or disadvantage of the women being hired.

Understanding which women will have the power to renegotiate their labor allocation and control over the output when new opportunities are created is a challenge. The empirical analyses of these outcomes usually do not ask the question as to which women benefit, other than to include some descriptive variables such as age, education level, or wealth.

Conclusion

It is challenging to target agricultural technologies, such as improved seeds or fertilizer, to improve the well-being of Africa's women farmers. Yet it is crucial that these new technologies do not simply bypass women farmers. It is hard to develop technologies, in the abstract, that will benefit women, although technologies that reduce women's workload and increase their productivity are certainly a start. In addition, it is important to think about how a technology will increase women's outside options and thus allow them to maintain control over their own labor and some of the benefits from the new technology.

The strategy proposed in *Engendering Development* is a general overall strategy. In implementing it, it will be critical to remember that all of the parts must go together. In particular, it is critical to remember that growth and development are necessary, but not sufficient conditions, to improve women's well-being. The other aspects, such as increasing women's control over their resources, will be important, especially in the agricultural sector. Translating this strategy into effective policies for African women farmers will continue to be a large challenge. We must find ways to both increase women's agricultural productivity and allow them to benefit from it.

Notes

1   See, for example, Marglin 1996.
2   Recent examples of the use of this quote are in *UN Wire*, *Ag Journal*, and *FAO News Highlights*.
3   This study does not look at the share of output or the share of the value of output produced by women since the data was not available to do this.
4   For a synthesis of the studies, see Doss *et al.* 2003.
5   For a synthesis of these studies, see Doss *et al.* 2003. For a critique of the studies and the methodology typically use in adoption studies, see Doss 2003.

References

Ag Journal (2003) "More Women Work the Land," Friday, October 3.

Bryson, J.C. (1981) "Women and Agriculture in Sub-Saharan Africa: Implications for Development (an Exploratory Study)," in N. Nelson (ed.), *African Women in the Development Process*, Totowa, NJ: Cass.

Burfisher, M.E. and N.R. Horenstein (1993) *Sex Roles in the Nigerian Tiv Farm Household and the Differential Impacts of Development Projects*, Case Studies of the Impact of Large-Scale Development Projects on Women 2, New York: Population Council.

Cloud, Kathleen (1985) "Women Farmers and AID Agricultural Projects: How Efficient are We?" in *Women Creating Wealth: Transforming Economic Development*, selected papers and speeches from the Association for Women in Development Conference, April 25–27, Washington, DC: AWID.

Doss, Cheryl (1997) "The Effects of Women's Bargaining Power on Household Health and Education Outcomes: Evidence from Ghana," paper presented at the Population Association of American annual meetings, New Orleans, LA.

—— (2002) Men's Crops? Women's Crops? The Gender Patterns of Cropping in Ghana," *World Development*, 30(11): 1987–2000.

—— (2003) *Understanding Farm Level Technology Adoption: Lessons Learned from CIMMYT's Micro Surveys in Eastern Africa*, CIMMYT Economics Working Paper, No. 02–05, Mexico, DF: CIMMYT.

Doss, Cheryl, Wilfred Mwangi, Hugo Verkuijl and Hugo de Groote (2003) *Adoption of Maize and Wheat Technologies in Eastern Africa: Synthesis of Eastern African Adoption Studies*, CIMMYT Economics Working Paper No. 03–06, Mexico, DF: CIMMYT.

Doss, Cheryl and Michael Morris (2000) "How Does Gender Affect the Adoption of Agricultural Innovations? The Case of Improved Maize Technology in Ghana," *Agricultural Economics*, 25: 27–39.

Economist, The (2001) "Keep it Simple," Dec. 10–16: 13.

Evenson, R. and D. Gollin (2003) "Assessing the Impact of the Green Revolution, 1960–2000," *Science*, 3000 (May 2): 758–62.

Ezumah, N.N. and C.M.D. Domenico (1995) "Enhancing the Role of Women in Crop Production: A Case Study of Igbo women in Nigeria," *World Development*, 23(10): 1731–44.

FAO News Highlights (1998) "Women Feed the World: FAO Announces Theme for World Food Day 1998," March 9.

Folbre, Nancy (2001) *The Invisible Heart, Economics and Family Values*, New York: The New Press.

Gladwin, Christina (ed.) (1991) *Structural Adjustment and African Women Farmers*, Gainesville, FL: University of Florida Press.

Jones, Christine (1993) "The Mobilization of Women's Labor for Cash Crop Production: A Game Theoretic Approach," *American Journal of Agricultural Economics*, 75: 1049–54.

Kumar, S.K. (1987) "Women's Role and Agricultural Technology," in J.W. Mellor, C.L. Delgado and M.J. Blackie (eds), *Accelerating Food Production in Sub-Saharan Africa*, Baltimore, MD: Johns Hopkins University Press.

—— (1991) *Adoption of Hybrid Maize in Zambia: Effects on Gender Roles, Food Consumption, and Nutrition*, Washington, DC: IFPRI.

Lastarria-Cornhiel, Susanna (1997) "Impact of Privatization on Gender and Property Rights in Africa," *World Development* 25(8): 1317–33.

Marglin, Stephen A. (1996) "Farmers, Seedsmen, and Scientists: Systems of Agriculture and Systems of Knowledge," in Frederique Apffel-Marglin and Stephen A. Marglin, *Decolonizing Knowledge*, Oxford: Oxford University Press.

Mehra, Rekha (1991) "Can Structural Adjustment Work for Women Farmers?" *American Journal of Agricultural Economics*, 73(5): 1440–55.

McPeak, John and Cheryl Doss (2003) "Are Household Production Decisions Cooperative? Evidence on Pastoral Migration and Milk Sales from Northern Kenya", mimeo, Department of Public Administration, Maxwell School, Syracuse University.

Poats, Susan V., Marianne Schmink and Anita Spring (eds) (1988) *Gender Issues in Farming Systems Research and Extension*, Boulder, CO: Westview Press.

Quisumbing, Agnes and John Maluccio (2003) "Resources at Marriage and Intra-household Allocation: Evidence from Bangladesh, Ethiopia, Indonesia, and South Africa," *Oxford Bulletin of Economics and Statistics*, 65(3): 283–327.

Saito, K.A. (1994) "Raising the Productivity of Women Farmers in Sub-Saharan Africa", World Bank Discussion Papers No. 230, Washington, DC.

Sen, Amartya (1990) "Gender and Cooperative Conflicts," in Irene Tinker ed. *Persistent Inequalities*, New York: Oxford University Press.

Staudt, K. (1987) "Uncaptured or Unmotivated? Women and the Food Crisis in Africa," *Rural Sociology*, 52: 37–55.

Udry, Christopher (1996) "Gender, Agricultural Production, and the Theory of the Household," *Journal of Political Economy*, 104(5): 1010–46.

UN Wire (2003) "Bush Must Address Gender During Africa Trip, Experts Say," July 3.

von Braun, Joachim and Peter Webb (1989) "The Impact of New Crop Technology on the Agricultural Division of Labor in a West African Setting," *Economic Development and Cultural Change*, 37(3): 513–34.

World Bank (2001) *Engendering Development*, New York: World Bank and Oxford University Press.

7 Taking gender differences in bargaining power seriously

Equity, labor standards, and living wages[1]

Stephanie Seguino

The relative wages of men and women . . . are . . . largely determined by the structure of markets . . . Firms operating in competitive environments discriminate less against women in hiring and pay practice than do firms with significant market power in protected environments . . .

(World Bank, *Engendering Development*, p. 17)

Making trade conditional on . . . [labour] standards may benefit many of the workers in the north and a few in the south but it is also likely to further marginalize large sections of the world's poor, particularly in the south. A win-win solution in international trade . . . is unlikely to arise out of ad hoc, piecemeal and self-serving demand for universal labour standards.

(Naila Kabeer, *Power to Choose*, p. 391)

Introduction

The World Bank Policy Research Report that is the focus of this book takes up the laudable task of assessing the relationship between gender equality in well-being and economic growth. The Bank argues that gender equality in well-being is improved by growth, and in turn, equity is an unequivocal stimulus to growth. The Bank narrowly defines well-being as capabilities, measured in terms of education and life expectancy. But well-being is a much broader concept, and includes female access to resources and opportunities, such as the means to generate a stable and sufficient income.[2] The World Bank report gives less attention to this aspect of well-being.

This may not be surprising since the policies needed to promote equity in access to income would require a rethinking of the Bank's support for neoliberal macroeconomic policies that constrain chances for gender wage equality. As this chapter argues, this tension suggests that there is an inverse relationship between gender wage equality and growth, implying that efforts to close wage gaps could slow economic growth. To advance gender equity, this constraint must be squarely faced and overcome with policy measures.

The Bank is silent on the policies that could make wage equality more compatible with economic growth. Instead, the Bank's prescriptions for narrowing gender gaps in income are based on proposals to level the playing field in institutions and human capital investment, and the promotion of economic growth based on principles of free markets and free trade. Despite the Bank's optimism, several factors weaken the link between economic growth and women's relative wages. Women's segregation in "mobile industries" – that is, labor-intensive manufacturing or service export industries – limits their bargaining power *vis-à-vis* employers, making it difficult for them to bargain for higher wages and job security, even as labor demand increases in the process of growth. This type of job segregation makes it particularly difficult to raise female wages without dampening female employment, given the growing mobility of firms.

This chapter provides evidence of women's weaker bargaining power in labor markets that sustains gender wage inequality, and I propose ways to overcome this impediment. I discuss two proposals that have recently received a great deal of attention. Labor standards and a global living wage have been proposed as a response to growing global inequality, and are seen as a means to put a floor under worker compensation, overcoming capital's increased bargaining power *vis-à-vis* workers. These strategies are likely to disproportionately benefit women who have typically occupied the lowest paid jobs (including those covered by minimum wage laws). Such policies can promote gender wage equality since they provide some (but not complete) equalization of female and male bargaining power *vis-à-vis* employers, and effectively raise the minimum wage.

These policy proposals are not uncontroversial. The Bank *a priori* opposes such efforts to interfere with market-determined wage outcomes, advocating instead that greater flexibility in labor market institutions and more female education are sufficient. But in so doing, the Bank appears not to recognize or take seriously women's relative lack of bargaining power in the workplace. Some from the global South, while recognizing the constraints on women's bargaining power in the workplace, argue that labor standards and living wage measures that are linked to trade agreements are a disguised effort to protect white northern male jobs. There is thus opposition to such policies on the grounds that, if enacted, they will lead inevitably to job losses for poor women from the global South (Kabeer 2000; Singh and Zammit 2000).

The concern over the potential negative employment effects of improving women's work conditions is related to a key question that this chapter explores: *can* enactment of labor standards and living wages be successfully implemented in export-oriented developing economies without producing negative effects on output and employment? The findings suggest that negative effects of improved labor standards and wages can be avoided, or at the very least, attenuated, through the adoption of development strategies that shift the export production mix to goods that are more price inelastic and income elastic. Under some conditions, higher wages may also stimulate increases in labor productivity, neutralizing the effect of wage hikes on unit labor costs, and thus leading to the avoidance of job loss. Further, if labor standards are enacted simultaneously among competitor countries, a country's relative competitiveness is not likely to deteriorate, with the result that negative employment effects are avoided. The mechanisms necessary to ensure these happy outcomes are dependent on an important role for the state in shaping the development and growth process, in direct contradiction to the Bank's policy proposals.

To elucidate these issues, I begin with a discussion of labor standards and living wages, followed by a discussion of trends in foreign direct investment (FDI) and their gender-related effects. I then discuss the possible pitfalls of labor standards and living wages in yielding unintended outcomes, and finally address means to overcome those constraints.

Labor standards and living wages: some background

Labor standards cover a variety of areas but for the purposes of this chapter, I refer to process-oriented core labor standards that can improve wages: freedom of association, abolition of child labor, and elimination of discrimination in respect to employment and occupation. Global living wages (an outcome-based standard) have also been advanced as a way to improve worker well-being, with living wages defined as a wage level sufficient for an adult to provide for the basic needs of self and dependants. While little has been said about viable mechanisms to enforce the payment of living wages, proponents argue such a policy can slow a "race to the bottom," acting as a global minimum wage, with the added benefit of being able to reflect country-specific cost of living differences. A global living wage has the potential to narrow gender wage gaps since those most affected by such a wage floor are women, particularly those in export industries who face limited bargaining power to negotiate higher wages. The effect of such a policy is to narrow the wage dispersion, where women are concentrated in the lower tail of the distribution and men in the upper.

This chapter focuses on the macroeconomic effects of both types of legislation, referring readers to a wide literature for consideration of the practical issues of implementation and enforcement.[3] Previous research on the macro effects of labor standards has not taken a gender perspective although some studies have attempted to include tests of the effects of reduced gender discrimination in employment. In empirical analyses, Kucera (2002) uses female share of industrial employment while Busse (2002) relies on female share of the labor force as a measure of gender discrimination. In both cases, a higher female share is assumed to be indicative of an improvement in labor standards. Measured in these ways, neither Kucera nor Busse find evidence of a negative effect of an improvement in labor standards on foreign direct investment (FDI) and comparative advantage, respectively.

While this might appear to be good news at first sight, the measures these authors use to capture improvement in gender equity are inadequate to reflect the way that investment, trade, gender, and labor standards interact. The problems that women face in improving their relative economic status is less a function of job access than of job segregation coupled with lack of bargaining power to raise their wages in the jobs they *can* get. Those issues are discussed in the next section as they relate to the current environment of globalized production processes.

Firm mobility, bargaining power, and gender

Efforts to promote gender equity via labor standards and living wages, to be successful, must take into account and overcome constraints imposed by the process of globalization. Of particular concern are the open-economy effects of higher production costs on investment and exports which influence output and employment. This section outlines some of these constraints and their relationship to gender-segregated labor markets.

Mobile capital and foreign direct investment

Investment liberalization has resulted in an increased ability of firms to respond to higher costs and more regulation (or the threat of these) by shifting production to countries with less regulation, lower costs, and in general, higher expected profits. The effect of reduced regulations on investment can be measured as the share of total foreign direct investment in gross fixed capital formation, or what I term *physical capital mobility*. This effect can be captured by summing inward and outward FDI, which is a quantitative assessment of the ability of firms to relocate across borders, should they face local cost increases, and thus reflects changes in their bargaining power *vis-à-vis* workers. This, in other words, is a proxy measure for the size of the "threat effect" that firm relocation poses to workers in wage or other labor-management negotiations.

The data in Table 7.1 indicate that physical capital mobility has been increasing in much of the developing world (see totals in bold italic type for each region) and indeed, the share of total FDI in gross fixed capital formation has more than doubled in the period 1987–2000. Of particular note is the rise in outward FDI, indicating that FDI is a more unstable capital inflow than it had been previously understood to be.[4]

The degree of physical capital mobility has implications for labor demand. As firms become more mobile across borders, they gain access to "substitutes" for domestic labor, and as a result, their demand for labor becomes more elastic. Except perhaps at high skill levels, labor has not become equally as mobile. Thus labor's options have not expanded.[5] The result of this asymmetry is an increase in capital's bargaining power *vis-à-vis* workers, both on the front of wages as well as other components of work conditions.[6]

Mobility and gender

This asymmetry suggests that investment now responds more strongly (negatively) to increases in labor costs than in the past. Further, capital's increased bargaining power has differential effects by gender. This can be traced to the

Table 7.1 Trends in FDI in developing countries (%)

Region	1987	2000	Change from 1987 to 2000
Latin America and Caribbean			
Inward	5.4	20.7	15.3
Outward	0.7	2.4	1.7
Total	**6.1**	**23.1**	**+17.0**
Sub-Saharan Africa			
Inward	7.1	10.5	3.4
Outward	6.9	1.2	−5.7
Total	**14.0**	**11.7**	**−2.3**
Asia			
Inward	3.3	11.6	8.3
Outward	1.6	7.4	5.8
Total	**4.9**	**19.0**	**+14.1**
Developing economies			
Inward	3.9	13.4	9.5
Outward	1.4	5.8	4.4
Total	**5.3**	**19.2**	**+13.9**

Source: United Nations (1999, 2002), *World Investment Report*.

practice of job segregation, with women in semi-industrialized economies typically concentrated in "mobile" industries and men in "immobile" or non-tradable industries.[7] (Mobile industries can be described as those for which sunk costs, including training costs, are limited and there is easy firm entrance and exit. These include labor-intensive manufacturing firms as well as services (such as informatics, data processing, and possibly tourism).[8] These industries are more likely to engage in vertical FDI, which is driven by firm efforts to locate labor-intensive segments of production in least-cost labor sites and capital-intensive production in countries where capital is relatively cheaper. Such firms tend to produce goods for export rather than sale to the domestic economy. In contrast, horizontal FDI occurs in immobile industries, that is, where firms locate production in a country to facilitate sales to that economy, due perhaps to import barriers. In the latter case, labor costs have a smaller effect on investment decisions.

Women are often the preferred labor force in mobile industries due to their lower wages and purportedly more limited resistance to poor working conditions, two factors which enhance firm profits.[9] The demand for female labor in mobile industries has risen, facilitated by trade and investment liberalization, leading Guy Standing (1989) to dub this period one of "global feminization."[10]

Men, on the other hand, tend to be concentrated in non-tradable industries and capital-intensive industries, even if these latter produce for export.[11] Men are also more concentrated in industries for which horizontal FDI is relatively high – such as, for example, automobile manufacturing in China or Indonesia. In general these tend to be "immobile industries," in part due to the limited role that labor costs play in affecting profitability and sales. In the case of non-tradables, the price elasticity of demand for such goods tends to be low, and higher wage costs can be passed on to consumers. In more capital-intensive industries, higher wages for men may reduce turnover, protecting the firm's investment in training. Industry structure and the price inelasticity of product demand thus ratify relatively higher male wages.

Firm mobility and capital–labor bargaining power

These stylized facts help to explain the persistence of gender wage inequality in a global economic environment that otherwise might promote a closure of the gender wage gap, as the demand for female labor rises relatively faster than for male labor. Because women are located in mobile industries in which the threat effect of firm relocation to lower wage sites is credible, women's bargaining power relative to that of capital does not rise, even as labor demand increases. Bhattacharya and Rahman (1999) have provided implicit evidence of this in the case of Bangladesh's female-dominated garment industry. The demand for female labor there has increased sharply in recent years. Despite that, female wages in that sector have not kept pace with rising productivity, so that the wage share of income has fallen – women workers are worse off relative to capitalists. The mobility of garment firms is a likely explanation for the power differential that has led to this outcome, in addition to other social and economic constraints on women's bargaining power.

In contrast, workers in immobile industries have more bargaining power to demand higher wages and better working conditions. Downward pressure on the wages of workers in mobile industries (in this case, women) can spill over into other sectors of the economy, insofar as jobs are gendered and men and women are not perceived to be substitutes. Thus low wages for women in mobile manufacturing firms serve to hold down female wages in non-tradable industries, such as retail sales, as well as social and community services. Men's wages are not similarly constrained.

One possible outcome of this process is growing wage inequality. Indeed, the polarization of wages in recent years is a well-documented phenomenon, although the role of gender in this process has received less attention. With regard to gender, we can hypothesize that as physical capital mobility increases, gender wage inequality worsens, even as trade expands and growth continues. There is some evidence of this in the case of Taiwan as compared to South Korea (Seguino 2000a).[12] During the period 1981–92, Taiwan liberalized rules on inward and outward foreign direct investment while, by comparison, South Korea, did not substantially alter rules on FDI. Figure 7.1 captures these trends, using the sum of inward and outward foreign direct investment, or total FDI, as a share of gross fixed capital formation. That figure also includes data on Singapore for comparative purposes.

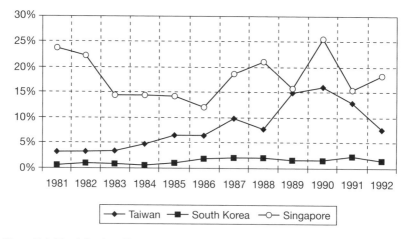

Figure 7.1 Total foreign direct investment as a percentage of gross fixed capital formation.

Interestingly, over the period 1981–1992, gender wage differentials in South Korea narrowed, while in Taiwan, they widened. One of the factors that explains this divergent outcome is the increase in physical capital mobility in Taiwan, as compared to South Korea.[13] The interpretation of these results is that women's bargaining power *vis-à-vis* capital decreased in Taiwan as female-dominated firms became more mobile, contributing to a widening gender wage gap. In fact, female wages fell from roughly 68 percent of average male wages in 1981 to 62 percent in 1992. In contrast, gender wage differentials improved slightly in South Korea over this period. These results imply that growth is not sufficient to close gender wage gaps (a point made in this volume by numerous authors, including Avin and Doss).

The inverse relationship between capital mobility and wages, coupled with gendered job segregation, suggests that efforts to raise female wages in semi-industrialized economies might result in reduced output and growth, and thus declining employment, particularly for women. There is thus potentially an inverse relationship between gender equity, measured as higher relative female wages, on the one hand, and growth of output on the other. Empirical analyses are consistent with this, and one study (Seguino 2000b) indicates that, among a set of semi-industrialized economies, those with the greatest gender wage inequality grew the most rapidly during the period 1975–95.

Higher relative female wages, then, appear to slow growth, at least for this set of countries, for two important reasons: (1) investment responds negatively to increases in female wages, and (2) exports fall as export prices rise, reducing the ability of an economy to import capital goods, thereby slowing productivity growth. The analytics of this problem are addressed in the appendix within the framework of a simple neo-Kaleckian model of an open developing macro economy (see also Seguino 2000b; Blecker and Seguino 2002).

Tai

These results stand in sharp contrast to the Bank study which argues that gender equity promotes economic growth. The Bank report focuses on educational gaps as a measure of inequality, and implies that those countries that treat women better grow faster. But as the preceding analysis suggests, the effect of gender inequality on growth depends on how inequality is measured. While closing educational gaps may potentially stimulate growth by improving the quality of the labor supply, wage inequality can and does co-exist with educational equality. The gap between educational attainment and wages signifies the degree to which women fail to be sufficiently compensated for their productive characteristics – in a word, it is a measure of the degree of exploitation. It is that exploitation which is a stimulus to growth, via its effect on firm profits and on prices that stimulate product demand.

These results suggest that the enactment of labor standards that lead to wage increases might stimulate outward FDI and a decline in exports of labor-intensive goods. A possible result would be employment losses for women, at least partially negating the beneficial effects of higher minimum wages. Kabeer (2000) argues that beneficiaries would be northern workers who would gain these jobs. The problem is more likely to be South–South job competition, however, since northern light manufacturing jobs all but disappeared a number of years ago, except in niche markets (Ross and Chan 2002; Polaski 2003). Thus the issue of concern is the effect of (and antidotes to) investment and export competition among a set of semi-industrialized economies. The next two sections consider those issues.

The potential for living wages to reduce gender wage inequality

While there are constraints on efforts to improve the living standards of low-wage workers by raising wages, as the previous section shows, there is room to maneuver in achieving this policy goal. This maneuverability is not obvious in World Bank analyses, which assume perfect competition in goods and labor markets, and infinitely price-elastic export demand.

An important component of arguments against labor standards is an assumption that wages rise only in one country. Thus, as with the model presented in the appendix, wages are assumed to rise in country A, while they are held constant in competitor countries so that the real exchange rate appreciates in country A. The application of global labor standards and living wage rules, however, implies the possibility of a simultaneous increase in female wages that may leave relative export prices among competitor countries unchanged, e.g. the relative price of garments produced in Bangladesh, say, and Thailand, remains unchanged. The effects of this policy shift would then be quite different than if wage increases occur only in country A.

I know of no research that examines the effects of a simultaneous wage increase among countries that are export competitors, but I will sketch what I think to be some important implications of such a strategy. First, insofar as wages rise in alternative or competitor production sites, there is little profit incentive for "footloose" capital to shift investment abroad (since, in effect, unit labor costs in competitor countries rise in tandem). Thus the negative employment effects, induced by higher wages on domestic economies, may be small.

Second, because the price of "substitute" export goods rises also, then the negative demand-side effect on exports will be smaller, although presumably this will still be negative. Together, these two possibilities suggest that, if enacted simultaneously amongst competitor countries, living wage effects (or labor standards) on employment may not be negative or only mildly so.

This is consistent with findings of a number of studies on employment effects of labor standards, including Kucera (2002) and Heintz (2002). In the latter study of a set of 49 countries from 1981 to 1996, Heintz finds that the elasticity of employment growth with respect to changes in the real wage is –0.61 – a 10 percent increase in real wages will lead to a 6.1 percent decline in employment, other factors remaining constant. Other factors may adjust when wages rise, however, including productivity, prices, and consumer demand. The effect of higher wages on productivity is taken up in the section below, but before that, it is useful to consider the effects of higher wages on prices and consumer demand.

Anti-sweatshop campaigns advertising the harsh working conditions faced by export workers in clothing industries, for example, reveal a disdain for such work conditions in the global South. In one study, northern consumers indicated they would be willing to pay 2–6 percent more for goods produced under more humane conditions, which would cover 100 percent of wage increases needed to bring workers up to a living wage (Pollin *et al.* 2001). It is thus conceivable that firms advertising the payment of living wages would experience little decline in product demand if prices were raised.

Of course, many goods of this kind are produced and marketed along a commodity chain, with multinationals subcontracting to smaller firms to produce small batches of goods. The subcontracting firm, often located in a developing country, is under great pressure to reduce costs. Labor standards and living wages that raise wages would force subcontractors globally to raise prices. But this may not have a large effect on product price if multinationals that market and distribute these goods were forced to squeeze their mark-ups, which have been shown to be very high in the case of goods in which brand name recognition is high (Heintz 2003). The result in both cases is a redistribution from the North (consumers or firms or both) to the South, in this case, southern female workers.

Assuming that women are the primary beneficiaries of such a policy, this implies an increase in the female wage bill, defined as the average female wage multiplied by female employment. Thus, total female income rises, and depending on the effect of living wages on male income, the female share of the total wage bill may also rise, contributing to greater gender income equality.

Enactment of living wages and labor standards would also require coordinated exchange rate adjustments between competitor countries that have experienced

wage increases, so that real exchange rates remain unchanged. That is, a sufficiently coordinated monetary policy would be required so that no country's
exchange rate movements could offset the effects of a wage increase any more
than in competitor countries. That is a big assumption, and suggests that any
effort to implement living wages would also have to consider coordination of
exchange rate policies among countries as well.

Wage-led productivity effects, gender equity, *and* growth: what are the chances?

Another important feature of the negative commentaries on labor standards (as
well as the model in the appendix) is the assumption that there is no link between
wages and productivity.[14] There is a possibility, however, that higher wages for
workers in labor-intensive manufacturing industries could stimulate productivity
growth, thereby neutralizing the effect of wage increases on unit labor costs and
prices. Empirical research on wage-led productivity effects in labor-intensive
manufacturing industries is scarce. This may be because we don't often see firms
in these industries using higher wages as a way to promote increased productivity
or quality improvements. In part, this may be because the firms do not *have*
to use wages as a tool to stimulate labor effort. Monitoring is easy; rapid turnover is not costly because of low levels of investment in training and worker
skills; and the target labor force is relatively powerless – women have few job
alternatives. Thus, firm strategy often involves a stick, rather than a carrot.

Further, if firms can rely on low wages to achieve a cost advantage, they feel
less pressure to raise productivity. Indeed, this might be described as a "low wage-
low productivity" trap where wages that are too low slow improvements in
productivity, output, and thus living conditions (Seguino 2004). In contrast,
externally induced wage increases (via government policy or labor organizing)
might, under the right conditions, spur firms to become more productive, to
innovate, to adopt more sophisticated technology – all of which serve to attenuate
the negative effect of higher wages on product price and therefore demand.[15]
Further, higher wages might induce improvements in product quality, again
offsetting negative effects of wage increases on demand. Finally, higher wages
may contribute to health and nutritional improvements that lead to improved
labor productivity on the job.

Unit labor costs and wage-led productivity effects

One might question why employers fail to raise wages on their own, if higher
wages, due to productivity effects, are cost-neutral and possibly even profitable.
One explanation is that the wage-led productivity effect described here suggests
multiple equilibria, as shown in Figure 7.2. Defining unit labor costs as:

$$C = w/b$$

where C is unit labor costs, w is the nominal wage, and b is labor productivity, then the rate of change of unit labor costs can be written

$$\hat{C} = \hat{w} - \hat{b}$$

(labor) labor prod .

where the "hat" signifies rate of change. Over a certain wage range,[16] productivity growth is a positive function of the rate of change of the nominal wage or

$$\hat{b} = f(\hat{w}).$$

Looking at Figure 7.2, the ray from the origin signifies constant unit labor costs. Note that the two wage-productivity equilibria (E_1 and E_2) reflect identical unit labor costs.

We can imagine a situation in which a developing economy finds itself at E_1, representing a low wage and low level of productivity. This is a stable equilibrium with no tendency for the wage, and thus productivity, to rise (Seguino 2004). An increase in the nominal wage however, *could* stimulate labor productivity growth. If the wage rose to $\hat{w}_2$, the wage-induced increase in productivity would be sufficient to compensate for the higher wage such that unit labor costs remain constant. As a result, prices are unchanged and thus higher wages do not generate employment losses.

What are conditions under which externally induced wage increases could induce productivity growth and quality improvements? While there may be several important conditions, of primary interest is the extent to which firms are "footloose," that is, the degree of physical capital mobility. If firms have few alternatives to domestic labor as wages rise, that is, if they are not easily able to relocate to lower wage sites, then they are disciplined by the higher wages. The

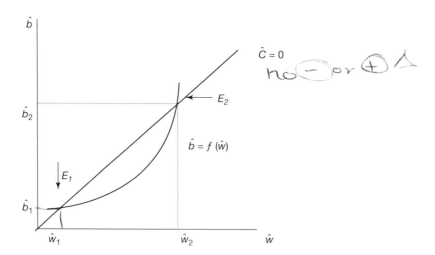

Figure 7.2 Wage-induced productivity growth.

dependent on demand?

effects of this discipline might take the form of increased corporate initiative to innovate and to improve productivity. They may take the form of more energetic efforts to market goods, or to reorient the product to niche markets where quality matters more and price less. Or simply, firms that are immobile may observe improvements in productivity and quality as labor effort increases in response to the wage incentive. The limitations on capital mobility force firms to stay around long enough to observe the productivity increases that would otherwise not have become apparent, had the firm relocated to lower wage sites.

South Korea and productivity growth in female-dominated industries

The case of South Korea is instructive. During the period 1975 to 1990, a time of limited inward and outward FDI, real wages more than quintupled in the manufacturing sector. There is evidence that real wage increases led rather than lagged growth, spurring labor productivity and firm efforts to innovate (Seguino 1999–2000). This period then appears to have been one of wage-led growth, with rising wages stimulating firms to invest in order to overcome the potentially negative effect of higher wages on export demand. In a sense, firms were squeezed by higher wages. To regain prior profit levels, firms were pushed to invest as a way to raise producivity.

An interesting feature of this period is that wages and productivity rose rapidly in female- as well as male-dominated industries. This is surprising, since it is often argued that wages are unlikely to produce significant increases in productivity in labor-intensive industries as compared to capital-intensive industries. The reasons advanced are that these industries simply do not lend themselves to greater mechanization, and most productivity gains resulting from process innovation have probably already occurred. The data from South Korea, however, suggest that wage increases stimulated productivity growth, even in labor–intensive female-dominated industries. The data in Table 7.2 are indices of labor productivity in selected female- and male-dominated manufacturing industries during

Table 7.2 Indices of labor productivity in selected South Korean manufacturing industries, 1976–1990

Industries	1976	1990
Female-dominated		
Wearing apparel	100	481
Footwear	100	562
Electronics	100	808
Male-dominated		
Iron and steel	100	483
Machinery	100	592
Transport	100	317

Source: Korean Productivity Center.

the period 1976–90. Note that productivity gains in female industries are similar to or exceed those in male industries.

The case of South Korea suggests that living wage standards that raise the wages of female manufacturing workers can stimulate productivity growth, either through increases in labor effort or because firms are prodded to become more efficient, and perhaps to increase investment in more sophisticated technology.[17]

This result is less likely to occur in an environment of footloose capital, it would seem, since firms can bargain down wages, using low wages as a cost advantage in lieu of productivity-enhancing investments. If that is the case, we would expect to see slower – not more rapid – productivity growth in countries for which physical capital mobility is high. That is, investment liberalization, because it reduces worker bargaining power and thereby depresses wages, can lead to a "low wage-low productivity growth" trap. In short, investment liberalization can make firms "lazy" in pushing for cost advantage via efficiency gains. The data presented in Figure 7.3 are consistent with this hypothesis, and show that those countries with the least physical capital mobility (total FDI as a share of investment) have had the most rapid productivity growth in recent years. This result has been confirmed in an analysis of 37 semi-industrialized economies for the period 1970–2000 (Seguino 2004). These results suggest that global labor standards, which essentially act as a constraint on capital mobility by reducing the incentive for firms to run from higher wages, may also induce higher rates of productivity growth.

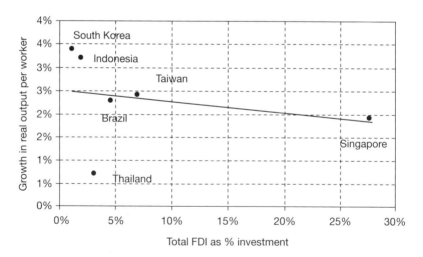

Figure 7.3 Average productivity growth and total FDI as percentage of gross fixed capital formation, 1972–1990.

Women move in small firms

Taking bargaining power differentials seriously: policy implications

The patterns of gender segregation and the differential bargaining power that arise in jobs in mobile vs. immobile industries underscore the need for intervention in labor markets as part of any effort to close gender gaps in well-being. A hands-off approach to labor markets will not suffice.

Focusing on labor standards and living wages as a means to close gender gaps, there are four related policies that can be adopted to make such a strategy work, in the sense that women's wages rise and job losses are avoided.[18] First, coordination among developing countries to ensure stable relative export prices would be necessary. In particular, monetary authorities would play a role in ensuring that no country's exchange rate movements offset the effects of a wage increase any more than in competitor countries.

Second, governments should develop industrial policies to move their labor-intensive sectors up the industrial ladder to the production of goods that are income elastic and where price matters less, and quality more. When this occurs, the price elasticity of export good demand is lowered, and the negative employment effects of wage hikes are attenuated. The role of the state is particularly important in the case where exports are largely produced by small firms since they often lack the technological expertise, or access to marketing and distribution networks that would permit them to shift to the production of more price inelastic export goods. Indeed, one reason why firms may have been able to respond to the wage-push stimulus in South Korea is that they possessed the internal resources, as large conglomerates, to purchase new technologies and to implement new processes that raise productivity.

Smaller firms may not be similarly equipped. Rama (2001) found, for instance, that when Indonesia doubled the real minimum wage in the early 1990s, productivity and employment rose in large manufacturing firms, but not in small firms. In fact, workers in small firms experienced substantial job losses as a result of the minimum wage hike. Why was this so? It may very well have been due to the technical and resource constraints small firms experience in attempting to raise productivity. This is a particularly important issue as regards the enactment of living wages and gender equity, since women workers tend to be more concentrated in small firms with informal work arrangements than men.

Third, anti-sweatshop campaigns have advanced a variety of mechanisms to link better labor practices with rewards in product markets. Heintz (2002) discusses these in detail. I simply note here that these campaigns have gender implications and efforts to improve gender equity should include ways to integrate such northern campaigns with efforts to improve work conditions and wages for women in the global South. The World Bank's support of such a strategy would be beneficial.

Finally, a major constraint on making living wage and labor standards work is firm mobility. There is increasing evidence that it is time to implement "speed bumps" for physical capital as has been done for financial capital in such countries

↓ firm mobility

as Chile. Reductions in firm mobility can permit wage-led productivity effects to emerge, thus producing a gain for workers, particularly female workers, in terms of higher wages while keeping unit labor costs low. How is this to be done? This is a question that requires some study and debate. I will point out here that South Korea, Taiwan, and Japan, and, more recently, China are examples of countries that have managed and constrained foreign direct investment to their advantage.[19] Controls on investment are not now in vogue. The current World Bank fashion, for example, emphasizes liberalization. But these winds of liberalization should not prevent those concerned with gender equality from arguing for more gender-equitable macro strategies and a debate on how to implement such policies.

A final note on the effects of labor standards on women employed in informal sector work: the effects of such standards on the work conditions and wages of those employed in the informal sector are ambiguous. Among informal sector workers are the self-employed and those working as home workers doing industrial piecework. The latter group may benefit indirectly, if formal sector work conditions improve, thus raising the wage floor. Further, technological improvements induced by higher wages as formal sector firms attempt to hold down unit labor costs would make those industrial piecework activities less profitable. An effort to organize home workers is likely to be necessary to prevent increased informalization of formal sector jobs. Because informal sector work is often residual employment, a more direct mechanism to improve the conditions of those who work as self-employed workers, such as street vendors, would benefit more from macroeconomic stimulus, and would be harmed by policies that increase formal sector unemployment.[20]

↑ w for informal → ↑ w informal

Conclusion

The World Bank PRR makes the important claim that gender equity is instrumental for economic development and growth. The Bank defines equity in terms of education, assuming that wage equality will automatically ensue, so long as liberalization of markets, trade, and capital flows yields competitive conditions and a "level playing field." The Bank's conclusion that equality unambiguously promotes growth suggests, however, the absence of a theoretical understanding of the linkages between gender, wages, economic structure, and macroeconomic outcomes.[21] The uncomfortable facts are that gender wage gaps can persist despite educational equality, and that attempts to close those gaps can slow, not stimulate, economic growth. Uncomfortable though this may be, proponents of gender equity should not shy away from these conclusions.

This chapter argues that gender wage gaps are in part the result of unequal female bargaining power *vis-à-vis* employers in the current globalized environment. The World Bank, in its analyses of gender, fails to note this constraint, in marked contrast to its willingness to acknowledge unequal female bargaining power within households, and the positive effect of outside options, such as human capital, earned income, and transfers, on women's access to household resources. As a result, the Bank's report thus fails to mount a broader consideration of the factors that lead to unequal gender outcomes in labor markets. But if we are to close gender gaps in well-being, unequal bargaining power within labor markets must also be acknowledged, and policies must be designed to ameliorate this condition without producing negative effects on women's access to income through employment.

Cognizant of these constraints, this chapter lays out some of the important macroeconomic considerations related to closing gender wage gaps in labor markets via enactment of labor standards and living wages. Such policies can improve the wages of those at the bottom of the wage distribution, where women are concentrated. In so doing, gender wage gaps can be narrowed and thus such policies not only improve women's absolute well-being but can also promote gender equality in incomes.

The evidence on wage-induced productivity growths suggests that higher female wages that approach living wages can provide a stimulus for firms to innovate. The result will be an increase in productivity, making wage increases cost-neutral and possibly even profitable, thus protecting against job loss. The realization of this positive effect of higher wages requires constraints on firm mobility. Even without restraints on firm mobility, the potential negative effects of higher wages on investment, when adopted in an individual country, can be lessened if implemented as a global labor standard. Industrial policies that shift production to income elastic and price inelastic exports will also help. All of these policy proposals suggest an important role for the state in managing the process of development and growth. Despite the Bank's resistance to state intervention in the production sphere of the economy, there is a clear connection between such intervention and improvements in gender equity. A virtuous cycle can be set in motion by reasoned state-level actions, with the resulting increase in gender equality further stimulating development and growth – a link the Bank does acknowledge.

[handwritten margin notes: "Must be managed by the state"]

APPENDIX

Wages in a two-sector macroeconomy with gender-segregated labor

A stylized characterization of developing country economies with a significant manufacturing or service export sector (that is, a semi-industrialized economy) is that these are two-sector economies, with a non-tradables sector producing "home" goods that employ male labor and a tradables (export) sector that employs female labor.[22] Assuming complete gender segregation, the mark-up price equations for the "home" and export goods sectors, respectively, can be written:

$$P_H = \tau(w_m a_H + eP^* n_H), \quad \tau > 1 \tag{1}$$

$$P_X = \varphi(w_f a_X + eP^* n_X),^{24} \quad \varphi > 1 \tag{2}$$

In these equations, τ and φ are the mark-up factors; w_m and w_f represent male and female wages, respectively; H is home goods and X is exports; the a_i ($i = H, X$) are the labor coefficients; the n_i are the intermediate input coefficients; P^* is the world price of intermediate inputs; and e is the exchange rate (domestic currency price of foreign exchange). The home sector mark-up (τ) is rigid due to high protectionist barriers, heavy subsidies, and a highly concentrated oligopolistic structure. The export-sector mark-up (φ) is assumed to be flexible in response to international competitive pressures and in particular, changes in the real exchange rate.[23]

The primary macroeconomic effects of any increase in female wages are exerted on export demand as well as investment in export industries. To see this, consider first the following expression for export demand:

$$E_X = A\left(\frac{eP_X^*}{P_X}\right)^{\psi}, \quad 0 < \psi < \infty \tag{3}$$

where E_X is export demand, A is a shift factor (such as foreign income), P_X^* is the price of competitive foreign exports, and ψ is the price elasticity of demand. Equation 3 implies that export demand can be stimulated by a devaluation and a decline in P_X. Further, it can be seen that a decline in the price elasticity of export demand will attenuate the negative effects of a rise in the domestic price of exports on export demand.

A simple reduced form investment function, with investment expenditures a function of profits in the two sectors, can be written:

$$I = I_0 + b_1 R_H + b_2 R_X \tag{4}$$

where I_H is home investment goods, and R_H and R_X are sectoral profits. The left-hand side is desired investment spending and the right-hand side is the investment demand function, in which I_0 is a constant term or shift factor (reflecting Keynesian "animal spirits") and b_1, $b_2 > 0$ measure the responsiveness of domestic investment to profits in the two sectors (call this the "profitability" effect). We can assume that $b_2 > b_1$ since the X sector is more "footloose," reflecting the greater ease with which such firms can move into or out of a country in response to changes in profitability.

These equations can be used to demonstrate the constraints on raising women's relative wages in an open economy. The effects of raising the female wage operate through two major channels: (1) *an export price effect* – the export price rises, causing the exchange rate to appreciate; and (2) *a class redistribution effect* – the firm-mark-up in the export sector is squeezed by higher wages, reducing the profit share from that sector. The first implies that higher female wages will cause export prices to rise, and export demand to fall (equations 2 and 3). Profits may also be squeezed, resulting in a decline in aggregate investment (equation 4). The combined negative demand-side effect is larger the more price-elastic exports (the larger is ψ). It is possible, of course, that a redistribution to women workers will induce an increase in consumption spending (if female workers' propensity to consume is higher than that of capitalists).[24] This effect would have to be quite large to overcome the negative effects on exports and investment, which are deflationary. This can be seen from the balance equation in an open economy (with the simplifying assumption that the government budget deficit is 0):

$$I_{W_F} + X_{W_F} < S + M \qquad (5)$$
$$(-) \quad (-) \quad (?)$$

where S is aggregate saving and M is imports demand. The price elasticity of export demand will influence the size of the effect of higher female wages on export demand. The "footlooseness" of capital will determine the extent to which higher female wages that squeeze profits also depress investment demand (as a result of physical capital flight or outward FDI). The difference in the propensity to consume out of wage and profit income will influence the effect of higher female wages on consumption demand for both the export good and the "home" good.

Higher female wages that lead to a decline in output and female employment is likely to occur if capital is footloose, if the price elasticity of exports is high, and if the spending propensities of workers and capitalists are similar. The first two conditions are likely to obtain in countries in the early stages of industrialization, and in that regard, the fears of Kabeer (2000) and others appear well-founded.[25]

An optimistic scenario – in which higher female wages result in little loss of export demand, little if any reduction in investment, and a boost to consumer demand, as income is shifted from those with a high propensity to save (capitalists) to those with a low propensity to save (female workers) – is likely to be possible only in those cases where capital is immobile (i.e. FDI faces restrictions), where export goods are price-inelastic (because they are skill-intensive, or because they are goods for which quality matters), or where export goods form a non-trivial share of wage goods. One can think of relatively few countries that fall into this category, but an important and instructive example is South Korea (discussed on pages 105–6). Nevertheless, under some conditions, higher female wages are consistent with increases in employment and output, even when there are no wage-led productivity effects.

Notes

1 I am grateful to astute and helpful comments from Christian Weller, Marilyn Power, and participants at the "Global Labor Standards and Living Wages" Conference at University of Massachusetts at Amherst, April 19–20, 2002.
2 Grown *et al.* (2003) and Malhotra *et al.* (2002) explore how to define and measure gender well-being in detail. They note that gender well-being also includes security and empowerment. I leave aside those issues here, focusing primarily on the contradictions evident in the Bank report between the goal of expansion of female opportunities while promoting economic growth under conditions of liberalized trade and capital flows.
3 See, for example, Brenner (2002) on issues related to calculating global living wages, Heintz (2002), Polaski (2003), and Sengenberger and Campbell (1994) on implementation concerns.
4 This is consistent with results presented in Rand and Tarp (2002), whose empirical analysis of business cycle data for a set of developing countries reveals that FDI inflows are very volatile, much more so than aid flows.
5 Thus, abstractly speaking, labor supply schedules have not become steeper to compensate as labor demand schedules have flattened.
6 See Zhao (1998) for a demonstration of the negative effect of physical capital mobility on wages within a Nash bargaining framework. Epstein (2000) explores these issues in further detail, exploring the effect of mobility on public finances as well as wages.
7 Semi-industrialized economies are those with a significant share of manufacturing in GDP and a correspondingly small share of agriculture. Manufacturing output tends to be labor-intensive as compared to industrialized economies, with a large share of manufacturing goods destined for export. Amongst this group can be included economies with a large export service sector, such as informatics and data processing. Examples of these include Jamaica and Barbados.
8 This phenomenon may not hold in countries of differing economic structures. For example, in the US, men have held the largest share of jobs in durable goods manufacturing industries where, in recent years, job losses have been high as firms have relocated to lower wage sites. We do see evidence of this pattern in service export-oriented economies, however, such as in the Caribbean where women are concentrated in "export" data processing jobs and in India, call centers.
9 For data on women's concentration in export production, see, for example, Standing (1989, 1999), UNDP (1999), and, for a set of semi-industrialized economies, Seguino (2000b). On services see, for example, Freeman (2000).
10 I refer here to the global phenomenon, since in some countries the demand for female labor in labor-intensive industries has fallen, either due to technological upgrading that excludes female workers, or because firms have relocated to lower wage sites. This process can be observed in the US and Europe, as well as some of the East Asian economies, such as Taiwan and Hong Kong (Kucera and Milberg 2000; Berik 2000).
11 A digression on gender and economic structure in sub-Saharan Africa (SSA) is in order. Unlike other regions, in the agricultural sector of many SSA economies, women are concentrated in subsistence food production, arguably a non-tradable industry, due to lack of internal transportation networks, and the perishability and types of food crops grown. Men are more likely to be involved in "cash" crop food production. Thus, the dichotomization of women as employed in tradables and men in non-tradables breaks down in the SSA. Nevertheless, cash crop production is often labor-constrained, with men depending on wives to provide labor. Rural African women's labor thus plays a role in generating foreign exchange, although in a different manner than in semi-industrialized economies or the manufacturing sector of African economies.

12 A widening wage gap has been noted in several other countries with strong growth as well – e.g. Chile, Mexico, and Hong Kong (UNIFEM 2000). Female relative wage trends may be faring worse in other countries as well, given the push toward subcontracting and home-based work where wages tend to be lower. But because most labor surveys cover establishments with a minimum of 10 workers, women's low wages in unsurveyed small shops may not show up in the official data, leading to artificially high estimates of average female wages.

13 In contrast, in the US, increased mobility in the 1990s was more pronounced in male-dominated industries, such as autos and machine tools, leading to a decline in male relative wages. On the "threat effect" in the US, see Brofenbrenner (2000). For a different view, see Black and Brainerd (2002) who attribute the closure of the wage gap to increased competition, rather than the threat effect of firm relocation holding down male wages.

14 In the model in the appendix, this is measured as the inverse of the labor coefficient (a_x) in equation 2.

15 This line of thought is not new. Power (1999) describes the use of parasitic-industries analysis as a motivating argument behind the push for a living wage for women in the early twentieth-century US. Based on Beatrice and Sydney Webb's analyses, activists argued that industries paying less than a living wage were parasitic on society, which was then required to take up the burden of providing for the additional costs of supporting women, via the family or through the net drain on women's health and well-being. Demands for a living wage in sweatshops addressed those concerns.

16 At some point, the wage-led productivity function may turn negative (not shown here). Bowles and Gintis (1985), for example, posit that when full employment is approached, and the "cost of job loss" falls, higher wages exert a smaller positive effect on productivity, which may eventually turn negative, if workers "shirk" or the costs of monitoring rise. Female-dominated labor intensive industries lend themselves to monitoring, however, and thus the conditions under which the wage-productivity function turns negative is more likely to be linked to technological constraints.

17 In another interesting study on minimum wage effects in developing countries, Saget (2001) estimates the effect of real wage increases on employment and finds little evidence of negative effects. This may be explained by non-compliance. It may also suggest that wage-led productivity effects are significant.

18 An obvious policy approach, not discussed here, would be to take steps to integrate labor markets.

19 A common reference on this topic is Alice Amsden (1989). See also Braunstein and Epstein (2002) and Ha-Joon Chang (2002).

20 This would not require direct policy action, if redistributions from capitalists to female workers led to a rise in the economy-wide marginal propensity to consume, thus stimulating aggregate demand. See Blecker and Seguino (2002) on this topic as well as the appendix.

21 This comment applies not only to the Bank report in question, but also to numerous Bank studies on the topic poverty and growth. Other authors in this volume address the Bank's failure to fully address the links between gender and macroeconomic outcomes as well (see, for example, Rose-Marie Avin and Cynthia Wood). The Bank is not the only entity that lacks such an understanding, which extends to other international financial institutions, bilateral agencies, as well as many otherwise progressive macroeconomists.

22 This formulation is from Blecker and Seguino (2002); see that paper for full details of this model.

23 Modelling price formation as a mark-up pricing process (reflecting oligopolisitic power) can in part account for the different viewpoint on the employment effects of labor standards as compared to neoclassical analyses. A neoclassical approach (e.g.,

Brown 2001), which assumes perfect firm competition, would imply an export price equation such as $P_X = wa_X + rk$ where P_X is the export product price, w is the wage rate, a_X is the labor coefficient, r is the profit rate, and k is the capital coefficient (ignoring intermediate goods for simplicity). Higher wages immediately result in higher prices, and given infinitely elastic demand for exports, demand falls and along with it, employment in the export sector.

24 Thus there is a third potential effect – *a consumption effect*. There is, however, little empirical evidence on which to base such an assumption about spending propensities, other than Seguino and Floro (2003), which considers only gender differences in saving propensities among workers.

25 Gibson and van Seventer (2000) point out, based on dynamic CGE simulations of the South African economy, that the effects of real wage increases on employment also depend on the macro policy environment. When there is monetary "policy dominance," efforts to raise wages can be frustrated by monetary authorities that respond to inflation (induced by higher wages) by raising interest rates, and thus engineering a contraction and a decline in employment. This is a point worth considering further in trying to anticipate the effects of enactment of labor standards and living wages.

References

Amsden, Alice (1989) *Asia's Next Giant: South Korea and Late Industrialization*, Oxford: Oxford University Press.

Berik, Gunseli (2000) "Mature Export-Led Growth and Gender Wage Inequality in Taiwan," *Feminist Economics*, 6(3): 1–26.

Bhattacharya, Debapriya and Mustafizur Rahman (1999) "Female Employment Under Export Propelled Industrialization: Prospects for Internalizing Global Opportunities in the Apparel Sector in Bangladesh," Occasional Paper No. 10, United Nations Research Institute for Social Development (UNRISD).

Black, Sandra and Elizabeth Brainerd (2002) "Importing Inequality? The Effects of Increased Competition on the Gender Wage Gap," NBER Working Paper No. W 9110, Cambridge, MA.

Blecker, Robert and Stephanie Seguino (2002) "Macroeconomic Effects of Reducing Gender Wage Inequality in an Export-Oriented Semi-Industrialized Economy," *Review of Development Economics*, 6(1): 103–19.

Bowles, Sam and Herb Gintis (1985) "The Production Process in a Competitive Economy: Walrasian, Neo-Hobbesian, and Marxian Models," *American Economic Review*, 75(1): 16–36.

Braunstein, Elissa and Gerald Epstein (2002) "Bargaining Power and Foreign Direct Investment in China: Can 1.3 Billion Consumers Tame the Multinationals?" Center for Economic Policy Analysis (CEPA) Working Paper 2002–13.

Brenner, Mark (2002) "Defining and Measuring a Global Living Wage: Theoretical and Conceptual Issues," mimeo, Political Economic Research Institute, University of Massachusetts at Amherst.

Brofenbrenner, Kate (2000) "Uneasy Terrain: The Impact of Capital Mobility on Workers, Wages, and Union Organizing," submitted to the US Trade Deficit Review Commission.

Brown, Drucilla (2001) "Labor Standards: Where Do They Belong on the International Trade Agenda?" Working Paper, Medford, MA: Tufts University.

Busse, Matthias (2002) "Do Labor Standards Affect Comparative Advantage in Developing Countries?" *World Development*, 30(11): 1921–32.

Chang, Ha-Joon (2002) *Kicking Away the Ladder: Policies and Institutions for Economic Development in Historical Perspective*, London: Anthem Press.

Epstein, Gerald (2000) "Threat Effects and the Impact of Capital Mobility on Wages and Public Finances: Developing a Research Agenda," Working Paper, Amherst, MA: University of Massachusetts at Amherst and Political Economy Research Institute.

Freeman, Carla (2000) *High Tech and High Heels in the Global Economy: Women, Work, and Pink-Collar Identities in the Caribbean*, Durham, NC: Duke University Press.

Gibson, Bill and Dirk Ernst van Seventer (2000) "Real Wages, Employment and Macroeconomic Policy in a Structuralist Model for South Africa," *Journal of African Economies*, 9(4): 512–46.

Grown, Caren, Geeta Rao Gupta and Sahia Khan (2003) *Promises to Keep: Achieving Gender Equality and the Empowerment of Women*, Washington, DC, International Center for Research on Women.

Heintz, James (2002) "Global Labor Standards: Their Impact and Implementation," Working Paper Series, No. 45. Amherst, MA: University of Massachusetts at Amherst and Political Economy Research Institute.

—— (2003) "The New Face of Unequal Exchange: Low-Wage Manufacturing, Commodity Chains, and Global Inequality," mimeo, Political Economic Research Institute, University of Massachusetts at Amherst.

Kabeer, Naila (2000) *The Power to Choose: Bangladeshi Women and Labour Market Decisions in London and Dhaka*, London: Verso.

Kucera, David (2002) "Core Labour Standards and Foreign Direct Investment," *International Labour Review*, 141(1–2): 31–70.

Kucera, David and William Milberg (2000) "Gender Segregation and Gender Bias in Manufacturing Trade Expansion: Revisiting the 'Wood Asymmetry'," *World Development*, 28(7): 1191–210.

Malhotra, A., S. Schuler and C. Boender (2002) "Measuring Women's Empowerment as a Variable in International Development," Working Paper, International Center for Research on Women.

Polaski, Sandra (2003) "Trade and Labor Standards: A Strategy for Developing Countries," mimeo, Carnegie Endowment for International Peace.

Pollin, Robert, Justine Burns and James Heintz (2001) "Global Apparel Production and Sweatshop Labor: Can Raising Retail Prices Finance Living Wages?" PERI Working Paper No. 19, University of Massachusetts at Amherst.

Power, Marilyn (1999) "Parasitic-Industries Analysis and Arguments for a Living Wage for Women in Early Twentieth-Century United States," *Feminist Economics*, 5(1): 61–78.

Rama, Martín (2001) "The Consequences of Doubling the Minimum Wage: The Case of Indonesia," *Industrial and Labor Relations Review*, 54(4): 864–81.

Rand, John and Finn Tarp (2002) "Business Cycles in Developing Countries: Are They Different?" *World Development*, 30(12): 2071–88.

Ross, Robert and Anita Chan (2002) "From North–South to South–South: The True Face of Global Competition," *Foreign Affairs*, 81(5): 8–13.

Saget, Catherine (2001) "Poverty Reduction and Decent Work in Development Countries: Do Minimum Wages Help?" *International Labour Review*, 140(3): 237–69.

Seguino, Stephanie (1999–2000) "The Investment Function Revisited: Disciplining Capital in Korea," *Journal of Post-Keynesian Economics*, 22(2): 313–38.

—— (2000a) "The Effects of Structural Change and Economic Liberalization on Gender

Wage Differentials in South Korea and Taiwan," *Cambridge Journal of Economics*, 24(4): 437–59.

—— (2000b) "Gender Inequality and Economic Growth: A Cross-Country Analysis," *World Development*, 28(7): 1211–30.

—— (2004) "Is More Mobility Good? Firm Mobility and the Low Wage–Low Productivity Trap," Working Paper, Burlington, VT: University of Vermont.

Seguino, Stephanie and Maria Floro (2003) "Does Gender Have Any Effect on Aggregate Saving?: An Empirical Analysis," *International Review of Applied Economics*, 17(2): 147–66.

Sengenberger, Werner and Duncan Campbell (1994) *International Labour Standards and Economic Interdependence*, Washington, DC: Brookings Institution.

Singh, Ajit and Anne Zammit (2000) *The Global Labour Standards Controversy: Critical Issues*, Geneva, Switzerland: South Centre.

Standing, Guy (1989) "Global Feminization Through Flexible Labor," *World Development*, 17(7): 1077–96.

—— (1999) "Global Feminization Through Flexible Labor: A Theme Revisited," *World Development*, 27(3): 583–602.

UNIFEM (2000) *Progress of the World's Women*, New York: UNIFEM.

United Nations Development Programme (UNDP) (1999) *1999 World Survey on the Role of Women in Development: Globalization, Gender, and Work*, New York: UNDP.

Zhao, Laxiun (1998) "The Impact of Foreign Direct Investment on Wages and Employment," *Oxford Economic Papers*, 50: 284–301.

8 World Bank discourse and World Bank policy in *Engendering Development*

A comment

Karin Schoenpflug

One of the difficulties feminists face when confronted with material such as the World Bank's report *Engendering Development: Through Gender Equality in Rights, Resource, and Voice* (World Bank 2001) is a conflict between perceptions: the World Bank's perception of gendered reality in developing countries versus the perspective feminists have developed from their sources of information. What makes this congregation of views – from my point of view – look more like a struggle than an enriching discussion is the reality of a multi-dimensional conflict of material interests behind the scenes of the report. The Bank shapes public discourse on development and gender, and its influence on policy-making has enormous consequences for the lives of millions of people in developing countries. *Engendering Development* is like a play being performed in order to conceal the economic drama behind the stage; now the show has gone on tour and is being performed in countries all over the world.

When evaluating the World Bank's descriptions of perceived realities and goals of social change, it seems beneficial to use some sort of proven systematic theory to help disentangle the interwoven realities created by language, definitions and arguments. (Hofmann 2004). I use Michel Foucault's discourse analysis to roughly categorize the arguments made by Avin, Doss and Seguino, and to outline the strategies necessary to deconstruct the Bank's conclusions. According to Foucault, discourses are collective ways of constituting reality by means of rules and conventions (Foucault 1972). Within discourses, agents refer to shared knowledge about differences and similarities. Discourses are never neutral or homogeneous; they are always practices of in- and exclusion (Foucault 1978). As a consequence, discourses – like the one led by the World Bank in *Engendering Development* – legitimate specific ways of perceiving reality and exclude others. Most importantly, the power of discourses comes from the order they create and their function in sense-making and legitimization.

Michel Foucault's theoretical approach towards discourse can be understood in terms of four localities. The first considers the role of discourse in the constitution of subjectivity and issues of voice. The second examines the processes of legitimization and the power of definition and brings to light the way power and knowledge are mutually constituted. The third notes that Foucault focuses on relations rather than dualisms, which permits a consideration of intersectionality.

The fourth explores the material or economic consequences of discourse. I will now consider these four localities in turn:

1. Foucault highlights the role of *discourse in the constitution of subjectivity and authorizing certain voices while silencing others.*

(Who is talking (loudest)?)

The ways in which the World Bank speaks *for* the (poor) people/women in developing countries has always been an issue of criticism. For instance, Joseph Stiglitz, in an interview by Greg Palast in the online London *Observer*, claims that "the Bank's staff 'investigation' consists of close inspection of a nation's 5-star hotels. The investigation concludes with the Bank staff meeting some begging, busted finance minister who is handed a 'restructuring agreement' pre-drafted for his 'voluntary' signature" (Palast 2001: online). In contrast, Rose-Marie Avin's chapter asks the bank to "acknowledge that Third World women, and especially women's organizations, have been and are agents of economic development", who have a voice of their own (this volume, page 65). This issue is acknowledged by the Bank, since the issue of a "political voice" is the third part of the World Bank's suggested three-pronged strategy: "take active measures to redress persistent disparities in command over resources and political voice" (World Bank 2001: 2).

Nevertheless under closer scrutiny it turns out that the issue of "agentification" through voice is used contrary to the feminist concept (as expressed in Virginia Woolf's *A Room of One's Own* in 1929): in the European Union, for example, the feminist agenda of empowering women by giving them economic independence and a voice has been replaced with the concept of *gender mainstreaming*. This strategy also seems to be employed by the Bank as well, even though the terminology is not mentioned explicitly in the report. Gender mainstreaming is a process implanted in bureaucracies which demands that gender equality needs to "always be taken into consideration" by policy-makers. Contrary to this, in a feminist sense, *empowerment* means that subjects may speak for themselves and alter existing institutional structures. In other words, instead of just adding women and stirring, feminists may want to change the cake recipe altogether.

Although gender mainstreaming purports to strengthen women in a patriarchal world by "considering them always" it fails to consider the conditions necessary for women to become agents and take responsibility for their own lives. In this way "the World Bank report does not directly address the . . . issues of power relations within households, communities, and countries" (Doss, this volume, page 80), the World Bank cannot "take active measures to redress persistent disparities" *for* someone as is suggested in the third strategy. Whether the Bank simply does not see the problem: "if only policy-makers and senior scientists understood that their clients were women, then . . . poverty would be reduced" (as Doss remarks cynically, page 81) or whether the Bank actually does not want to change women's position in developing countries is the Gretchen Question in this regard.[1]

2. Foucault focuses on *processes of legitimization* and the *power of definition*. This brings to light the way power and knowledge are combined in a certain society.

(What is the language of the discussion?)

The issue here is the power of definition in World Bank terminology. First consider the distinction between *growth* and *development*. Avin, Doss and Seguino all note the fact that the World Bank report does not distinguish between economic growth and economic development. As Rose-Marie Avin points out, there are definitions for the multi-dimensional process of development such as the ones by Michael Todaro, who lists three "core values of development" or by Amartya Sen, who defines development as "a process of expanding the real freedoms that people enjoy" that take into consideration an array of factors that are integral to a nation's development (Avin, this volume, page 66). They are completely ignored (although five pieces of Sen's work are nevertheless quoted in the literature section of the report) in favor of the simplistic and incorrect view that growth is equal to development.

The focus on growth rather than development results in two distortions in the World Bank report. First, Avin points out that "the three-part strategy proposed by the report is inconsistent with the neoliberal agenda of international lending organizations, including the World Bank" (Avin, page 77) This means that the three-part strategy suggested does not seem to fit the overall goals, or might even work contrary to them.

Another problem lies in the Bank's static world view that considers only movements or interactions used in standard macroeconomic theory (i.e. sinking interest rates will lead to increased (foreign) investment). It does not consider a fluid reality nor the impacts of gender on macroeconomic processes. Seguino finds for instance that mobile industries (measured by FDI movements) make it more difficult to close gender wage gaps and diminishes the bargaining power of workers. So to the extent that growth is dependent on FDI, it will exacerbate rather than ameliorate gender inequalities.

3. Foucault emphasizes *relations* rather than dualistic concepts. This makes it possible to consider not only gender, but its intersections with class, race, ethnicity, sexuality, age, nationality, and other categories of difference.

(Who remains invisible?)

One of the most severe criticisms of the World Bank report centers around the exclusion of certain categories. The Bank's focus on dualistic concepts such as male–female, developed–developing, etc. reinforces and reproduces socially constructed binary differences. The intersectionality that is so central to feminist scholarship today is ignored. As Avin points out, the report "fails to take into consideration the issues of class, race, and ethnicity, a very important omission [. . .] It is important to acknowledge differences among women in terms of race and ethnicity" (Avin, page 65).

This leads us to seriously question their interpretation of the definition of "engendering." Most surprisingly, the report does not offer a single hint on what the Bank exactly means by "engendering." I am left to interpret engendering as gender mainstreaming. But instead of "taking gender into consideration" it seems that the Bank is (unconsciously?) strengthening binary gender categories; by not differentiating among women it reifies gender difference.

Avin, in contrast, demonstrates an example of a more nuanced approach towards gender when describing the effects of the Sandinistas' institutional reform in Nicaragua of the 1980s. She explains how different modes of access for women from different classes and cultural backgrounds made it possible for more than the most privileged sub-group of the category "women" to become empowered.

> Women also played a significant role in the political arena. . . . While many poor women entered the political arena at the grassroots level by joining popular organizations, middle- and upper-class women achieved high positions such as ministers or regional party coordinators . . . Working-class and peasant women increased their rights, their access to resources, and for the first time had a voice in their community.
>
> (Avin, page 72)

Doss provides a concrete example of the importance of differentiating within categories. She points out that there are three definitions for a "female farmer." "The gender of the farmer may be defined as the gender of the head of the household, the holder of the land, or the one who has the right to keep the proceeds" (Doss, page 86). The definition depends on particular legal and cultural norms that are highly contextual. The report's missing differentiation within the category "female farmer" makes its findings for those women farmers rather useless, since policies' consequences differ greatly for each sub-group of women working in agriculture.

This takes us directly to the next locality:

> 4. Foucault is interested in the *practices of inclusion and exclusion*, the processes occurring between subjects, by which dominant groups control social discourse, policy-making and therefore distribution and economic well-being. This focus on the *material consequences* of discourses is, for economists, certainly the most important issue. The material or economic consequences are the manifestation of unjust social relations naturalized through discourse.
>
> *(Who wins/loses materially?)*

The specific effects of development policies on sub-groups of considered groups is pointed out by Avin who states that

> some empirical studies . . . have shown that the poorest members of society may become worse off with economic growth . . . So there is no trickle

down with economic growth as this report seems to imply . . . economic growth is necessary but not sufficient to improve the lives of the vast majority of people and to improve gender equality.

(Avin, page 67)

She challenge the Report's overall conclusions that "on balance the evidence suggests that females' absolute status and gender equality improved, not deteriorated during the structural adjustment period of the 1980s and 1990s in Latin America" (Avin, page 65). She concludes that the neoliberal policies of the 1990s have not led to greater economic growth and gender equality.

In her chapter Seguino goes even as far as to argue that not only have the predicted successes of World Bank policies failed to materialize, but that the outcomes are actually contrary to contrary to the Bank's predictions. For example, she argues that "there exists an inverse relationship between gender wage equality and growth, implying that efforts to close wage gaps could slow economic growth." As evidence she notes that "those [countries] with the greatest gender wage inequality grew the most rapidly during the period 1975–1995" (Seguino, page 100).

Material consequences are easily uncovered when empirical tools are applied. Many feminist economists have so far concentrated on proving the effects of gender-blind or gender-adverse policy; now the task seems to have been expanded to demonstrate the adverse effects of allegedly gender-inclusive policy.

The uncovering of material consequences allows alternative solutions with more favorable economic outcomes to be offered. For instance, empowering the silenced has always been large on the feminist agenda. Avin, Doss and Seguino offer various strategies ranging from empowerment through technology (in the African context), through institutional reform (in the Latin American context) or through restricting capital mobility (in the Southeast Asian context). All three authors stress the need for international cooperation among developing and developed countries when employing measures such as speed bumps for physical capital, or global actions, such as anti-sweatshop campaigns.

In order to leave the dualistic framework of North–South, where the focus is on the World Bank "doing something to" developing countries, I will now briefly aim to demonstrate that this process of deconstruction of powerful institutions' rhetoric and policy is also taking place in the European Union.

In a recent project, Roswitha Hofmann uses a Foucauldian framework to deconstruct the process of knowledge creation and policy-making for the European Union's Lisbon Process (Hofmann 2004).[2] The Lisbon strategy, with its seemingly progressive agenda includes ten explicit commandments for employment reform, such as promoting gender equality in employment and pay and combating discrimination against disadvantaged groups.[3] Unfortunately, the primary goal of the EU's overall economic policy (the "Broad Economic Policy Guidelines") is the Stability and Growth Pact (SGP), which demands balanced budgets and debt reduction (Euro Papers 2002). The SGP has been signed in order to enable European monetary union (the Euro) and it disables member states' ability to conduct either monetary or fiscal policy. Ironically, the Lisbon goals are organized in such a way that all measures for achieving those goals have to be taken nationally. This restriction makes it impossible to actually increase resources for socially and economically marginalized groups given the dominant goal of budget consolidation and shrinking power of national governments.

The European Union situation with the formerly ten commandments is analogous to the World Bank's three-pronged strategy goals. Both sets of goals sound progressive but are subordinated to larger, opposing goals. For the European Union this is the SGP, for the World Bank, it is SAPs. The same political context of neoliberalism is prevalent in both cases. The redistributive power of governments is turned upside down; tax systems are reversed from progressive to regressive, social assistance and public goods are being replaced by competing private enterprises selling their services (i.e. retirement schemes, water, and education) to those who can afford them.

It is necessary for feminists to always bear in mind that policy-making in developing countries is connected to policy-making in "the first world." This connection demonstrates that a differentiated, inclusive feminist approach (one takes in as much of the whole picture as possible) is essential in order to challenge institutional operations such as those of the World Bank. As the feminist theorist bell hooks points out: "globally, women and children are the new proletariat and white women in the so-called developed countries support the enslavement of lower-class and poor women around the world" (hooks 1996: online). That's an indictment that is hard to hear. But if we really want to talk about the liberation of women, then we've got to talk about the investment that bourgeois women of all races have in the social structure. Not only is the political practice of "first world" institutions in developing countries post-colonial at best, disparities of wealth, income, and opportunity are increasing both between the developed and developing worlds, and also within geographic boundaries, between men and women and other (marginalized) groups.

In the European Union, double talk results from the power struggle between labor unions, the "left" and their employment commandments versus banks/large businesses and their neoliberal agenda (Jenson and Pochet 2002). Unions in the first world are trapped into protecting their employed workers at the expense of the unemployed, protecting the wages of male workers at the expense of female workers, and protecting domestic workers at the expense of those in developing countries.

Similar power conflicts may exist in the World Bank and this leads to the question, who within the Bank is interested in gender equality? Basically no one and everyone is the answer. The process of engendering development is only one device in the larger context of internationalizing suppression and enhancing the processes of neocolonization.

Feminist deconstruction and analysis has revealed the World Bank report *Engendering Development* as a powerful piece of institutional sweet-talking aimed at creating its own sense-making and legitimization for World Bank policies.

Similar processes can be observed worldwide, as has been pointed out in the context of the European Union. All three authors have concluded that the Bank's policies have not had the positive effects on gender equality as has been claimed. The analysis of *Engendering Development* from a feminist point of view finds that gender equality cannot and will not be reached, given the conflicting strategies recognized in the report. To conclude with Seguino's words: "the policies needed to promote equity . . . would require a rethinking of the Bank's support for neo-liberal macroeconomic policies" (Seguino, page 94). Since this may not happen in the near future, a way to implement alternative feminist policy solutions will need to be found.

Acknowledgments

Thanks to Nicky Imre for proofreading, Roswitha Hofmann for discussing and sharing her work on Foucault and the Lisbon strategy and to Drucilla Barker for her enormous help in wording this piece.

Notes

1 The "Gretchen Question" is a parable for questioning someone's dubious religious or political convictions, using a slightly naïve slant. Asking the "Gretchen question" refers to a passage in Goethe's *Faust*. Faust has long sold his soul to the devil, which his young and pure lover Gretchen certainly does not know. Then in one scene Gretchen innocently asks Faust if he really believes in God, a question poor Faust can only dodge.
2 In 2000 the European Council decided that the EU should become the "most competitive and dynamic knowledge based economy in the world, capable of sustainable economic growth with more and better jobs and greater social cohesion" (European Parliament 2000).
3 In 2005 the European Union has altered its failing Lisbon Strategy. There are currently seven guidelines for employment instead of ten and the promotion of gender equality has been taken off the (explicit) agenda. Growth and sustainability seem to be of equal importance in the new "Interpreted Guidelines for Growth and Employment (2005–2008)"; the Stability and Growth Pact has been extended by multiple cases of exceptions.

References

Euro Papers (2002) *Co-ordination of Economic Policies in the EU: A Presentation of Key Features of Main Procedures*, Paper No. 45, Brussels: Directorate General for Economic and Financial Affairs.
European Parliament (2000) *Lisbon European Council 2000: Presidency Conclusions*, Strasbourg. http://www.europarl.eu.int/summits/1is1en.htm (accessed October 11, 2005).
Foucault, M. (1972) *The Archaeology of Knowledge*, London: Routledge.
—— (1978) *Dispositive der Macht*, Berlin: Merve.
Hofmann, R. (2004) "Divides of the European 'Knowledge Society'," Vienna: University of Economics and Business Administration Working Paper.

hooks, b. (1996) "Tough Talk for Tough Times," in *On the Issues*, December 1, 1996, online, available http://static.highbeam.com/o/ontheissues/december011996/tough talkfortoughtimes/ (accessed August 24, 2004).

Jenson, J. and P. Pochet (2002) "Employment and Social Policy since Maastricht: Standing up to the European Monetary Union" Paris: University of Notre Dame, online, available http://www.cevipof.msh-paris.fr/rencontres/colloq/palier/Full%20 paper/Palier%20FP.doc (accessed August 24, 2004).

Palast, G. (2001) *The Globalizer Who Came In From the Cold*, in the London *Observer*, Wednesday, October 10, online edition: http://www.gregpalast.com/detail.cfm?artid =78&row=1 (accessed October 14, 2005).

World Bank (2001) *Engendering Development*, New York: Oxford University Press.

Part III

Disciplinary paradigms/ development paradigms

9 Colonizing knowledge

Economics and interdisciplinarity in *Engendering Development*

Suzanne Bergeron

Setting the disciplines in motion at the World Bank: adding the social and cultural to the equation

One of the features that distinguishes the emerging post-Washington consensus from the neoliberal agenda that proceeded it is the attention that has been given to social issues in development. The dislocations caused by two decades of economic restructuring, along with pressure from anti-poverty, women's, environmental and indigenous people's movements, have prompted development institutions such as the World Bank to be more responsive to social concerns such as poverty and inequality. Under President James Wolfensohn, the Bank has undertaken a self-proclaimed "paradigm shift" that includes a commitment to helping marginalized groups such as women and indigenous minorities, promoting an equitable distribution of income, working to promote democratic participation with the people directly affected by its projects, protecting the environment, and increasing its lending for health and education. This stated change in direction marks a break from the neoliberal, economistic approach taken by the Bank during the past 20 years, exemplified most famously in a memo signed by former chief economist Lawrence Summers on the efficiency of shipping toxic waste to Africa, which dismissed potential criticisms as likely to be based on some fuzzy set of "social concerns" and "moral reasons" that had no legitimate place in the development conversation (Summers 1992: 66). Now, social concerns seem to be taking center stage at the Bank.

However, increased attention to social development at the Bank also needs to be placed in the context of the development community's current fascination with theoretical innovations in economics that are adding cultural and social factors to the equation (Fine 2001; Bergeron 2002). These new approaches allow economists to take into account the impact of social and cultural forces on economic outcomes without sacrificing the core ideas of economic analysis. For example, in contrast to the growth theories that dominated development thinking 25 years ago, today's theories contend that social relations, culture, and institutions matter for economic growth. This creates a space for examining how formerly neglected social aspects of development, such as gender inequalities, might interfere with the goal of growth (Klasen 1999). Another innovation which has caught on in development circles is the concept of social exclusion. This concept links poverty to social and political as well as economic factors, particularly in terms of how socially excluded groups are denied access to resources that would affect their economic well-being. The related concept of social capital has of late received significant attention from economists, sociologists, and political scientists working in development in general (Woolcock 1998) and gender and development in particular (Rankin 2002).

Because of economic theory's influence on development research and practice, these theoretical innovations have made it more legitimate for the "epistemic community" (Haas 1992) of development thinkers to take social and cultural factors into account, and embrace new models based on multidisciplinary approaches. It is not surprising that the Bank's paradigm shift has been accompanied by the entry of increasing numbers of anthropologists, sociologists, and political scientists into an institution that until recently had been the almost exclusive territory of neoclassical economists (Cernea 1991). Even though these non-economists remain only a small percentage of the total research staff, a cursory examination of the Bank's research output ten years ago versus today suggests that the disciplines are in motion at the Bank, with increased exchange of disciplinary knowledges creating fresh space for understanding the relationship between social institutions, culture, and economy.

At first blush, this recent paradigm shift at the Bank, and the increased dialogue among the disciplines that has accompanied it, seems to represent the kind of changes in development theory and practice which political economists, feminists, and others on the margins of the profession have long called for. The acknowledgement that development problems do not come in discipline-shaped boxes has allowed for a more multi-dimensional analysis of existing research issues than was allowed by the economistic framework that dominated the field during the past 20 years. Inequality is a good example. The recognition that inequalities are based on differences which contribute to social exclusion, for instance by gender, has created openings for multidisciplinary approaches to understanding poverty, as mainstream economics by itself hasn't much to offer with regard to theorizing social roles, relationships, and resistance to exclusion (Jackson 2002: 500). Such analytical breakthroughs also support policy initiatives, for instance government programs to address exclusion issues such as discrimination in labor and credit markets. This acceptance of the existence of market failures, and the need for intervention to resolve those failures, can be contrasted with the free-market orthodoxy of the Washington consensus years (Stiglitz 1998).

Comparing frameworks: multidisciplinarity at the World Bank and the critical transdisciplinary approach of women's studies

The focus on the social that characterizes feminist scholarship, combined with the ongoing debates on the cultural character of economic processes within feminist theory, would seem to place it in a position to make a significant contribution to development theory and policy at this juncture (Jackson 2002: 499).

However, the sort of critical and transdisciplinary approach that feminist theory can bring to the development conversation might not get much of a hearing in development institutions such as the World Bank due to a variety of structural, epistemological, and institutional factors. For one thing, attempts to bridge disciplinary divides are somewhat fraught because in addition to the constraints associated with the political economy of knowledge production in the academy (where many face pressures to hew to the line of disciplinary boundaries), institutions like the World Bank continue to be dominated by economics. These pressures are exacerbated by the fact that development economists at the Bank have historically not take seriously those knowledges that, in their view, fail to achieve the same standard of rigor as economic theory. As William Ascher puts it:

> Many professionals in the World Bank have been reluctant to incorporate new considerations in formulating development strategies if they require modes of analysis less rigorous than the traditional economic framework. Unless and until development strategies can be converted into decision making procedures acceptable to the professional norms of those entrusted with using them, the implementation of these strategies is bound to meet resistance.
>
> (Ascher 1983: 417)

So what tends to get a hearing in the post-Washington consensus Bank are those insights about social institutions, cultural norms, and politics from non-economics fields which can be fitted to the existing model. The new emphasis on institutions, and thus the level of disciplinary interchange, relies not so much on contingent sociopolitical and cultural analysis as much as it does on theoretical notions dear to mainstream economists' hearts such as individual optimization. For example, as one World Bank researcher notes:

> What distinguishes new institutional economics from previous "institutional" or "historical" schools is that the former has more theory behind it. That particular theory has two interdependent components: first, a reliance on competition as the condition that induces efficiency, and second, the belief that the right incentive structure is the best answer to the restrictions that arise from the neoclassical model.
>
> (Wiesner 1998: 114)

Adding culture, social factors, and institutions to the equation, in other words, is within the bounds of acceptable practice only if it is framed in terms of preserving core ideas of neoclassical economics such as methodological individualism and a focus on market efficiency.

A story told by Cecile Jackson in a recent *World Development* article gives one example of how the economics-centered approach of the Bank in the current conjuncture frames the ways that disciplinary encounters are conceived.

A well-known World Bank economist, when asked about his vision of inter-disciplinary research, said that his ideal was to be able to call up a similarly well-known social anthropologist when he came across questions that puzzled him (Jackson 2002: 500). As Jackson explains, this perspective fails to value the modes of inquiry and insights of anthropology. It is at best an attempt to expand the tool kit of the discipline of economics, rather than fostering a true interdisciplinary engagement that would value and connect different ways of working and thinking.

The view of other disciplines serving as handmaiden to economics, allowing for better explanations of problems as they are framed by the Bank's pre-existing research agenda, provides a very limited sort of exchange, and one that falls far short of the ideal of feminist theory and women's studies research. Different disciplines bring new issues, new questions, and different conceptual frameworks to the table, and feminist research at its best tends to take more of a trans-disciplinary approach, one that not only broadens knowledge production but reorganizes it along new lines. Instead of viewing disciplinary border-crossing as adding to one's disciplinary toolkit, or a happy exercise in bridge-building, an apt analogy for the approach most valued in women's studies might, as Marjorie Pryse (1998) suggests, be Gloria Anzaldua's idea of "mestiza conciousness" – the coming together of two or more self-consistent but habitually incompatible frames of reference that causes a cultural collision. Thinking about it in this way suggests connecting different ways of thinking and working, and acknowledges the different modes and disparities among disciplinary knowledges (versus a more utopic bridge-building approach which would wish these disparities away). Further, if certain disciplines have in some sense colonized knowledge – and what better example of this is there than economics, which has increasingly been characterized by imperialism, the effects of which have been felt quite keenly in academic fields of political science and sociology in recent years – then to the extent which women's studies constitutes a challenge to disciplinary models we might consider it as a particular sort of postcolonial strategy.

The World Bank's approach to adding social and cultural factors to the equation, in contrast, does not challenge the core of economics or its imperialistic tendencies. The recent paradigm shift at the Bank is certainly multidisciplinary, in the sense that it adds insights from a variety of disciplines to expand the tool-kit used to make sense of social factors in development while retaining the core of economic disciplinarity. The reframing of development suggested by the women's studies approach would be more of a transdisciplinary method that brings the disciplines together in ways that challenge their cores, while reshaping the very boundaries that organize disciplinarity itself.

Thus, while border-crossing is a usual characteristic of knowledge growth, one that has characterized the development of all disciplines (including economics), much women's studies research is based on the more critical premise that disciplinary organization is contested (Klein 1993). This sort of critical transdisciplinarity, while likely quite productive in terms of generating knowledge that can serve as a basis of social change and empowerment for women, might not be an easy sell for institutions such as the World Bank where expertise still tends to be constructed along disciplinary (economic) lines.

The multidisciplinary approach of *Engendering Development*

The World Bank's policy research report on *Engendering Development* reflects the more general paradigm shift of the post-Washington consensus Bank toward social concerns and multidisciplinary approaches. The goal of the report is to understand the links between gender, public policy, and development by bringing a gender perspective to bear on the analysis and design of development policies and projects. In pursuit of that goal, *Engendering Development* adopts a self-consciously multidisciplinary approach that draws upon literature from economics, anthropology, sociology, political science, and education disciplines. In its conclusions, the report proposes a strategy based on reforming institutions to establish the legal and economic conditions for equality, fostering economic development to strengthen incentives for equal pay, and improving women's access to resources and political voice to reduce gender disparities (ibid.: 16–26, 231). The report's emphasis on the social and cultural factors that influence women's capabilities and agency, along with its focus on social development concerns such as education and health care, represent a real improvement over the earlier efficiency and growth-fetishized approach of the Bank. The emphasis on issues such as social norms, women's autonomy, and voice, because of the complexity of the issues raised by these concepts, shows a recognition and concern for creating the conditions in which women can influence social change, and the importance of asking key questions about what voices will be heard, how participation is fostered, and whether women will be able to represent and articulate the interests of other women. This suggests a great salience for the sort of transdisciplinary approaches that the best of women's studies scholarship can offer (Jackson 2002: 501). Understanding the ways that social institutions impede gender equality, for example, would entail a close study of the following: how cultural norms about gender interact with the construction of the self and subjectivity; gender relationships in social institutions such as the family and education; political life such as community engagement, government policies, and the legal structure; economic processes including the globalization of markets and local provisioning. It would also entail an analysis of how all of these interact with each other. This is the sort of complex, multilayered analysis suited to creative and critical exchange across and between the disciplines.

But while the report does make an attempt to bring these different factors to bear on the analysis of how gender disparities persist, there is in general not much analysis about how these factors work together to produce the outcomes they do. When there is such an attempt, disciplinary knowledges and insights that might challenge the Bank's attachment to the core ideas of economics are pushed to the margins. The multidisciplinary approach taken in the report, while a positive step compared to the narrowness of earlier economism, remains a limited perspective on gender and development by failing to pursue insights that a genuinely transdisciplinary approach would enable. Among other things, this would include drawing upon social constructivist and postcolonial insights to analyze the sources of difference among women and how these relate to women's agency. While it would certainly challenge the core neoclassical story in which individual agents are born and not made – as Julie Nelson (1996) has observed, neoclassical theory tends to see economic agents as Hobbesian "mushroom men" who emerge fully formed – grounding the report in these aspects of feminist theory would help to avoid the obscuring of difference created by universalistic accounts of women's behavior and experience which I examine below. Instead, the report's view of women's agency and its account of outcomes by gender (e.g. the idea that all women in a particular country benefit from economic growth) are a reflection of its continued attachment to rational choice theory on the one hand and macroeconomic representations which link GDP growth to national collective well-being on the other.

This has implications for how policy solutions are framed as well. For example, when the question is first raised regarding why gender disparities exist and are worse in some places than others (World Bank 2001: 97–9), the answer provided fails to incorporate insights from disciplines that have attempted to theorize social agency and social movements. In the absence of a richer theory of gender and agency, increased output and modernization are offered as the answers. Like earlier World Bank approaches to inequality, growth and marketization are consistently presented throughout the report as the great levelers, and deviant local "culture" as the constraint that keeps women from achieving empowerment through markets (see also Barriteau, this volume).

Unlike the strict neoliberal approach taken by the Bank in the 1980s and early 1990s, the report does specify a role for government policy in improving both efficiency and equity. Many of these policy prescriptions (e.g. affirmative action, equal pay laws) are grounded in theories of market failure that acknowledge such concerns as monopoly power and information problems which could result in statistical discrimination and impede optimal outcomes in markets (World Bank 2001: 126–42). This is at least in part due to the innovations in economics discussed in the first section. In the past, there was little room to theorize the problems of discrimination in mainstream neoclassical thought, which made it difficult for such concerns to have a voice at the Bank (Kardam 1991: 72). But as mainstream economics has embraced new models such as social exclusion theory, the discourse of the Bank has changed as well. Combining the individual-rationality approaches of neoclassical economics with sociological insights about discrimination by race and gender, a new information-theoretic approach to understanding labor market outcomes can explain not only why discrimination might exist, but also why it might be pervasive and in need of correcting via policy. Analyzing the social and cultural factors that contribute to peoples' exclusion, and designing projects aimed specifically at including these formerly marginalized groups in the development process (which, since this is the World Bank, means integrating them into the global capitalist economy) form an integral part of the Bank's new anti-poverty initiative (World Bank 1998) and this is reflected in the *Engendering Development* report as well.

Some implications of the colonizing knowledge of economics in *Engendering Development*

While this paradigm shift at the Bank can be seen as a positive step in that it is putting the question of gender inequality on the World Bank's map, there is also a need for caution. This shift remains within the general framework of neoclassical thought as it maintains an analytical separation of the social and cultural from the economic, and therefore tends to make sense of social norms and culture as things that interfere with the universal (culture-free) market economy. In this sense, the insights gleaned from sociology, anthropology and political science do not challenge as much as expand the toolkit of an existing discipline. The report might have included some of the recent literature on gender and global economics, which argues that the economy itself is deeply cultural (e.g. Benería 1999). But this sort of story is unlikely to get a hearing in the neoclassically centered approach of the report, which tends, except in the most limited of cases, to see culture and social relations as the "traditional" constraints on women's empowerment, which, in its modernization tale, occurs through integration into the global market.

A story that underscores this point is told by Joanna Kerr, who attended a summit on gender and structural adjustment in Africa, at the end of which one World Bank economist said, "I'm still not convinced that structural adjustment has a negative impact on women, but I am convinced that women's inequality has a negative impact on economic growth." This frames the social and economic as separate, and the economic as universal. What needs to be changed is not the Bank's relatively pro-market policy, but only the barriers that hinder women from contributing to the market. "Women are seen as an 'untapped' labor resource – as merely instruments of growth" (Kerr 1999: 197).

The policy implications of maintaining an analytical separation between the economic and the social are in fact quite deep. For example, Elson and Çagatay's analysis of recent attempts to integrate social content such as gender equity into development macroeconomic policies suggests that the promises of Bank President Wolfensohn to make gender central to such policies have not yet been met. In part, this is because the Bank continues to envision the social and the economic as two separate spheres, and gives priority to the latter. "Sound" monetary and fiscal policy are viewed by the Bank as the "essential backdrop" against which social goals must accommodate themselves (World Bank 2000: 21, cited in Elson and Çagatay 2000). Similarly, the analytical approach of the *Engendering Development* report continues to give priority to economic "fundamentals" such as expanding markets and growth, both of which it deems to be beyond discussion. As Elson and Çagatay suggest, an approach aimed at truly integrating social concerns (including gender equity) into economic policy would include analyses that might call into question what should count as fundamentals, or "sound" economic policy (Elson and Çagatay 2000: 1353). Unfortunately, the new economics' tendency to separate the economic from the social has given priority to economic fundamentals at the expense of a more transformative approach.

While there is a tendency for analyses to remain within the general discursive frame of mainstream economics in the report, it is certainly not completely dominated by economics. There are, in fact, entire sections of the report that do rely specifically on non-economic knowledges to explain certain aspects of gender subordination. In chapter 3, for example, there is an extended discussion of how gender-related norms and customs affect women's equality. This section describes differences in women's experiences across cultures using an anthropological frame. It is a welcome addition to the analysis of this question in the report, being attentive to, among other things, the inner workings of kinship, religious systems, and social norms as factors that contribute to gender disparities. For example, the section discusses the custom of brides moving to their husband's village upon marriage in parts of Southeast Asia, which explains their families' unwillingness to send them to school, whereas in other parts of Southeast Asia, women are expected to play a more important economic role in the family, thus creating an incentive to send them to school (World Bank 2001: 110–11). It also discusses how *machismo* in Latin America contributes to occupational segregation by gender, as well as to gendered violence (ibid.: 111–12). This section provides an alternative to the general thrust of the Bank's economic/social theorizing, which reduces everything to individualistic, rational, self-interested behavior. It opens the door to a more complicated historical and cultural narrative of women's oppression that eschews the universalizing tendencies of neoclassical economics.

Still, it remains problematic that a set of concerns related to the production of such knowledge about gender roles and traditional culture in anthropology are not included here, or in any other part of the report. For example, anthropologist Ruth Behar's *Translated Woman: Crossing the Border with Esperanza's Story* (1993) provoked a great deal of discussion among feminist anthropologists regarding the representation of the "other" in their work, and Behar's influence has led to more nuanced attempts to define the subject position of Western anthropologists, particularly as they view themselves as the "liberated" modern other against whom the "traditional" non-Western woman is judged (see Mohanty 1991 and Marchand and Parpart 1995 for examples of how feminists working out of other disciplines have tackled this issue). Integrating these insights would be useful because they would contribute to an understanding that traditional social norms are not always constraints on gender equality. For example, a participant in an online discussion of a draft of the report suggested as an example the Islamic concept of repudiation which has been used by some women to empower themselves.

As Avin (this volume) points out, the theoretical framework of the report is not able to address the problem of work not empowering women. Its universalizing, naturalistic portrayals of the economy impede it from imagining the ways that increased integration into the formal labor market might interfere with women's well-being. The flip side of this is that the report can not easily imagine how non-market social processes might potentially act as sites of negotiation and women's agency – with the exception of a handful of arguments that rely on essentialism, for example, the claim, discussed below, that women have more potential social capital because women as a group are naturally more cooperative. By maintaining the economy/culture dichotomy in which the universal market provides salvation from the backwardness of local culture, the report tends to entrench the image of the vulnerable, pre-modern Third World woman who is limited by social norms which are "slow to change," and it pushes to the margins those narratives of strategies for empowerment in which these women may already be involved on a daily basis.

This reflects a more general tendency of the report to present its findings and solutions within the growth-oriented modernization framework of neoclassical economics. One of the effects of taking this road is the report's tendency to see women's rights and empowerment in an instrumental manner: they matter only because inequalities by gender interfere with modernization goals such as growth. In chapter 3, the report states that equal rights for women are viewed as an important development goal because "legal social and economic rights provide an enabling environment in which women and men can participate productively in society, attain a basic quality of life, and take advantage of the new opportunities that development affords" (World Bank 2001: 116). Similarly, the argument in favor of providing more education to girls is instrumental. Educating girls leads to multiple "payoffs" including later marriages, increased contraceptive usage, reduced infant mortality and higher earnings (ibid.: 196). It is justified on the grounds that it will increase productivity and decrease birth rates. This sort of argument views gender equity as a means to an end, not as a goal unto itself (Baden and Goetz 1998: 24). Further, the objectives are rendered as technical (efficiency, birth rates) rather than political, which means that they may ultimately fail to address the systematic nature of gender and social injustices.

The rhetorical strategy of tying the goals of women's equality instrumentally to achieving the goals of economic growth needs to be made sense of in institutional context – it may, as Nukut Kardam (1991) suggests, give feminists some leverage within the growth-centered discourse of the Bank. The reticence of economists and other Bank staff to seriously consider the gender implications of their policies has caused some gender entrepreneurs inside and outside of the Bank to utilize arguments that it can understand. However, this approach, by staying inside the dominant disciplinary discourse of the Bank, may cost more than it is worth. As Diane Elson (1998: 155) puts it, "if we only work on the 'inside' we run the risk of merely achieving small improvements in the formu-lation of models or collection of statistics which do not actually transform women's lives." While focused on the question of cross-cultural knowledge, David Crocker's discussion of the relative merits of "insider" and "outsider" knowledge is relevant here as well, especially when we recognize that the World Bank has an institutional culture that in part frames its knowledge production. Crocker argues that insiders face social pressures that might inhibit their ability to develop alternative ways of thinking (Crocker 1991).

This seems to be the case in *Engendering Development*, which does not address the more contingent sociopolitical and cultural dimensions associated with improving women's lives and instead relies on the World Bank's well-worn script of modernization and marketization as the key to improvement. Examples of more integrated, transdisciplinary approaches to these issues include the essays in the edited collections by Afshar and Barrientos (1999) and Chang and Ling (2000) among others. These authors view women's struggles for rights and resources in a context that suggests a much more contested relationship with the growth of the market and modernization, as well as a complex renegotiation of their places in the household, workplace, and community.

The implicit and explicit equating of women's empowerment as economic empowerment via integration into the market economy can also be seen in *Engendering Development*'s discussion of reproductive labor. The report should certainly be commended on its inclusion of non-market labor as an important factor in women's lives. However, its focus on reproductive labor as something that should be substituted with market labor is quite limiting. Here, among other things, there may be space for a postmodern critique, as the report's analysis relies on a dualistic formulation of market versus non-market, reproductive versus productive labor, in which, like all dualistic frameworks, one term (in this case, the market) is the privileged term. I can imagine this dualism being exploded in a number of different ways, for instance by including the insight that it leaves out an important third term, community labor, which has become an important part of women's resistance and survival strategies during the current era of economic restructuring (Pardo 1998).

Still another aspect of the neoclassical framing of the report that would likely be eschewed by a more transdisciplinary women's studies approach lies in its representation of progress in such a way that the North is continually held out as the highest stage of development and liberation for women. At the end of chapter 3, for instance, the authors suggest that Third World countries might take heart at the progress made by the United States, which experienced gender inequities that were even "more severe than developing countries today":

> Take also the case of colonial America, where women were essentially the property of men, either their father or their husband. Women could not own property or enter contracts independent of their husband, and they had to relinquish property and wages to him. They had no custodial rights to their children, could not vote or hold political office, and were routinely excluded from social and professional organizations. These restrictions, common in 1776 – and more severe than those in developing countries

today – no longer exist in the United States. Why? Increases in per capita wealth, women's activism, and women's education all contributed to broadening women's rights.

(World Bank 2001: 144)

Similarly, the discussion of the gender gap in work on pages 184–5 contends that in countries that experience growth, the gender gap in total hours worked will fall. This is done by comparing hours worked by men and women in richer and poorer countries, and showing that in richer countries it is more equal. By taking this stance, the report suggests that all countries are marching along the same path, some are simply behind others and need to catch up to those countries where economic development has liberated women. This seems to replicate precisely the sort of "stages of development" modernization approach that fails to capture the contingent realities that different countries face. This approach has come under criticism from multiple quarters, including what was certainly one of the most vibrant debates in the gender and development literature in the 1990s (Connelly *et al.* 1995).

In addition to its general neoclassical adherence to the view of development as growth, and attachment to outdated notions of linear progress, the report also tends to trade in essentialistic portrayals of women. There is a strong tendency in *Engendering Development* to use gender as a monolithic category despite the existence of multiple analyses of the complex realities and difference among women that exist in the gender and development literature more broadly. While some attempts are made to differentiate women in the report, usually via a listing of characteristics such as age, race, ethnicity, religion, etc. in different sections of the text (e.g. p. 112), most of the analysis seems to take a more flattened approach. Some examples of this include the following. First, the general thrust of the book seems to posit that even while there are differences among women, women are, as a group, relatively worse off than men (see especially chapter 1). To be fair, one exception to this is found in the discussion of adjustment on page 211, where it is pointed out that men, especially young men, were hit harder by unemployment than women during Thailand's economic crisis in the 1990s. Similarly, the general argument of chapter 5 is that development makes women as a group better off. This second formulation (relating to chapter 5) seems to come from the somewhat universal neoclassical economic assumptions regarding growth lifting all boats. But arguing that social arrangements affect women more adversely than men, or that development improves the lot of women generally, is problematic for several reasons. Such representations do not allow for differentiation among women and men in terms of class, race, ethnicity, age, nationality, and education. As such they do not provide a very useful basis for theorizing feminist activism or gender-sensitive policy-making.

Some specific examples of essentialism in the report include the section on corruption and gender on pp. 92–6. Summarizing a growing body of research on the subject, the text states that "there may be intrinsic differences in the behavior of women and men" that cause governments to be less corrupt when women are in power, and that "gender differentiated attitudes toward corruption seem to be more or less a worldwide phenomenon" (World Bank 2001: 93). While these differences might bear out empirically, their origins could be treated in a more nuanced way in the report. While the existing literature utilizes psychological, sociological, and criminal justice perspectives to explain these differences in terms of women's role in reproduction and/or or gender social-ization, the report simply offers them as "intrinsic." This representation of women as if they embody a set of given characteristics is troubling not just because it obscures differences among women, but also because it suggests generalized gender differences in behavior that, as Jackson puts it, "can be relied on in gender differentiated policy" (Jackson 2002: 502).

The tendency to theorize that women are universally disadvantaged *vis-à-vis* men and the reliance on generalized gender differences to imagine policy scenarios are carried over into the discussion of social exclusion and social capital. Women, it is argued, have less social and political capital than men, thus putting them at a disadvantage (World Bank 2001: 97, 101). Interestingly, in the past couple of years, the World Bank has taken a slightly different view from what is presented in the report, imagining on the one hand contexts in which women suffer from social exclusion, but increasingly making the argument that women are better at social networking, and thus have more (or particularly distinct and more useful) social capital than men. This, for instance, is the basis of the World Bank's microcredit lending programs, in which women's social cohesion is viewed as a substitute for collateral. As Robert Picciotto of the World Bank puts it, "co-operation is more of a female attitude," making women a particularly good credit risk for these loans. Note that this essentialist characterization is one that depends on gender subordination, for the argument is that women are better at cooperating because they don't have access to resources like well-paid jobs (World Bank 2002).

Another example of essentialism occurs on page 186 of the report. In the discussion of how economic growth can contribute to the deepening of markets, which in turn will lighten women's load, the report states that "where available, hired labor can substitute for family labor on farms or in care activities, thus easing the workload of family members." It goes on to say that "a market for farm workers enables households to cope with peak season labor demand without pulling children out of school or adding excessive hours to women's work." In this section the clear implication is that the "women" benefiting from these labor market arrangements are the ones doing the hiring. This represents a combination of the "integrate, integrate, integrate" approach of liberal feminism along with the class-blindness associated with adherence to a more or less neoclassical framework that has been challenged in feminist circles (especially feminist development circles) in the past twenty years. The class, ethnic, age, and other differences that might underlie this market arrangement (what will be the impact on the well-being of the person – woman? – being hired, what circumstances might have brought her to the labor market as a household worker or "peak season" farm worker in the first place?) are thus pushed to the margins in such an analysis, which, as we know from many previous cases, has often resulted in policies that attempt to deal with gender inequalities but only serve relatively well-off and educated women, leaving poor women behind.

Conclusion

The shift towards a greater appreciation of the social, cultural and political aspects of development, and thus towards interdisciplinary approaches, has led to some interesting and refreshing insights into the relationship between gender and development as presented in the World Bank's *Engendering Development* report. However, much of the analysis of the report has remained within the disciplinary framework of neoclassical economics that continues to dominate institutions such as the World Bank. Here, the other social sciences serve primarily as hand-maidens to the Bank's already established assumptions and agendas. A more critical transdisciplinarity, one that builds on the knowledge-producing strategies of women's studies research in general and recent debates in gender and develop-ment in particular, would create the conditions for less instrumental and more transformative approaches to both knowledge production and development policy.

Acknowledgments

The author would like to thank two anonymous referees and the editors of this collection, Edith Kuiper and Drucilla K. Barker, for their helpful comments and suggestions.

References

Afshar, Haleh and Stephanie Barrientos (eds) (1999) *Women, Globalization and Fragmentation in the Developing World*, New York: St. Martin's Press.

Ascher, William (1983) "New Development Approaches and the Adaptability of Internation Agencies: The Case of the World Bank," *International Organization*, 37(3): 415–39.

Boden, Sally and Ann Goetz (1998) "Who Needs (Sex) When You Can Have (Gender)? Conflicting Discourses on Gender at Beijing," in Cecile Jackson and Ruth Pearson (eds), *Feminist Visions of Development*, London: Routledge.

Behar, Ruth (1993) *Translated Women: Crossing the Border with Esperanza's Story*, Boston, MA: Beacon Press.

Benería, Lourdes (1999) "Globalization, Gender and the Davos Man," *Feminist Economics*, 5(3): 61–83.

Bergeron, Suzanne (2002) "Challenging the World Bank's Narrative of Inclusion," in Amitava Kumar (ed.), *World (Bank) Literatures*, Minneapolis, MN: University of Minnesota Press.

Cernea, Michael (1991) "Using Knowledge from Social Science in Development Projects," World Bank Discussion Paper Series, Washington, DC: World Bank.

Chang, Kimberly and L.H.M. Ling (2000) "Globalization and Its Intimate Other: Filipina

Domestic Workers in Hong Kong," in Marianne H. Marchand and Anne Sisson Runyan (eds), *Gender and Global Restructuring*, London: Routledge: 27–43.

Connelly, M. Patricia, Tania Murray Li, Martha MacDonald and Jane M. Parpart (1995) "Restructured Worlds/Restructured Debates: Globalization, Development and Gender, *Canadian Journal of Development Studies* (special issue).

Crocker, David (1991) "Insiders and Outsiders in International Development," *Ethics and International Affairs*, 5: 149–73.

Elson, Diane (1998) "Talking to the Boys: Gender and Economic Growth Models," in Cecile Jackson and Ruth Pearson (eds), *Feminist Visions of Development*, London: Routledge.

Elson, Diane and Nilufer Çagatay (2000) "The Social Content of Macroeconomic Policies," *World Development*, 28(7): 1347–64.

Fine, Ben (2001) *Social Capital Versus Social Theory*, London: Routledge.

Haas, Peter (1992) "Introduction: Epistemic Communities and International Policy Coordination," *International Organization*, 46 (Winter): 1–36.

Jackson, Cecile (2002) "Disciplining Gender?" *World Development*, 30(3): 497–509.

Kardam, Nükut (1991) *Bringing Women In: Women's Issues in International Development Programs*, Boulder, CO: Lynne Rienner Publishers.

Kerr, Joanna (1999) "Responding to Globalization: Can Feminists Transform Development?" in M. Porter and E. Judd (eds), *Feminists Doing Development: A Practical Critique*, London: Zed Press.

Klasen, Stephan (1999) "Does Gender Inequality Reduce Growth and Development? Evidence from Cross-country Regressions," Background paper for *Engendering Development*, World Bank, Washington, DC, available online at http://www.eldis.org/static/DOC8972.htm (accessed October 11, 2005).

Klein, Julie Thompson (1990) *Interdisciplinarity: History, Theory and Practice*, Detroit, MI: Wayne State University Press.

—— (1993) "Blurring, Cracking, and Crossing: Permeation and the Fracturing of Discipline," in Ellen Messer-Davidow and David R. Shumway (eds), *Knowledges: Historical and Critical Studies in Disciplinarity*, Charlottesville, VA: University Press of Virginia.

Marchand, Marianne and Jane Parpart (1995) *Feminism/Postmodernism/Development*, London: Routledge.

Mohanty, Chandra Talpade (1991) "Cartographies of Struggle: Third World Women and the Politics of Feminism," in C.T. Mohanty, A. Russo and L. Torres (eds), *Third World Women and the Politics of Feminism*, Bloomington, IN: Indiana University Press.

Nelson, Julie (1996) *Feminism, Objectivity and Economics*, New York: Routledge.

Pardo, Mary (1998) *Mexican American Women Activists*, Philadelphia, PA: Temple University Press.

Pryse, Marjorie (1998) "Critical Interdisciplinarity, Women's Studies, and Cross-Cultural Insight," *NWSA Journal*, 10(1): 1–22.

Rankin, Catherine (2002) "Social Capital, Microfinance, and the Politics of Development," *Feminist Economics*, 8(1): 1–24.

Stiglitz, Joseph (1998) "Towards a New Paradigm for Development: Strategies, Policies, and Processes," Prebisch Lecture, UNCTAD, Geneva.

Summers, Lawrence (1992) "Let Them Eat Pollution" (excerpt of Lawrence Summers' internal memo to the World Bank), *The Economist*, February 8: 66.

Wiesner, Eduardo (1998) "Transaction-Cost Economics and Public-Sector Rent-

Seeking in Developing Countries: Toward a Theory of Government Failure," in E. Weisner and R. Picciotto (eds) *Evaluation and Development: The Institutional Dimension*, New Brunswick, NJ: Transaction Publishers for the World Bank: 108–23.

Woolcock, Michael (1998) "Social Capital and Economic Development: Towards a Theoretical Synthesis and Policy Framework," *Theory and Society*, 27(2): 1–22.

World Bank (1998) "Social Development Update: Making Development More Inclusive and Effective," Social Development Department, Paper No. 27, May 28, Washington, DC: World Bank.

World Bank (2000) *Entering the 21st Century: World Bank Development Report 1999/2000*, New York: Oxford University Press.

—— (2001) *Engendering Development: Through Gender Equality in Rights, Resources, and Voice*. Washington, DC: World Bank.

World Bank (2002) "Social Capital" and "Social Capital and Gender." On the World Bank website http://worldbank.org/poverty/scapital, accessed March 17, 2002.

10 Adjustment with a woman's face

Gender and macroeconomic policy at the World Bank

Cynthia A. Wood

The World Bank's policies for structural adjustment have been consistently criticized for the unequal distribution of their negative effects, or "social costs." Two major strands of this criticism are the poverty critique, articulated in UNICEF's *Adjustment with a Human Face* (Cornia *et al.* (eds) 1987, 1988), and the gender critique, put forward in *The Invisible Adjustment* (UNICEF 1989; see also Commonwealth Secretariat 1989).[1] However, the World Bank has responded to these critiques very differently. The Bank's many published analyses of the social costs of adjustment since 1987 deal almost exclusively with the poor. Gender inequalities in the costs of adjustment have not been addressed. While the poverty and gender critiques have much in common, they are not identical. The Bank's different responses to them thus have important implications for policy.

Because the Bank has shown increasing commitment to issues of gender and development in other areas of policy, the persistent lack of attention to gender in its analysis of structural adjustment requires an explanation. Much of this explanation must come from institutional and political analyses of the Bank which are beyond the scope of this chapter (see O'Brien *et al.* 2000: 24–66; Women's Eyes 1997).[2] However, such analyses are not enough; conceptual issues must also be addressed. I argue in this chapter that criticisms of the social costs of adjustment are given credence by macroeconomic policymakers at the Bank only to the degree that they can be framed in terms of the neoclassical economic paradigm which has dominated Bank lending for so many years (Kapur *et al.* 1997; Murphy 1995: 35). Arguments in *Adjustment with a Human Face* which were so framed were quickly addressed in official discussions of adjustment. In contrast, the gender and adjustment critique is not framed in neoclassical terms, and suggests instead that the paradigm is problematic. Consequently, the Bank disregards this literature even in its discussions of social costs and of compensatory measures to ameliorate those costs. The few Bank documents which discuss gender in the context of structural adjustment generally present only issues compatible with the paradigm and do not refer to the gender critique.

With continued pressure from critics, gender is beginning to enter Bank analysis of structural adjustment. However, many gender inequalities resulting from adjustment emerge in areas likely to be marginalized in neoclassical economics. I focus on one such area, unpaid domestic labor (or housework), to show that the failure to consider issues excluded by the paradigm makes it likely that future macroeconomic policy emerging from the Bank will continue to be gender-biased.[3] Furthermore, without attention to unpaid domestic labor and other issues incompatible with neoclassical theory, compensatory programs are unlikely to counter many gender inequalities in the effects of structural adjustment, and may worsen them in some cases. As long as the neoclassical paradigm dominates macroeconomic policymaking at the Bank, institutional changes and political pressure which encourage greater attention to gender will not, by themselves, eliminate gender bias in adjustment policies.

I base my argument on an examination of publicly available World Bank documents – formal publications, technical notes, and material on the Bank's external web site – analyzing structural adjustment, the social costs of adjustment, and gender. I also analyze Bank documents that mention gender in the context of adjustment, and other publications which demonstrate the Bank's position particularly well. My goal is to present an accurate picture of the Bank's analysis of structural adjustment and social costs using documents which together constitute its public discourse on the topic.[4]

After a description of structural adjustment policies, I briefly review the gender and adjustment literature. Next, I document the absence of gender in Bank analyses of structural adjustment and social costs, including a review of exceptions to this rule. I then illustrate the overall lack of discussion of adjustment in the Bank's gender analyses until the publication of *Engendering Development* (World Bank 2001b). I explain the Bank's failure to incorporate gender in macroeconomic policymaking through an exploration of the neoclassical paradigm, focusing on its exclusion of unpaid domestic labor. Finally, I discuss the success of the poverty critique in attracting Bank attention and implications for the future of gender analysis in Bank macroeconomic policy.

Structural adjustment and compensatory programs

From a neoclassical economic perspective, the problems faced by less-developed countries beginning with the debt crisis in the early 1980s were due to long-term interference with the market by individual governments (Mosley *et al.* 1991: 4–9; Commonwealth Secretariat 1989: 19–22). "Structural adjustment" was the process of correcting these market imbalances (Mosley *et al.* 1991: 23). Successful adjustment was signaled by market criteria: low inflation, competitive exchange rates, reductions in government spending, and a "microeconomic environment that is favorable to new investment" (World Bank 1990: 11).

Policies to achieve macroeconomic "stabilization" devalued exchange rates, cut consumption and government spending, and tightened monetary policy. The World Bank made loans conditional on changes in national economies which increased the role of the market through trade liberalization, privatization, reducing state involvement in the economy, and eliminating exchange rate controls and subsidies on consumer goods and services (Mosley *et al.* 1991: i, 34).

From the Bank's perspective, short-term recessional effects resulting from adjustment policies were transitional costs necessary to achieve the conditions necessary for long-term growth (World Bank 1987: 6).

Rising unemployment, falling wages, widening income inequality, and increasing morbidity and mortality rates devastated countries which applied structural adjustment policies during and after the 1980s. Many argue that the long-term effects of these policies will be equally damaging (see Cornia *et al.* (eds) 1987, 1988; Oxfam Policy Department 1995; SAPRIN 2001). In response to criticisms such as these, the Bank developed "compensatory programs" such as social emergency funds, which were designed to accompany adjustment and compensate vulnerable groups through targeted provision of income and social services (Vickers 1991; Benería and Mendoza 1995). The Bank eventually made social protection a condition of further loans (World Bank 1996). However, gender is not yet a factor in Bank evaluations of the social costs of adjustment, despite a substantial literature on the topic.

Gender critiques of adjustment

Numerous presentations, articles, and books on gender and adjustment have appeared since 1987, several published by respected international agencies.[5] Most authors of these works are development practitioners or Ph.D. economists at universities, international agencies, or non-governmental organizations (NGOs). Overviews of the literature highlight a few major points (see Çagatay *et al.* (eds) 1995; Sparr (ed.) 1994; Blackden and Morris-Hughes 1993; Vickers 1991: 15–42):

1 Structural adjustment policies are biased against women in conception, implementation, and evaluation;
2 The invisibility of this bias to policymakers at international agencies such as the World Bank is part of the problem and is reflected in the paucity of statistical data on the issue;
3 Evidence consistently shows that women suffer more and gain less than men from adjustment policies.

At the conceptual level, many argue that the neoclassical underpinnings of adjustment policies are a major source of gender bias. There are many threads of this argument which I shall be unable to discuss here. I focus on unpaid domestic labor because I believe that in defining economic analysis in market terms, neoclassical theory is particularly resistant to the inclusion of such labor as an economic activity (see Wood 1997).

Critics argue that because neoclassical economics does not include unpaid domestic labor in its definition of economic activity, the effects of adjustment on such labor are invisible to Bank policymakers. Yet this labor is an important household resource and must be considered if the effects of adjustment are to be understood fully. The substitution of unpaid domestic labor for market income and social services, in particular, is a major factor in the "success" of structural adjustment policies as defined by neoclassical policymakers (see Elson 1989: 57–8). This substitution occurred routinely as a direct result of structural adjustment policies in the 1980s and after; poor households used all available resources to adapt to worsening economic conditions. Since unpaid domestic labor is socially defined as "women's work," this particular effect of adjustment was not gender neutral. Women's workloads increased more than men's.

Quantitative data is difficult to find on unpaid domestic labor. Since it is not considered an economic activity, it is not measured in conventional economic surveys.[6] However, case studies and anecdotal evidence from NGOs and other sources suggest that adjustment increased the quantity and intensity of unpaid domestic labor. Women compensated for falling income by spending more time on day-to-day management of the household and by substituting unpaid work for commodities they could no longer afford. Searching for lower prices and cheaper substitutes to make a smaller income go further, women in Argentina, Mexico, and elsewhere went to more shops or markets, shopped more frequently, traveled further from home, and spent more time checking prices (Feijoó and Jelin 1989: 39; Benería 1991: 175). Time spent seeking out loans or selling assets such as jewelry in response to lower income also increased (Moser 1989: 149; Stewart 1991: 1853). Women worked longer hours producing what they could once buy, with a lower quality of domestic equipment (Feijoó and Jelin 1989: 39; Benería 1991: 175; Waylen 1992: 158). They bought food that was less processed, which required that the processing be done at home, and spent more time gathering firewood and water (Commonwealth Secretariat 1989: 65). Repairs not made on items such as refrigerators increased cooking time (Benería 1991: 175; Moser 1989: 148).

Many adjustment policies directly increased women's domestic labor by cutting government funds to social services. Decreasing public expenditures on water, sanitation, and sewerage made the search for potable water and the disposal of waste more difficult (Rocha *et al.* 1989: 27). As a result, illness became more common. Since many countries also cut spending on health care and subsidies on food as part of their adjustment program, women spent more time caring for the sick (see Cornia 1987: 29, 39; Commonwealth Secretariat 1989: 42; Waylen 1992: 159–60). Cutting clinic hours or shutting down clinics meant that women spent more time traveling or waiting in line with sick children. Raising or introducing charges for clinic visits meant that many could not afford to go at all.

Poor women found innovative ways to cope with reduced income and social services, such as communal kitchens in Peru, but these also often required increases in unpaid domestic labor (Jacobs 1991; Waylen 1992: 170–1; Commonwealth Secretariat 1989: 42). Even outside assistance to address the effects of structural adjustment on the poor increased women's unpaid work (Moser 1989: 158). Increases in adult women's workload overall resulted in girls staying home from school to take on domestic labor (Moser 1989: 154–5; Cornia 1987: 40).[7]

While the breadth and complexity of gender critiques of adjustment cannot be pursued here, this summary is enough for an examination of the World Bank's treatment of gender in its evaluation of structural adjustment policies. Almost without exception, Bank policymakers evaluating structural adjustment and their social costs do not measure, or even recognize, the effects of adjustment on women described in these critiques.

Gender in the Bank's analysis of structural adjustment

The Bank has not addressed gender critiques of its policies in publications devoted to adjustment or social costs. It fails for the most part even to acknowledge the existence of these critiques, in stark contrast to its response to *Adjustment with a Human Face*. Gender itself is marginal to the Bank's discussions of structural adjustment, as even some within the Bank have noted (Blackden and Morris-Hughes 1993: 16).

Consider a paper on the "Structural-Adjustment Debate" given in 1993 by Lawrence Summers, then Chief Economist of the World Bank. According to Summers and his co-author, the paper "distill[s] the main lines of criticism levied against structural-adjustment programs to four critiques and assess[es] the validity of each" (Summers and Pritchett 1993: 383). Summers discusses the poverty critique, but does not refer either to gender or to the literature criticizing adjustment's effects on women. Since Summers was a major figure in the development of Bank policies for structural adjustment at the time, the absence of gender in his presentation is especially significant. His lack of attention indicates the Bank's general position.

A review of more recent Bank publications on structural adjustment and social costs demonstrates the continued failure to address gender in this area of analysis. In the overview *Structural and Sectoral Adjustment: World Bank Experience 1980–92*, there is only one brief reference to women (Jayarajah and Branson 1995: 177). The study *Social Dimensions of Adjustment: World Bank Experience, 1980–93*, supposedly a review document on social costs, "looks at all the evaluated adjustment operations supported by the Bank . . . and tracks what happened to poverty and income distribution" (Jayarajah *et al.* 1996: xi). The review never refers to gender in the context of structural adjustment, nor does it analyze gender in terms of social costs. It mentions women only briefly in isolated comments (see ibid.: 107, 111, 114, 118). While it is difficult to document the absence of attention, I have found no Bank analysis of adjustment or the social costs of adjustment which makes more than a passing reference to gender, with the exception of the documents discussed below.

The first exception is Paul Collier's work, which explains the impact of adjustment on women in terms of the constraints they face in earning income and differences in their consumption of certain public services (Collier 1993). Collier's essay is significant in defining a legitimate space for gender in the World Bank's structural adjustment literature, as demonstrated by its appearance in a

[handwritten margin note: no reference to gender or literature]

publication edited by senior economists, but this space is telling for what it excludes. He does not refer to the literature on gender and adjustment, which is important because it allows him to define both the problem and the solution to it in neoclassical terms, as I discuss below.

The second exception is an Africa Region Technical Note by C. Mark Blackden and Elizabeth Morris-Hughes entitled *Paradigm Postponed: Gender and Economic Adjustment in Sub-Saharan Africa* (Blackden and Morris-Hughes 1993). Blackden and Morris-Hughes not only refer to gender critiques of adjustment, but take this literature (and feminist economic theory) as their primary frame of reference in analyzing policies for structural adjustment. Research and policy recommendations of the multi-donor Special Program of Assistance for Africa (SPA), including a pilot Structural Adjustment and Gender in Africa (SAGA) initiative funded by the World Bank, are based in part on *Paradigm Postponed* (World Bank 1996; Blackden 1998).

However, no other publication in the Bank's literature on adjustment and social costs to date refers to *Paradigm Postponed*, nor does it appear in a collection or series indicating general acceptance among Bank economists responsible for macroeconomic policy, as Collier's work does (see also O'Brien *et al.* 2000: 56). Even *Adjustment in Africa*, a formal Bank publication produced by the office of the Chief Economist in "close collaboration with the World Bank's Africa Region," fails to cite Blackden and Morris-Hughes, and makes only two brief comments on gender in the context of structural adjustment (World Bank 1994a: xv, 167–8, 174). In light of these indications of marginality, I consider *Paradigm Postponed* an "outlier" in the Bank's analysis of structural adjustment. Nevertheless, it is important as a published alternative to Collier's approach to gender and adjustment appearing within the Bank, and the application of this work by the Africa Region and the SPA models innovative macroeconomic analysis responsive to the gender critique of adjustment (see Blackden 1998).

Examining the exceptions to the general absence of gender in the Bank's macroeconomic analysis runs the risk of overstating their importance. Bank overviews of adjustment and social costs cite neither Collier's work nor *Paradigm Postponed* (e.g. Jayarajah and Branson 1995; Jayarajah *et al.* 1996; World Bank 2001a). Even combined with the work of the Africa Region and the SPA, these documents were not enough to bring about the incorporation of gender in the Bank's overall analysis of structural adjustment.

At the United Nation's 1995 Fourth World Conference on Women held in Beijing, James D. Wolfensohn, President of the World Bank, stated:

A priority concern must be to ensure that women are not hurt by structural adjustment programs. I am well aware of the wide criticism of the Bank on this subject. I believe that a macroeconomic plan is crucial to development, but I will be vigilant and more sensitive to arguments which relate to disproportionate adverse social impacts on women.

(Wolfensohn 1995)

Wolfensohn is known to be concerned with the social costs of adjustment and "is regarded by gender equity advocates both within and outside the Bank as a tremendous positive resource for change" (O'Brien *et al.* 2000: 53). Nevertheless, some years after Beijing there is little evidence that macroeconomic policy-makers are paying serious attention to the effects of structural adjustment on women, except in the Africa Region, where interested and committed staff responded very early to the gender critique (see Women's Eyes 1997; O'Brien *et al.* 2000: 24–6).

Structural adjustment in the Bank's analysis of gender

Corresponding to the absence of gender from the Bank's analysis of structural adjustment is the lack of discussion of adjustment in its now extensive work on gender. Bank staff working on gender are not directly involved in macro-economic policymaking, so this is the less important of the two in the design of policies for structural adjustment. However, pressure exerted by staff interested in or mandated to promote gender issues at the Bank could, at least theoretically, affect macroeconomic policy.[8] Unfortunately, serious pressure to incorporate gender in the Bank's analysis of structural adjustment is not obvious in Bank publications on gender. While unpublished internal pressure certainly exists, to date these efforts have failed to "engender" macroeconomics at the Bank. The recent publication of the Policy Research Report *Engendering Development* (World Bank 2001b) actually undermines the impetus to do so.

The Bank's literature on gender is devoted almost exclusively to project-based lending in areas of "social development," such as education, population, and health, so much so that adjustment policy must be seen as outside the purview of gender analysis as defined by the Bank, at least until *Engendering Development* (see Buvinic *et al.* 1996: 2–4). In two World Bank studies, Josette Murphy reviews the Bank's "record of incorporating gender issues in the operations it supports" and discusses a total of 800 projects either implemented or approved between 1967 and 1996 (Murphy 1995: xi, 1; 1997: 1). Neither study considers macroeconomic lending, and other than a brief comment on the work of the SPA, Murphy does not mention structural adjustment (1995: 54; 1997: 15–16). Indirectly, she suggests that gender and macroeconomics are mutually exclusive: "The Bank's shift toward macroeconomic policy during the early 1980s made such issues as poverty alleviation and gender less immediate Bank concerns" (1995: 35).

A few exceptions to the general absence of structural adjustment in Bank discussions of gender exist before *Engendering Development*. In 1994, the first World Bank policy paper on women appeared, *Enhancing Women's Participation in Economic Development* (World Bank 1994b). Policy papers must be approved by the Board of Executive Directors and represent the Bank's official position, so it is especially significant that this document explicitly addresses the effects of structural adjustment on women: "In some countries and situations, . . . short-term adverse effects [of adjustment policies] may fall disproportionately on women" (World Bank 1994b: 66–7). It also suggests that "the beneficial effects of adjustment may be slow in reaching women" (ibid.: p. 68). These remarks constitute the Bank's first acknowledgment in an official document that adjustment may have had adverse effects on women. Coupled with the statement that "[g]ender issues will be systematically addressed . . . in the design and implementation of lending programs, including adjustment operations" (ibid.: p. 13), they justify and even mandate analysis of gender and adjustment. Unfortunately, follow-through on this particular aspect of the policy paper has not been forthcoming. Even the Operational Policy statement accompanying the paper summarizes recommended policy changes without mentioning structural adjustment (World Bank 1994c).

Two Bank publications prepared for the UN's Beijing conference mention macroeconomic policy in the context of gender, but neither comments on actual or potential negative effects (see World Bank 1995a, 1995b). A progress report following Beijing devotes a section to "integrating gender into adjustment operations and economic reform" (World Bank 1996). This report acknowledges the gender critique of Bank policies, and suggests that "the design and implementation of [economic reform] programs . . . should take gender differences in needs, constraints and resources into consideration." However, the SPA's work is the only concrete example offered to support the assertion of Bank progress in this area. The majority of this section discusses poverty.

Again, documenting exceptions to the general absence of adjustment in the Bank's gender analysis makes them appear more important than they are. The Bank itself does not take these exceptions seriously. In *Mainstreaming Gender and Development in the World Bank*, Caroline Moser and her co-authors do not refer to structural adjustment in their comments on the documents analyzed above (Moser *et al.* 1999).[9]

The most recent publication on gender, *Engendering Development*, presents several pages on gender differences in the effects of structural adjustment, finally breaking the silence on this issue in gender analysis at the Bank (World Bank 2001b: 212–19). However, despite several promising suggestions for engendering macroeconomics and a call for more research, it seems likely that policymakers will find ample reason to ignore gender in the design and evaluation of adjustment policies in this statement: "While there is evidence to support both sides of the debate about the impact of structural adjustment, on balance the evidence suggests that females' absolute status and gender equality improved, not deteriorated, over the adjustment period" (ibid.: 215).

Further investigation is necessary to understand how the authors of the report come to a conclusion so contrary to the negative effects "exhaustively documented" in the existing gender and adjustment literature (World Bank 1998). It seems to be based primarily on the Bank's own research conducted for purposes of the report.[10] Despite acknowledging the existence of a debate and the legitimacy of many of its arguments, the report does not actually respond to specific gender critiques of adjustment. This is certainly due in part to the Bank's consistent dismissal of qualitative research as legitimate evidence (see World Bank

2001b: xiv). The conclusion bears scrutiny, in any case. For example, while the report finds that changes in women's life expectancy and girls' school enrollments over the adjustment period were more positive for adjusting than for non-adjusting countries, it assumes that these positive outcomes resulted from adjustment policy. Other potential explanations would suggest that these outcomes occurred despite rather than because of adjustment.[11]

Explaining the absence of gender in the Bank's analysis of structural adjustment

Why does the Bank fail to consider gender or the gender critique in its analysis of structural adjustment and social costs? My answer to this question is based on an analysis of the economic paradigm dominating macroeconomic policy-making. Neoclassical theory excludes or marginalizes issues central to a complete understanding of the effects of adjustment on women. As a result, even Bank economists committed to the elimination of gender inequality will produce gender-biased macroeconomic policies. Further, they will be unable to recognize that their policies are gender-biased. This not only explains the absence of gender in the Bank's discussions of structural adjustment throughout the 1990s, but also predicts the outlines of gender bias in future macroeconomic policies which recognize gender as a topic relevant to discussions of adjustment.

According to the World Bank charter, "it must lend only for productive purposes and must stimulate economic growth in the developing countries where it lends" (World Bank 1985: 3). The apparent neutrality of this goal obscures the implicit assumption of market criteria for defining legitimate boundaries for economic analysis and policy evaluation. In practice, for policymaking and lending at the Bank, "economic growth" refers to growth in the market sector, and market indicators are the only evidence necessary for measuring economic advance or decline. Neoclassical approaches to macroeconomics assert that free prices are the most efficient and desirable means to policy goals (World Bank 1991: 1). This approach has not been altered by the Bank's recent attention to poverty reduction and sustainable development, both of which it sees as defined by and best achieved through the market.

In light of gender critiques of the neoclassical paradigm, an evident problem with this focus on the market is that it ignores or marginalizes nonmarket economic activity such as unpaid domestic labor in the creation and evaluation of policy. Since the Bank defines productivity and economic growth in market terms, attention to unpaid labor in Bank policy would be incompatible with its goals. The emphasis on "getting prices right" also ensures that such labor remains invisible to policymakers. Macroeconomists do not look at unpaid domestic labor in their analyses of economic policy except in a few cases as a noneconomic factor explaining market behavior, because the paradigm does not allow them to do so.

Institutionalized attention to women in the analysis of development and policy does not prevent this exclusion. According to Nüket Kardam, policymakers within the Bank who wish to promote policy benefiting women have "taken care to make WID issues acceptable by framing them within economic rather than social welfare and equity arguments" (Kardam 1991: 79; see also Razavi and Miller 1995: iv–v, 40; Murphy 1995: 44; Buvinic *et al.* 1996: 73; Women's Eyes 1997; O'Brien *et al.* 2000: 48).

Gender research at the Bank is thus devoted to proving economic (market) benefits of projects targeting women or taking gender into account. For example, in 1992, Chief Economist Summers spoke at the Bank's annual meeting on the importance of girls' education in the process of development (1994). Summers suggests that "investment in girls' education may well be the highest return investment available in the developing world" (Summers 1994: 1).[12] However, the focus of this analysis is still the market, since "education is positively correlated with overall economic growth, with one year of schooling . . . leading to as much as 9 percent increase in GDP for the first three years of schooling" (ibid.: v). A primary argument in *Engendering Development* is that "[g]ender inequalities undermine the effectiveness of development policies" (World Bank 2001b: xiii) and that gender inequality "diminishes an economy's capacity to grow" (ibid.: p. 11).

If gender achieves legitimacy at the World Bank by being made acceptable to neoclassical economists, it follows that gender analysis which is not framed in neoclassical terms will be excluded. The theoretical framing of much of the gender and adjustment literature requires analysis of unpaid domestic labor as an economic activity. Since the neoclassical paradigm assumes a market definition of economic activity, discussions that analyze unpaid domestic labor in economic terms (i.e. as itself an economic activity rather than subsidiary to economic activity) will be marginalized.[13] Both because it is critical of the neoclassical paradigm and because it focuses on nonmarket issues, the gender critique is necessarily excluded from the Bank's analysis of structural adjustment.

More telling, perhaps, is the absence of gender itself. This absence cannot be completely explained by hostility to the gender and adjustment literature, because the topic could be discussed without reference to the literature. But if, as many gender critiques suggest, understanding the effects of structural adjustment on women requires a look at unpaid domestic labor, economic analyses of adjustment based on the neoclassical paradigm are hard-pressed to address the topic at all.

The few Bank documents which look at gender in the context of adjustment do not refer to unpaid domestic labor. In keeping with neoclassical economic analysis, these documents focus almost exclusively on the market repercussions of adjustment, differentiated by gender. According to *Enhancing Women's Participation in Economic Development*, for example, "[a]djustment policies typically remove price distortions and restore profitability of certain crops and activities, but women may not be able to take advantage of such beneficial changes unless their particular constraints are removed" (World Bank 1994b: 68). Similarly, most of Paul Collier's work analyzes the impact of adjustment on women in terms of the market (Collier 1983: 185–93). He looks at unpaid domestic labor only as it affects the allocation of women's time to market work, and gives no indication that structural adjustment has any effect on unpaid domestic labor itself (ibid.: 193–6). In its discussion of structural adjustment, *Engendering Development* refers to domestic labor only in terms of the impediments such labor imposes on women's ability to "participate fully in longer term economic opportunities associated with adjustment" (World Bank 2001b: 214).

While it is important to look at the market effects of structural adjustment policies on women, gender critiques highlight the centrality of unpaid domestic labor to understanding gender bias in adjustment. In this context, the absence of any reference to such labor in the Bank's few analyses of gender and adjustment is striking. Even if Bank policymakers believe these critiques to be flawed, their analyses should at least address the effects of adjustment on unpaid domestic labor, if only to give solid reasons for dismissing the importance of these effects.

Paradigm Postponed suggests that for the Bank, "[t]he critical question is whether the distribution of costs (and benefits) of adjustment between men and women . . . is sufficiently important to make a difference to economic outcomes and prospects" (Blackden and Morris-Hughes 1993: 16). In other words, the Bank will show serious concern for gender inequality in the effects of adjustment only if an economic justification for such concern is provided. Since "economic" in a neoclassical context refers to the market, Bank statements to the effect that "the effective integration of gender concerns into the design and implementation of reform measures can lead to improved performance outcomes" do not imply that the Bank will consider the effects of adjustment on unpaid labor, except perhaps as instrumental to improving market indicators (World Bank 1996). To the degree that the gender bias of structural adjustment policies derives from their effects on unpaid domestic labor or some other topic excluded from neoclassical economics, future policy will thus remain gender-biased.

Adjustment with a human face

The World Bank addressed the poverty critique of structural adjustment policies almost immediately, and in most ways the social cost literature can still be seen as defined by that critique. How can this difference in reception be explained? According to Joan Nelson, *Adjustment with a Human Face* "focused and legitimized concerns that had been mounting in many quarters" (Nelson 1989: 95). For the Bank's macroeconomic policymakers, legitimization entailed making concerns over the effects of adjustment policy on the poor consistent with neoclassical economic theory.

Adjustment with a Human Face was intentionally framed to appeal to a neo-classical perspective: "From the start, it was clear that practical advance toward adjustment with a human face would only be possible if it attracted the under-standing and support of those in the mainstream of economic policy-making" (Cornia *et al.* 1987b: 3). The authors did not question the need for structural adjustment, and they highlighted the "economic" reason for their concern – the long-term and irreversible damage to "human resources" which occurs with increasing poverty (ibid.: 5–6). Concern over the social costs of adjustment from this perspective is legitimized by the potential for falling rates of growth resulting from lost (human) resources.

However, criticisms of structural adjustment policy which were not translated into the neoclassical economic paradigm were not addressed. The Bank never took seriously, for example, the argument that "the appropriate adjustment may not be . . . in the national economies where the major and unsustainable imbalances emerge, but in the international conditions which give rise to them" (Cornia *et al.* 1987c: 133). From the Bank's perspective, *Adjustment with a Human Face* was a warning about the dangers of disinvestment in human capital which demanded no more than minor changes in the design of adjustment policy. This is the only aspect of its analysis that had "economic" significance within the neoclassical paradigm.

Many policymakers see no problem with discussing the social costs of adjustment exclusively in terms of poverty, since policies which benefit the poor necessarily benefit women (e.g. World Bank 1996). This argument ignores issues crucial to understanding gender inequality in the effects of structural adjustment. An analysis of gender bias in compensatory programs will illustrate this point further.

Compensatory programs

Because the World Bank's analysis of social costs does not currently incorporate gender, compensatory programs are designed without attention to gender inequality and are themselves gender-biased.[14] The neoclassical paradigm establishes theoretical constraints on the evaluation of policy which make it likely that gender bias in structural adjustment will persist despite greater emphasis at the Bank on addressing social costs, even as this comes to include attention to gender (e.g. see World Bank 2001b: 227).

Safety net and social emergency programs have reduced the negative effects of adjustment on vulnerable groups, but while women tend to benefit from income and employment programs designed for the poor, they do not necessarily benefit equally. Lourdes Benería and Breny Mendoza argue that gender inequality in Emergency Social Investment Funds (ESIFs) in Honduras and Nicaragua can be explained in part by (neoclassical) conceptual biases which ignore gender issues in income distribution (1995: 65; see also Buvinic *et al.* 1996: 64).[15]

The exclusion of unpaid domestic labor from economic analysis is a less obvious source of gender inequality in compensatory programs. In accordance with the neoclassical paradigm, the Bank's analysis of social costs is limited to market effects. *Protecting the Poor During Periods of Adjustment* asserts that "[a]nalyzing the effects of a policy change on the poor involves assessing the effect of that change on real purchasing power by determining the impact on the disposable income of the group and the prices and quantities of the goods and services the group consumes" (World Bank 1987: 36). From this perspective, decreases in market consumption define the possible negative effects of adjustment, and directing monetary income to households is the best compensation. Again, changes in unpaid domestic labor (or in nonmarket consumption derived from such labor) resulting from structural adjustment policies or compensatory programs will not be visible to policymakers in this context. Nor will they be compensated for in future policy.

In one World Bank Living Standards Measurement Study (LSMS) study, Paul Glewwe and Gillette Hall report that during the late 1980s, female-headed households in Peru were no more vulnerable to macroeconomic shocks produced by structural adjustment than male-headed households (Glewwe and Hall 1995). These results are "contrary to the common assertion that female-headed households, and women *per se*, are one 'vulnerable group' in periods of . . . structural adjustment" (ibid.: 31). It follows that attention to gender in adjustment policy is not justified even on the basis of equity.

But this report, like most LSMS studies, measures household welfare strictly in terms of market consumption (ibid.: 5). Female-headed households in Peru may have maintained their market consumption by increasing paid labor time but also increasing the intensity of time spent on unpaid domestic labor. Or time spent on food preparation, repair of clothes, and childcare at home may have increased in intensity or been shifted on to young daughters. Other than the increase in paid labor time, none of this would be captured by an LSMS survey. How valid, then, is Glewwe and Hall's conclusion? Evidence of structural adjustment's effects on unpaid domestic labor suggests that it is at least problematic. Policy will nevertheless be based on this conclusion, which ignores a persistent source of gender inequality. Glewwe and Hall argue that while "similarity in structural adjustment policies across many countries may produce the same 'vulnerable' groups in those countries, . . . in principle, these groups can be made 'invulnerable' by corresponding policy changes" (ibid.: 3). This is true only if neoclassical policymakers recognize and measure all aspects of vulnerability. Since they do not, it is unlikely that women will be made "invulnerable" to the negative effects of structural adjustment by future policy changes.

The relationship between unpaid domestic labor and social services is another potential source of gender bias in Bank policies unlikely to be addressed in compensatory programs, again because issues outside the neoclassical paradigm are not considered. For example, a cut in subsidies decreases the number of days spent at the hospital by increasing costs to the consumer. According to the neoclassical paradigm, fewer scarce resources are used as a result of the increased price. However, Diane Elson points out that "in reality there has been a transfer of the costs of care for the sick from the paid economy to the unpaid economy of the household. The financial costs fall but the unpaid work of women in the household rises. This is not a genuine increase in efficiency . . . " (Elson 1991: 178).

Due to the effects of policy on unpaid domestic labor, compensatory programs which increase household income will not necessarily compensate women for cuts in social programs that do not have an affordable and readily available market substitutes. Cutting clinic hours in rural areas is likely to increase women's unpaid domestic labor (by increasing waiting at the clinic, travel time to another clinic, or time spent caring for the sick), whether or not her household has been compensated with increased income to cover the higher cost of health care elsewhere. Supplementary feeding programs, a common component of compensatory programs, may also increase unpaid domestic labor by requiring women's direct involvement in providing food (see Vilas 1996: 24).

Structural adjustment policies shaped by neoclassical economics produce gender inequalities likely to be invisible to policymakers. Compensatory measures, which also derive from neoclassical theory, fail to address these gender inequalities and may actually compound them whether or not gender is accounted for in implementation. Conformance with the neoclassical paradigm limits the potential both for adjustment policies to be gender neutral and for compensatory programs to correct the policies' gender biases.

Conclusion

There is no doubt that over the past ten years the World Bank has increased its commitment to gender issues in development. That its attention to the social costs of adjustment increased simultaneously only highlights the lack of intersection between these two areas of policymaking. Macroeconomics at the Bank remains devoid of gender analysis, despite gender critiques of adjustment. Because Bank lending continues to focus on policies for structural adjustment, the failure to incorporate gender in its analysis of adjustment and social costs is likely to affect women in economies in the process of being "reformed" for years to come.

The Bank is likely to include gender as a component of macroeconomic evaluations of "reform" relatively soon.[16] However, my analysis of the reasons for the absence of gender in the design and evaluation of policies for structural adjustment suggests that the terms of this incorporation are predictable and will be limited by the neoclassical paradigm. The Bank will continue to consider only market aspects of gender differences in the effects of structural adjustment and ignore or marginalize nonmarket effects, especially those on unpaid domestic labor. Other issues incompatible with neoclassical economics but vital to gender analysis of macroeconomics will also be excluded, and any conflict between market growth and women's welfare will be decided in favor of the market. Under these conditions, it is doubtful that "engendering" macroeconomics on the Bank's terms will eliminate gender bias in adjustment policies.

The implications of this analysis go beyond the Bank. The shared approach to policy defined by the "Washington consensus" of mainstream economists in the US government and international financial institutions suggests that gender is similarly absent in macroeconomic policies promoted by the IMF, the US Agency for International Development (USAID), the Inter-American Development Bank (IDB) and other agencies affiliated with, influenced by, or dependent on these institutions (see Williamson 1996). It follows that economic policies prescribed by these agencies are no less gender-biased than the Bank's, and for similar reasons.[17]

If the neoclassical paradigm is a primary source of gender bias in policies for structural adjustment, then improved training for policymakers and increased accountability on gender issues will not be enough to eliminate gender inequality from macroeconomics at the Bank and elsewhere. The economic theory on which policy is based must be transformed. Feminist economists underscore the sweeping changes necessary for new economic paradigms to include gender as a fundamental category of analysis. Women's nonmarket activities must be recognized as economic and valued equally with market aspects of the economy. Differences in household organizations of production and conflicts over distribution not governed by the market must be built into the theory as well. Method can challenge or reinforce fundamental concepts, so traditional approaches to how economics is done must also be interrogated. These ideas are difficult to grapple with, but essential to explore if gender equity in economic policy is to be achieved.

Notes

1 UNICEF published the first edition of *The Invisible Adjustment* in both English and Spanish in 1987, the same year as the first volume of *Adjustment with A Human Face*. Note that while this chapter emphasizes academic and development practitioner critiques of Bank policies, grassroots opposition stimulated these critiques and has been vital in bringing pressure to bear on the Bank to reevaluate structural adjustment.

2 See Kapur *et al.* (1997) and Mosley *et al.* (1991) for histories of the World Bank.

3 I use the term "unpaid domestic labor" to refer to those unremunerated activities performed in maintenance of households and their residents, such as cooking, cleaning, and childcare. Other activities such as childbirth, emotional caretaking, and sex should possibly be included as well. However defined, unpaid domestic labor is predominantly women's work. See Wood (1997) for an analysis of the importance of definitions and First World bias in how such labor is conceptualized.

4 The World Bank is a large and complex institution, with internal conflicts which are not necessarily reflected in public documents. There are Bank professionals currently working to promote gender analysis in macroeconomic policy. There is also external political pressure to do the same. While these are very important, I believe that the Bank's public documents reflect who is "winning" struggles over the direction of its policies for structural adjustment.

5 In addition to UNICEF (1989) and Commonwealth Secretariat (1989), see Afshar and Dennis (eds) (1992), Palmer (1991),Vickers (1991), Benería and Feldman (eds) (1992), Sparr (ed.) (1994), Bakker (1994), Elson (1989, 1991, 1998), and Çagatay *et al.* (eds) (1995). There are differing approaches among these authors, which should not be overshadowed by my brief literature review.

6 Feminist activists and development practitioners working on gender have sought the inclusion of unpaid domestic labor in official data for well over two decades, with little success (see Benería 1992).

7 Women's paid labor force participation also increased more than men's (Cornia 1987: 22; Stewart 1991: 1853; Moser 1989: 144–7, 153; Benería 1991: 172–3).

8 See Murphy (1995), Women's Eyes (1997) and O'Brien *et al.* (2000) for accounts of the evolution of Bank approaches to gender.

9   This is especially significant because before her tenure at the Bank, Moser was a prominent critic of Bank policies. Attributing many of the negative economic changes in a *barrio* of Guayaquil, Ecuador directly to structural adjustment, her work focused on the effects of these policies on women (1989). In another study done for the Bank, Moser discusses the economic changes in Guayaquil only in terms of "external shocks" and "economic crisis," with no comment on the relationship between structural adjustment policies and the worsening economic environment (Moser 1996).

10 The Bank often uses its own data to support arguments, and ignores critical external research. For example, the Structural Adjustment Participatory Review Initiative (SAPRI) was a joint World Bank/civil society project. A Bank SAPRI report was positive in its evaluation of adjustment policies (World Bank 2001a). The final SAPRI summary by the NGO SAPRIN, in contrast, "present[s] evidence from studies in which the Bank was involved of the negative impacts of its policies" and suggests that systematic Bank resistance to the SAPRI process demonstrates "the disingenuousness of . . . claims that they are interested in engaging civil-society groups in meaningful endeavours to attend to the issues that have driven so many to the streets" (SAPRIN 2001: 7).

11 Less positive results for life expectancy in non-adjusting South Africa, for example, might result from civil war, transitional governance, or the escalating AIDS epidemic among women during the "adjusting period."

12 Summers' speech on girls' education was given the year before his talk on structural adjustment, which omitted discussion of gender. This reinforces my argument that the Bank's failure to analyze gender in the context of adjustment cannot simply be explained as a lack of knowledge or commitment to gender issues generally.

13 Economists do discuss some forms of unpaid labor such as subsistence agriculture. However, the System of National Accounts, which ostensibly measures all forms of economic activity, explicitly excludes unpaid domestic labor. See Wood (1997) for an analysis of causes and implications of this.

14 Issues of implementation are also important to understanding gender bias in compensatory programs. See Benería and Mendoza (1995). Note that a rising commitment to social protection has not altered structural adjustment policies substantively. Compensatory programs are meant to counter policies which are otherwise unproblematic (World Bank 1987; 1994b: 68; Razavi and Miller 1995).

15 For example, 75 percent of jobs created through the ESIF funded by the World Bank in Honduras went to men (Benería and Mendoza 1995: 58). Income directed toward men is unlikely to be distributed equally within households or to compensate fully for an equal amount of income lost to women due to adjustment policies, since men tend to keep a proportion of their income for personal use (see Dwyer and Bruce 1988; Benería 1992).

16 There are many indications of this. In July 1999, for example, Mark Blackden ran a session on "tools for engendering adjustment" for the Bank's Poverty Reduction and Economic Management (PREM) network, which is directly involved in macroeconomic policymaking (personal communication, June 18, 1999). The Bank's recent SAPRI report commented on the negative effects of adjustment cuts in public sector employment on women (World Bank 2001a: 27). In addition, an upcoming *World Development Report* will be devoted to gender, in anticipation of the fifth UN Conference on Women to be held in 2005 (O'Brien *et al.* 2000: 47). Pressure on the Bank to demonstrate some change in response to demands made at Beijing to address the disproportionate effects of structural adjustment on women will be very high.

17 The same argument applies to the rising "post-Washington consensus," which is only a refinement of neoclassical approaches to policy and will not contribute to the incorporation of gender in macroeconomics (see Stiglitz 1998).

Acknowledgment

Thanks to Derek Stanovsky, Kay Smith, Susan Eckstein and Jay Wentworth for comments, and to Daryl Sink for assistance in researching this chapter.

References

Afshar, Haleh and Carolyne Dennis (eds) (1992) *Women and Adjustment Policies in the Third World*, London: Macmillan.

Bakker, Isabella (ed.) (1994) *The Strategic Silence: Gender and Economic Policy*, London: Zed Press.

Benería, Lourdes (1991) "Structural Adjustment, the Labor Market and the Household: The Case of Mexico," in G. Standing and V. Tokman (eds), *Towards Social Adjustment: Labor Market Concerns in Structural Adjustment*, Geneva: International Labour Office: 161–83.

—— (1992) "Accounting for Women's Work: The Progress of Two Decades," *World Development*, 20(11): 1547–60.

Benería, Lourdes and Shelley Feldman (eds) (1992) *Unequal Burden: Economic Crises, Persistent Poverty, and Women's Work*, Boulder, CO: Westview Press.

Benería, Lourdes and Breny Mendoza (1995) "Structural Adjustment and Social Emergency Funds: The Cases of Honduras, Mexico and Nicaragua," *European Journal of Development Research*, Spring: 53–76.

Blackden, C. Mark (1998) "Integrating Gender Into Economic Reform Through the Special Program of Assistance for Africa (SPA)," presented at the Symposium on Economie et Rapports Sociaux entre Hommes et Femmes, January 28–29, Geneva, Switzerland. Retrieved January 11, 2002. (http://www.unige.ch/iued/new/information/publications/pdf/yp_silcence_pudique/8-Eco-Blackden.pdf).

Blackden, C. Mark and Elizabeth Morris-Hughes (1993) *Paradigm Postponed: Gender and Economic Adjustment in Sub-Saharan Africa*, Africa Technical and Human Division (AFTHR), Technical Note No. 13, Washington, DC: World Bank.

Buvinic, Mayra, Catherine Gwin and Lisa M. Bates (1996) *Investing in Women: Progress and Prospects for the World Bank*, Policy Essay No. 19, Washington, DC: Overseas Development Council.

Çagatay, Nilüfer, Diane Elson and Caren Grown (eds) (1995) "Gender, Adjustment and Macroeconomics," Special Issue, *World Development*, 23(11).

Collier, Paul (1993) "The Impact of Adjustment on Women," in L. Demery *et al.* (eds), *Understanding the Social Effects of Policy Reform*, Washington, DC: World Bank: 183–97.

Commonwealth Secretariat (1989) *Engendering Adjustment for the 1990s*, Report of a Commonwealth Expert Group on Women and Structural Adjustment, London: Commonwealth Secretariat.

Cornia, Giovanni A. (1987) "Economic Decline and Human Welfare in the First Half of the 1980s," in Cornia *et al.* (eds), *Adjustment with a Human Face, Vol. I, Protecting the Vulnerable and Promoting Growth*, Oxford: Clarendon Press: 11–47.

Cornia, Giovanni A., Richard Jolly and Frances Stewart (eds) (1987a) *Adjustment with a Human Face, Vol. I, Protecting the Vulnerable and Promoting Growth*, Oxford: Clarendon Press.

—— (1987b) "Introduction," in Cornia *et al.* (eds), *Adjustment with a Human Face, Vol. I, Protecting the Vulnerable and Promoting Growth*, Oxford: Clarendon Press: 1–8.

—— (1987c) "An Overview of the Alternative Approach," in Cornia *et al.* (eds), *Adjustment with a Human Face, Vol. I, Protecting the Vulnerable and Promoting Growth*, Oxford: Clarendon Press: 131–46.

—— (eds) (1988) *Adjustment with a Human Face, Vol. II, Country Case Studies*, Oxford: Clarendon Press.

Dwyer, Daisy and Judith Bruce (eds) (1988) *A Home Divided: Women and Income in the Third World*, Stanford, CA: Stanford University Press.

Elson, Diane (1989) "The Impact of Structural Adjustment on Women: Concepts and Issues," in B. Onimode (ed.), *The IMF, The World Bank and African Debt*, Vol. 2, Atlantic Highlands, NJ: Zed Books Ltd: 56–74.

—— (1991) "Male Bias in Macro-economics: The Case of Structural Adjustment," in D. Elson (ed.), *Male Bias in the Development Process*, New York: Manchester University Press: 164–90.

—— (1998) "The Economic, the Political and the Domestic: Businesses, State and Households in the Organisation of Production," *New Political Economy*, 3(2): 189–208.

Feijóo, María del Carmen and Elizabeth Jelin (1989) "Women from Low Income Sectors: Economic Recession and Democratization of Politics in Argentina," in UNICEF, *The Invisible Adjustment: Poor Women and the Economic Crisis*, Santiago: UNICEF, The Americas and the Caribbean Regional Office: 29–58.

Glewwe, Paul and Gillette Hall (1995) "Who Is Most Vulnerable to Macroeconomic Shocks? Hypotheses Tests Using Panel Data from Peru," World Bank Living Standards Measurement Study No. 117, Washington, DC: World Bank.

Jacobs, Beryl K. (1991) "Lima's Communal Kitchens," *Women in Action*, 2: 16–17.

Jayarajah, Carl and William Branson (1995) *Structural and Sectoral Adjustment: World Bank Experience, 1980–92*, Washington, DC: World Bank.

Jayarajah, Carl, William Branson and Binayak Sen (1996) *Social Dimensions of Adjustment: World Bank Experience, 1980–93*, Washington, DC: World Bank.

Kapur, Devish, John P. Lewis and Richard Webb (eds) (1997) *The World Bank: Its First Half Century, Vols 1 and 2*, Washington, DC: Brookings Institution Press.

Kardam, Nüket (1991) *Bringing Women In: Women's Issues in International Development Programs*, Boulder, CO: Lynne Rienner Publishers.

Moser, Caroline O.N. (1989) "The Impact of Recession and Adjustment Policies at the Micro-Level: Low Income Women and Their Households in Guayaquil, Ecuador," in UNICEF, *The Invisible Adjustment: Poor Women and the Economic Crisis*, Santiago: UNICEF, The Americas and the Caribbean Regional Office: 137–66..

—— (1996) *Confronting Crisis: A Comparative Study of Household Responses to Poverty and Vulnerability in Four Poor Urban Communities*, Washington, DC: World Bank.

Moser, Caroline O.N., Annika Tornqvist and Bernice van Bronkhorst (1999) *Mainstreaming Gender and Development in the World Bank: Progress and Recommendations*, Washington, DC: World Bank.

Mosley, Paul, Jane Harrigan and John Toye (1991) *Aid and Power: The World Bank and Policy-based Lending, Vol. 1, Analysis and Policy Proposals*, New York: Routledge.

Murphy, Josette L. (1995) *Gender Issues in World Bank Lending*, Washington, DC: World Bank.

—— (1997) *Mainstreaming Gender in World Bank Lending: An Update*, Washington, DC: World Bank.

Nelson, Joan (1989) "The Politics of Pro-poor Adjustment," in J. Nelson (ed.), *Fragile Coalitions: The Politics of Economic Adjustment*, Washington, DC: Overseas Development Council: 95–113.

O'Brien, Robert, Anne Marie Goetz, Jan Aart Scholte and Marc Williams (2000) *Contesting Global Governance: Multilateral Economic Institutions and Global Social Movements*, Cambridge: Cambridge University Press.

Oxfam Policy Department (1995) *A Case for Reform: Fifty Years of the IMF and the World Bank*, Oxford: Oxfam Publications.

Palmer, Ingrid (1991) *Gender and Population in the Adjustment of African Economies: Planning for Change*, Geneva: International Labour Office.

Razavi, Shahra and Carol Miller (1995) *Gender Mainstreaming: A Study of Efforts by the UNDP, the World Bank and the ILO to Institutionalize Gender Issues*, Geneva: United Nations Research Institute for Social Development.

Rocha, Lola, Eduardo Bustelo, Ernesto López and Luis Zuñiga (1989) "Women, Economic Crisis and Adjustment Policies: An Interpretation and Initial Assessment," in UNICEF, *The Invisible Adjustment: Poor Women and the Economic Crisis*, Santiago: UNICEF, The Americas and the Caribbean Regional Office: 9–27.

SAPRIN (Structural Adjustment Participatory Review International Network) (2001) "The Policy Roots of Economic Crisis and Poverty: A Multi-Country Participatory Assessment of Structural Adjustment," Washington, DC: SAPRIN, retrieved January 11, 2002 (http://www.saprin.org/SAPRIN_Synthesis_11-16-01.pdf).

Sparr, Pamela (ed.) (1994) *Mortgaging Women's Lives: Feminist Critiques of Structural Adjustment*, London: Zed Press for the United Nations.

Stewart, Frances (1991) "The Many Faces of Adjustment," *World Development*, 19(12): 1847–64.

Stiglitz, Joseph (1998) "More Instruments and Broader Goals: Moving Toward the Post-Washington Consensus," retrieved August 13, 1999 (http://www.wider.unu.edu/stiglitx.htm).

Summers, Lawrence H. (1994) *Investing in All the People: Educating Women in Developing Countries*, EDI Seminar Paper No. 45, Washington, DC: World Bank.

Summers, Lawrence H. and Lant H. Pritchett (1993) "The Structural-Adjustment Debate," *The American Economic Review*, 83(2): 383–9.

UNICEF (1989) *The Invisible Adjustment: Poor Women and the Economic Crisis*, Santiago: UNICEF, The Americas and the Caribbean Regional Office.

Vickers, Jeanne (1991) *Women and the World Economic Crisis*, London: Zed Books.

Vilas, Carlos M. (1996) "Neoliberal Social Policy: Managing Poverty (Somehow)," *NACLA Report on the Americas*, 29(6), May/June: 16–25.

Waylen, Georgina (1992) "Women, Authoritarianism and Market Liberalisation in Chile, 1973–1989," in H. Afshar and C. Dennis (eds), *Women and Adjustment Policies in the Third World*, London: Macmillan: 150–78.

Williamson, John (1996) "Lowest Common Denominator or Neoliberal Manifesto? The Polemics of the Washington Consensus," in R. M. Auty and J. Toye (eds), *Challenging the Orthodoxies*, New York: St. Martin's Press: 13–22.

Wolfensohn, James D. (1995) "Women and the Transformation of the 21st Century," Address to the Fourth UN Conference on Women, retrieved July 8, 1999 (http://www.worldbank.org/gender/how/womenand.htm).

Women's Eyes on the World Bank – US (1997) "Gender Equity and the World Bank Group: A Post-Beijing Assessment," Washington, DC: Oxfam America.

Wood, Cynthia A. (1997) "The First World/Third Party Criterion: A Feminist Critique of the Production Boundary in Economics," *Feminist Economics*, 3(3): 47–68.

World Bank (1985) *The World Bank Annual Report*, Washington, DC: World Bank.

—— (1987) *Protecting the Poor During Periods of Adjustment*, Washington, DC: World Bank.

—— (1990) *World Development Report 1990*, Washington, DC: World Bank.

—— (1991) *World Development Report 1991*, Washington, DC: World Bank.

—— (1994a) *Adjustment in Africa: Reforms, Results, and the Road Ahead*, Washington, DC: World Bank.

—— (1994b) *Enhancing Women's Participation in Economic Development: A World Bank Policy Paper*, New York: Oxford University Press.

—— (1994c) "The Gender Dimension of Development," World Bank Operational Policy 4.20, retrieved July 8, 1999 (http://www.worldbank.org/gender/how/termr2.htm).

—— (1995a) *Advancing Gender Equality: From Concept to Action*, Washington, DC: World Bank.

—— (1995b) *Toward Gender Equality: The Role of Public Policy*, Washington, DC: World Bank.

—— (1996) "Implementing the World Bank's Gender Policies," retrieved July 1, 1999 (http://www.worldbank.org/gender/how/report.htm).

—— (1998) "Selected Comments on the Concept Note from External Readers," retrieved July 8, 1999 (http://www.worldbank.org/gender/know/comment.htm).

—— (2001a) "Adjustment from Within: Lessons from the Structural Adjustment Participatory Review Initiative," retrieved January 7, 2002 (http://www.worldbank.org/research/sapri/).

—— (2001b) *Engendering Development*, Washington, DC: World Bank.

11 Gender and intrahousehold decision-making

International migration and other frontiers for development policy

Aida Orgocka and Gale Summerfield

For more than two decades feminist economists have criticized neoclassical concepts of the household and recognized the unequal gender relations in intrahousehold decision-making and allocation of resources (see Woolley 1999; Summerfield 1998; Benería 1995). Negotiation within the household affects the well-being of all its members and influences the effectiveness of development policies. *Engendering Development: Through Gender Equality in Rights, Resources, and Voice*, a Policy Research Report (PRR) of the World Bank, includes an entire chapter on these dynamics (2001: 147–80).[1]

Our chapter addresses whether the PRR presents sufficient material on gender and intrahousehold decision-making for policy-makers to consider in making, implementing, and revising development policies. Our main critique of the PRR is that it does not push ahead to reflect cutting-edge approaches to work being done now or look toward the future. It also is rather selective in what it considers even of work from the recent past; it stresses econometric studies rather than including other approaches or the theoretical literature. Our critique is organized into two main sections. The first section examines key factors for the analysis of intrahousehold decision-making including functions and structure of households, policy areas that could contribute to a more equitable alloca-tion of resources within the household, the need to include theoretical and conceptual contributions to the study of intrahousehold dynamics, and use of qualitative methods as part of an interdisciplinary analysis of these dynamics. The second section utilizes an example from our research on international migration to illustrate how factors overlooked in the discussion in the PRR are needed to understand some frontier issues in intrahousehold aspects of develop-ment policy. In particular, the section examines the context of cross-border development issues that exist in the North (in this case, through immigrants from Muslim countries to the USA) and intergenerational interactions within the household regarding young women's sexuality education, a part of health policy.

Key factors for analysis of intrahousehold decision-making

A summary of gender aspects of intrahousehold decision-making needs to include relevant theoretical material as well as empirical studies. It should provide an understanding of the dynamics of households and families and the importance of embedding the studies in particular contexts. Understanding gender aspects of power in the household requires studying not only spouses or adult partners but also relationships between generations, between siblings, and within the same sex (since those also reflect and reproduce the biases of society). Taking some material from the work on families in fields outside economics can build an interdisciplinary analysis that is useful in understanding how development policies affect individuals within families.

Functions and structures of households

PRR

The PRR chapter on intrahousehold power, incentives, and allocation of resources begins with a description of the functions and structures of households around the world. It notes that households are context-specific and dynamic and that members do not necessarily share responsibilities and resources equitably. Households reproduce gendered relations and outcomes by socializing children into gender-specific roles, including making gender-specific investments in human capital and perpetuating a gendered division of time and tasks. The PRR authors then discuss resource control, bargaining power, and household allocations in detail. They criticize the conceptualization of the household as a unitary model and pinpoint the pitfalls of (1) looking at a household as one in which common preferences are the basic characteristic of household decision-making, and (2) concentrating only on the total level of household resource allocations and investments instead of including the distribution of resources within households as well. The lengthy discussion of intrahousehold issues in the chapter is a refreshing change from the traditional, economic/survey definition of a household as a stable unit over time and space with a cooperative, unitary approach to decision-making.

While the PRR devotes some attention to bargaining power and the divergent interests within households, its main theoretical/conceptual discussion is a brief presentation of the inadequacy of the unitary model of the household and some empirical tests of the model's implications (starting on p. 154). A wealth of material exists that elaborates on alternatives to the unitary model and would add to understanding the gendered distribution of resources within the household. Familiarity with these ideas is especially important for formation and implementation of development policy.

Especially notable is the absence of any reference to capability approach concepts, especially Sen's discussion of the family as a site of cooperation and conflict (Sen 1990, 1999; Nussbaum 2000). These concepts have informed numerous studies dealing with intrahousehold bargaining power in recent years

Capabilities + Sen

(and they implicitly seem to inform the PRR also because of the stress on going beyond the unitary model). The conceptual framework of the family as a unit that embodies both cooperation and conflict (as opposed to a completely co-operative family of the unitary model) assumes that the relationships between individuals in a household are based both on common interests and areas of conflicting goals (Sen 1990). Agency, status, and bargaining power at home are influenced by opportunities outside the family and a complex of other factors including the different perceptions of individuals regarding their position in and contribution to the family. In making decisions about resource allocation, individuals have to factor in what the outcomes will do to their relative positions in the household. Bargaining is partly shaped by how much risk individuals are willing and able to undertake in the process.

Relationships within the household in addition to the ones between wives and husbands are important in determining household resource allocation. The PRR discusses the relationships between parents and children briefly, but the discussion is incomplete and raises some questions about the implications of other sections (see PRR: 164). Allocation of children's work is determined not only by traditional gender roles but also by age, birth-order, and sibling composition (Punch 2001; Blanchet 1996; Adagala 1991). Moreover, generational and gender relationships are constantly changing and negotiated against a backdrop of children's acquiring skills and shaping a sense of autonomy from their family as well as other socioeconomic conditions (Finch and Mason 1993). The PRR misses a discussion on children's agency in shaping the allocation of resources. They are seen mainly as recipients of benefits coming from the parents (and investments for future support of the parents). Examination of these dynamics would contribute to a deeper understanding of household power distribution and use of resources.

The relationships between mothers and daughters provide a good illustration of these dynamics. Studies have shown complex and diverse relations among female family members, from mothers or grandmothers passing down hurtful traditions such as foot-binding in China before it was banned in the 1950s (Papanek 1990) to mothers being more likely to spend their income on assuring the education of daughters as well as sons (as the PRR discusses). In conveying gender roles to their daughters, mothers are usually caught in the double bind of assuring daughters' economic and social well-being while adhering to patriarchal gender norms. Such contradictions appear in both developing and more industrialized countries. A close relationship with their mothers, for example, influences the development of Korean daughters' career orientation outweighing other factors such as gender inequality in formal education (Song 2001). Researchers also show, however, that South African mothers' commitments related to fertility, child-rearing and schooling are at times more influential in explaining daughters' propensity to leave school than the family economy (Fuller *et al.* 1995). Although men frequently have a strong influence on major decisions, women are responsible for a steady flow of smaller decisions that may generate major societal impacts (Cloud 2002). Furthermore, as women-headed households are increasing throughout the world, reference to studies that focus on intergenerational dynamics would aid in understanding how policies will play out within families.

Policies and incentives: equitable allocation of resources within the household

The PRR maintains the policy-oriented focus of the Bank and also focuses on policies and incentives that could contribute to a more equitable allocation of resources within the household, with particular attention to how these policies improve women's and girls' lives. Three different types of policy incentives where gender influences women's agency within the household are discussed: appropriate pricing policy, accessibility to services that support girls' health care, nutrition and education, and availability of low-cost childcare.

While the PRR recognizes that policies and programs outside the household affect bargaining power and opportunities within the household, its coverage is very narrow. Although microcredit programs and education are important influences on overall agency and intrahousehold bargaining, they are over-emphasized. Health care, nutrition, farming, and childcare are only briefly addressed. The PRR should expand its coverage of these topics and at least point out the forward-looking work that researchers are doing on how caring labor, housing and property rights, informal sector work, and formal employment opportunities influence intrahousehold decision-making.

The changes associated with the increasingly rapid processes of globalization are straining the traditional system of caring labor. Typically, women have increased their unpaid labor to provide security for the family during crises and adjustment periods, but women are less available for this function. The discussion of childcare is much too brief, and other aspects of caring labor, including care of the elderly and the ill, should be examined. Recent work such as Folbre (2000) that explores these changes and their implications for the family should be discussed.

Researchers have also recognized that housing and other property rights have strong gender equity effects within the household, and policy alters these rights. Property rights influence the ability of poor women to contribute monetarily to the household through home-based businesses and rental of rooms and to support themselves if divorced or widowed. The ability for women as well as men to hold rights to property and the current income generated from property affect the allocation of investment by parents to girls and boys and other intrahousehold decisions (Tinker 1999).

Formal-sector employment is changing, with greater flexibilization of the labor force and risk for workers and growing opportunities for women in foreign-funded export-processing work. The intrahousehold effects of these formal-sector employment changes should be examined more. Kabeer's significant contribution on women's work in Bangladesh and the UK would be a useful example (2000). Equally important are effects of microcredit on intrahousehold bargaining and decision-making. The reason microcredit is so crucial is that millions of women have turned to self-employment – at the microenterprise level because of their meager resources. Efforts of groups such as SEWA and BRAC should be mentioned here, especially their use of a whole-sector approach to development rather than a narrow focus on the microcredit component.[2]

The economic transformation policies promoted by the IMF and the World Bank since the late 1970s and the processes of globalization have had numerous gendered impacts, and researchers have taken up the task of analysis (see, for example, Benería 2003; Aslanbeigui and Summerfield 2000; Benería and Feldman 1992). The pressures of globalization in recent years have led development specialists to focus more on topics that cross borders in terms of (1) examining similar development issues that occur in more developed as well as developing countries, and (2) studying flows of people through international migration as well as flows of physical and financial capital (Pyle 2001; Kaul *et al.* 1999).[3] The influences of the processes of economic restructuring and globalization on family dynamics, however, are not explored.

As the PRR states, changing institutional and policy environments "inevitably alter the constraints, opportunities, and incentives that women and men face and respond to in their households" (p. 147). International migration creates an instant transformation in these areas, but if the migrants live in the West, the explorations into such intrahousehold issues are more likely to be considered part of ethnic studies rather than a gender and development issue. This break is artificial because the ties between the migrants and their home countries often remain strong and they continue to be so for the second generation of migrants (see, for example, Levitt and Waters 2002). Furthermore, household formation and access to and allocation of resources in the host society impact women and men differently (Pessar 1999; Hondagneu-Sotelo 1994).

Migration affects both internal and external resources that define economic power within the domestic group. Changes in gender relations in the new environment are likely to lead to changes in intrahousehold bargaining power. Sometimes women obtain the better-paying, more prestigious jobs while their husbands have to settle for a step down in opportunity (Kibria 1993). Sometimes women are kept from most outside work or other contacts by language and cultural limitations, but other women who do not work outside the home may establish support networks that increase their agency and bargaining power at home. In a globalizing world where international migration is on the rise, these factors need to be addressed. The second part of our chapter uses an international migration setting to explore gendered aspects of intrahousehold dynamics outside the usual spousal bargaining, drawing on our research on Muslim immigrant mothers and daughters in the USA. Some discussion of methodology for intrahousehold analysis is useful before beginning the application.

Δ^s environment $\rightarrow$ Δ^s intrahousehold

Qualitative methods for understanding intrahousehold dynamics

The PRR draws on numerous empirical studies from developing countries to discuss intrahousehold concerns. These studies are carefully constructed using econometric techniques, and provide a growing collection of data broken down by gender. Quantitative data and empirical analyses, however, have their limitations in doing intrahousehold analysis. For example, gathering accurate quantitative data on allocations of labor, leisure, food consumption, and decision-making within the family is difficult if not impossible since people are likely to alter their behavior when observed. Although the PRR discusses this problem to some extent, the chapter relies too heavily on this single approach to gender analysis while overlooking other contributions to the literature.

Women's and men's roles and relations within the household are culturally constructed phenomena, and qualitative methods such as focus groups and small surveys generated through snowball sampling can be useful in getting at the richness and depth of people's experiences. Qualitative methods are commonly used in fields outside of economics and are an important component of creating an interdisciplinary approach to a topic such as intrahousehold decision-making. Cultural convictions, norms, ideas, and values may constrain the activity of all members in the household. Conversely, individuals change culture through means such as language and art. By paying attention to such dynamics, qualitative methods may help draw a fuller picture of intrahousehold behavior.

Critics of single-method research suggest that using both qualitative and quantitative methods of data collection and analysis together yields more than the sum of the two approaches used independently. Studies combining qualitative and quantitative methods are common, such as Madhavan (2001) who uses qualitative and survey data from two ethnic groups in Mali to study the relationship between household discord and child survival. Likewise, Ene-Obong *et al.* (2001) examine the effects of socioeconomic and cultural factors on the health and nutritional status of women of childbearing age in two rural farming communities in Enugu, Nigeria. One of the most important reasons for including some qualitative material is to give voice to those being studied.

International migration and intrahousehold dynamics

This section explores several frontier issues in intrahousehold analysis for development using an interdisciplinary framework that draws on the capability approach (Sen 1999; Nussbaum 2000) and qualitative methods.[4] It illustrates the value of addressing some of the factors identified above as neglected in the PRR, namely, intergenerational negotiation in intrahousehold decision-making in the context of international migration. Specifically, this section examines intrahousehold negotiations between mothers and daughters regarding sexuality education programs for adolescent girls in Muslim immigrant families in the Midwest in the United States.[5] Sexuality education decisions are related to health care and human security, and the negotiations between mothers and daughters reflect gender relations in the family and in both the host community and country of origin. Our goals are to improve the understanding of factors influencing intrahousehold decision-making in order to increase women's and girls' agency and inform policy-makers of ways to be more responsive to intrahousehold dynamics in designing and revising sexuality education programs that bear relevance for immigrant families.

Appropriate sexuality education for adolescents is a significant development policy issue in these days of HIV/AIDS. Education (in general, including sexuality education) increases agency and benefits both women and men (Sen 1995). Education of women tends to lower the fertility rate, which is a social goal in most countries (World Bank 2002). If girls and women are provided with specific sexuality education about their reproductive health, they improve not only their own well-being – for example, through prevention of unintended pregnancy and infectious diseases – but also the health of their children. Better access to this body of knowledge helps women participate in household decision-making about spacing childbearing and influencing childrearing. Learning about reproductive health through formal channels helps women build that knowledge base. Thus, the issue of women's access to and use of educational resources is of paramount importance.

The challenge of providing appropriate sexuality education exists for all countries, but it is complicated by cultural differences such as those associated with international migration. While parents move to the US to better their lives economically, they often try to distance themselves and their children from the moral values that are taught through school-based education programs. The message given in schools may conflict with what children are taught at home (Reese 2001) and thus contribute to a dubious access and use of knowledge. School-based sexuality programs are the case in point. Traditionally these programs aim to provide youth with the knowledge, attitudes, and skills to avoid sexual intercourse or to use contraception properly in case they decide to engage in sexual intercourse. They address antecedents to sexual behavior such as values, beliefs, perceived norms, and intentions regarding sexual behavior related to pregnancy and childbearing. We contend that such programs, by distributing *accurate* information, can assist women and girls in making better decisions about their reproductive health.

However, participation in these programs is influenced by parental concerns on whether girls should learn about sex and through what means.[6] Access to school sexuality education programs is determined partly by what is available and partly by intrahousehold negotiation (since courses are usually optional and require parental permission).

This study highlights intrahousehold negotiations between mothers and daughters to contrast with the usual studies that center on wives and husbands. Among Muslims, maintaining family honor through women's guarded sexual behavior is of primary importance. Mothers are particularly responsible for guarding that honor and any teaching that they impart to their daughters may be in the shape of moral interdictions to safeguard social order. Mothers'

norms + values

relationships with daughters are also regulated by norms and values that condemn premarital sex as sinful. Among Muslims, values associated with modesty imply that one should not learn about one's sexuality until just before entering the marital union. This leaves many girls misinformed. In compliance with these values, mothers have a significant input into decisions about the type of sexuality education girls receive. The girls can negotiate with their mothers, and this interaction is likely to change both mothers and daughters (see discussion of interviews below).

For this study, we used qualitative research methods to interview Muslim immigrant mothers and daughters about their perceptions of the usefulness of sexuality education programs in public high schools and how those perceptions are affecting decision-making about participation in the classes.[7] During the period of May 2001 and March 2002, we conducted separate sessions of group discussions (three to five participants) and individual in-depth interviews with 30 mothers (with a mean age of 43 years) and 38 of their daughters (with a mean age of 16 years).[8]

We asked both mothers and daughters whether they ever talked about sex. Only a few mothers mentioned that they had talked to their daughters about sex. Their communication was limited to technicalities of managing menstruation and the threats that came to social order and family honor from daughters' unguarded sexual behavior. Girls avoided talking to mothers about sexual issues because, in their view, if they brought up the topic, their mothers might think that they wanted to have sex. Furthermore, girls were not very hopeful that their mothers could satisfactorily respond to questions that dealt with reproductive health. Nor did some want the mothers to teach them the technicalities of sex.

We also asked both mothers and daughters whether the daughters should attend sexuality education classes and what they thought about the quality of the classes.[9] Most girls and mothers favored some attendance at sexuality education classes. Somewhat surprisingly, mothers favored their daughters' participation more than the girls did; almost one-third of the mothers wanted their daughters to have sexuality education throughout their high school years, while only 10 percent of the girls favored this possibility. Country of origin, length of stay in the US and/or educational level were not significantly related to these answers.

The main reason some mothers and daughters objected to these classes was that they perceived a conflict between their religious beliefs and the content of the classes. They argued that these classes, by showing videos and promoting condom use even as prevention, promoted a lifestyle of premarital sex that was not acceptable to Muslims. While research shows that attendance in sexuality education classes is not associated with increase in teenage sexual activity and pregnancy (see Kirby and Coyle 1997 for a review), these mothers, like many non-Muslim parents, still worried that the girls would become sexually active after attending the classes. As a preventive measure, six of the mothers interviewed had decided not to allow their daughters to attend the sexuality education classes.[10] Mothers who allowed (or would allow) their daughters to attend the sexuality education classes, carefully reviewed (or planned to review) the class content by reading the course description and sometimes attending one or more classes. They supplemented the information given in the classes by talking with their daughters about the threats that premarital sex brings to social order and told them that most of the information from the classes should be used only after marriage.

Daughters criticized the classes for different reasons from mothers. The girls complained that the classes were oblivious to differences in experiences. A good majority of the girls were of the opinion that these classes were useless because they put too much emphasis on prevention of pregnancy and illness for those who engage in premarital sex. The classes were perceived as insensitive to girls who had had no experiences of sexual encounters and marginalized their decisions to not engage in premarital sex. Moreover, the quality of the information given to the girls in class was questionable because the classes focused mainly on biology and technicalities of a topic. They rarely covered how emerging sexuality impacts an individual's social and emotional development.

The girls had few alternatives to the classes for getting information on sensitive issues. Outside the classes, many girls resorted to books. An 18-year-old girl expressed this succinctly when she commented that "as a Muslim, I should not be ashamed to discuss sex, or marriage, or issues of menstruation or anything, because we have the religious obligation to know this." Others turned to their peers and relatives for information. A 17-year-old said that she "learnt about it on the street, my friends, both female and male. My male friends say 'chicks are so nice' and most of them are carrying condoms in their pockets all the time."

Although mothers and daughters differed in their support of sexuality education in schools, the differences in their views were not extreme and did not lead to negotiation problems at home about attending the classes. However, the concerns of some mothers about the information given in these education classes required their daughters to justify attending the classes. These daughters emphasized that it was very important to them that their mothers were not worried about what they were learning in school. They stressed the value of familial bonds (i.e. keeping their mothers happy). Daughters brought home their books and assured their mothers that there was nothing immoral about these classes. They stated that other teenage girls in the USA might need the classes because they were engaged in premarital sex and getting pregnant, but the classes discouraged sexual activity. Although this reassured them somewhat, mothers never lost guard of the ideas their daughters brought home.

This example illustrates that sexuality education programs can reach populations considered to be likely to refuse to have their daughters participate in the classes. From a gender and development perspective, these classes are not only important for health but also for increasing girls' agency in ways that can benefit men as well as women. They may contribute to greater decision-making about spacing of pregnancy and avoidance of HIV/AIDS and other sexually transmitted diseases. The discussions also illustrate that these women would like to see changes in the content of the classes to address their concerns more. This example shows that accessing information about sexuality is not simply an issue of how much information these girls receive. Preparing for the future involves not only the amount but also the quality of information girls receive. Mothers in Muslim families play a definite role in the decision to allow the girls to attend the classes and in discussing the issues from class at home. Although within this group there was not much intrahousehold conflict to resolve about participation in the classes, the talks opened the door for further discussions and negotiation between mothers and daughters about more sensitive sexuality issues (such as attending events with boys as well as girls).

Conclusion

This chapter addresses how the World Bank considers gender in intrahousehold aspects of development policy by examining the discussion in the PRR. It also illustrates key factors that have been omitted that could provide a much more current and thorough base for policy-makers and others reading the report. The PRR inclusion of a chapter on the gendered power dynamics of intra-household resource allocation is a progressive step by the gender division of the Bank; many World Bank studies still omit gender analysis, much less the attempt to understand the intrahousehold dynamics related to their policies. Having a whole chapter of the PRR focused on intrahousehold resource allocation and investment reflects the importance of these areas to human development. At the same time, the relatively narrow focus of the PRR chapter is a concern. It summarizes what is known about a core group of issues, heavily relying on econometric studies, but it does not take account of some of the more recent policy-related changes of economic restructuring and globalization. Nor does the PRR address intrahousehold aspects of many important frontier issues in the gender and development field.

Using an example from a recent study, we explore some of these frontier issues. The example addresses intrahousehold dynamics in the context of international migration as Muslim immigrant mothers in the USA make decisions about allowing their daughters to take sexuality education classes in high school, a health policy issue. The analysis focuses on international migrants – one of the increasing flows associated with globalization – and brings gender and development issues across borders into the United States; it focuses on the mother–daughter dyad in intrahousehold decision-making instead of the usual analyses of bargaining between spouses; it brings in a health policy issue set in the specific context by examining perceptions of mothers and daughters about attending sexuality education classes in public schools; and it draws on other disciplines by using qualitative methods as well as considering the interaction between mothers and daughters.

The interaction between mother and daughter over sexuality education does not involve transfer of money or other types of payments, but – at its best

– the outcome can have a substantial positive impact on girls' agency and social policy goals, such as reducing fertility rates, unwanted pregnancies, or the incidence of sexually transmitted diseases. Furthermore the interaction between mothers and daughters is likely to change not only the daughters but the mothers too as they adjust to a new society. This feedback loop is especially strong for international migrants.

The example touches on only a few areas often overlooked in studying intra-household aspects of economic development policies, but it illustrates key issues that are being addressed in current research and the need for policy-makers to understand the specific context and different expressions of agency in the groups they serve. As a basis for development policy-making, the PRR should expand to indicate cutting-edge issues such as those discussed in this chapter.

Acknowledgments

This study was supported by the Cooperative State Research Grant, Education and Extension Service, US Department of Agriculture, under Project No. ILLU-45-0358 to Gale Summerfield. The authors wish to thank Drucilla Barker and Edith Kuiper for their useful suggestions on an earlier version of this paper.

Notes

1 See PRR, Chapter 4, "Power, incentives, and resources in the household," pp. 147–80. The PRR chapter examines "how economic incentive, public investment, and the distribution of power within the household affect family resource allocations and investments by gender" (p. 148). The chapter provides an overview of empirical research from numerous developing countries on gender aspects of household decision-making. It also recommends policy incentives that can reduce gender inequalities in allocations within the household.

   While this chapter and the PRR use the terms *households* and *families* interchangeably, it is important to note that there are distinctions between the two. Historians show that by the nineteenth century the word *family* commonly described a married couple with their co-resident children, distinguished from household residents or more distant kin, the latter being qualified as extended family (Coontz 2000). A definition of household is given in the PRR, noting that the conditions of the definition are not usually satisfied (PRR: 150). Use of one term instead of the other becomes less pressing as families and households change over time; both concepts are socially and historically constructed as the many attempts to define the two illustrate (e.g. Demo *et al.* 2000). This is especially obvious in the case of migration where family members in the city or other countries send remittances back home or maintain two residences, spending only part of the year living away from the original home (PRR: 150; Rahman 2000).

2 SEWA (Self-Employed Women's Association) in India and BRAC (Bangladesh Rural Advancement Committee) support a range of employment and education activities in addition to providing microcredit programs. More information on the broader approach can be found in *Beyond Credit* (Chen 1996).

3 These changes have also generated a growing literature on human and social capital (Marger 2001; Portes 1995).

4 Summerfield *et al.*, in progress. The project on gender and human security of immigrants uses the capability approach to examine income, health, and housing

security. We devote particular attention to immigrants' access to public services such as health care; sex education is part of our focus on preventive health care availability.

5 We recognize that Muslims are an ethnically diverse group crosscut by all kinds of indicators such as country of origin, family background, time spent in the USA and place of residence.

6 As Bergeron (in this volume) contends, the West is held over as a model to follow and policies sometimes hardly recognize the problems that the people from the developing world face. What happens when one imposes the Anglo-Saxon view on migrant populations in the USA may bear some resemblances to what may happen to policies designed in Washington, DC and carried out in the country intended to use these policies.

7 The fieldwork for this project was carried out in Central and Northeast Illinois by Aida Orgocka, with support from the Kathleen Cloud International Research Grant administered by Women and Gender in Global Perspectives Program at the University of Illinois at Urbana-Champaign. Fifty-seven percent of the participants lived in DuPage and Cook counties in Northeast Illinois and 43 percent in Peoria, McLean and Champaign counties in Central Illinois.

8 Participants were recruited by snowball sampling techniques and by frequent visits to the local *masjid-s* (mosques) and the Islamic Centers. Four criteria for selection were established based on the previous literature and consultation with local key informants: (1) Both mothers and daughters identified themselves as Muslim; (2) Both mothers and daughters belonged to the first and/or second generation of immigrants to the USA; (3) Daughters were between the age of 14 and 20; (4) Participants lived in the state of Illinois. For a more in-depth report on these data see Orgocka (2004).

9 This study does not evaluate specific school-based sexuality education programs. Instead it explores participants' opinions about the programs offered through their local high schools, which can be used by school officials to construct more effective ways to reach these groups.

10 This applies to the optional sexuality education classes, which were available in Champaign, Peoria, Bloomington, and Naperville, Illinois. (The classes were mandatory only in Chicago.)

References

Adagala, K. (1991) "Households and Historical Change on Plantations in Kenya," in E. Masini and S. Stratigos (eds), *Women, Households, and Change*, Tokyo: United Nations University Press.

Aslanbeigui, N. and G. Summerfield (2000) "The Asian Crisis, Gender, and the International Financial Architecture," *Feminist Economics*, 6(3): 81–104.

Benería, L. (1995) "Towards a Greater Integration of Gender in Economics," *World Development*, 23(11): 1839–50.

—— (2003) *Gender, Development, and Globalization: Economics as if All People Mattered*, London and New York: Routledge.

Benería, L. and S. Feldman (eds) (1992) *Unequal Burden: Economic Crises, Persistent Poverty, and Women's Work*, Boulder, CO: Westview Press.

Blanchet, T. (1996) *Lost Innocence, Stolen Childhoods*, Dhaka: University Press.

Chen, M. (1996). *Beyond Credit: A Subsector Approach to Promoting Women's Enterprises*, Ottawa, Canada: Aga Khan Foundation Canada and the Harvard Institute for International Development (HIID).

Cloud, K. (2002) "How Mothering Behaviors Change during Structural Transformation," *Journal of Socio-Economics*, 31(1): 3–14.

Coontz, S. (2000) "Historical Perspectives on Family Diversity," in D.H. Demo, K.R. Allen and M.A. Fine (eds), *Handbook of Family Diversity*, New York: Oxford University Press.

Demo, D.H., K.R. Allen, and M.A. Fine (eds) (2000) *Handbook of Family Diversity*, New York: Oxford University Press.

Ene-Obong, H.N., G.I. Enugu and A.C. Uwaegbute (2001) "Determinants of Health and Nutritional Dtatus of Tural Nigerian Women," *Journal of Health Population and Nutrition*, 19(4): 320–30.

Finch, J. and J. Mason (1993) *Negotiating Family Responsibilities*, London; New York: Tavistock/Routledge.

Folbre, N. (2000) *The Invisible Heart: Economics and Family Values*, New York: The New Press.

Fuller, B., J.D. Singer and M. Keiley, M. (1995) "Why Do Daughters Leave School in Southern Africa? Family Economy and Mothers' Commitments," *Social Forces*, 74(2): 657–81.

Hondagneu-Sotelo, P. (1994) *Gendered Transitions: Mexican Experiences of Immigration*, Berkeley, CA: University of California Press.

Kabeer, N. (2000) *The Power to Choose: Bangladeshi Women and Labour Market Decisions in London and Dhaka*, London: Verso.

Kaul, I., I. Grunberg and M. Stern (eds) (1999) *Global Public Goods: International Cooperation in the 21st Century*, New York and Oxford: Oxford University Press.

Kibria, N. (1993) *Family Tightrope: The Changing Lives of Vietnamese Americans*, Princeton, NJ: Princeton University Press.

Kirby, D. and K. Coyle (1997) "School-based Programs to Reduce Sexual Risk-taking Behavior," *Children and Youth Services Review*, 19(5–6): 415–36.

Levitt, P. and M.C. Waters (2002) *The Changing Face of Home: The Transnational Lives of the Second Generation*, New York: Russell Sage Foundation.

Madhavan, S. (2001) "Female Cooperation and Conflict in Rural Mali: Effects on Infant and Child Survival," *Journal of Comparative Family Studies*, 32(1): 75–98.

Marger, M.N. (2001) "The Use of Social and Human Capital Among Canadian Business Immigrants," *Journal of Ethnic and Migration Studies*, 27(3): 439–53.

Nussbaum, M. (2000) *Women and Human Development: The Capabilities Approach*, Cambridge: Cambridge University Press.

Orgocka, A. (2004) "Perceptions of Communication and Education About Sexuality among Muslim Immigrant Girls in the US," *Sex Education*, 4(3): 255–71.

Papanek, H. (1990) "To Each Less Than She Needs, From Each More Than She Can Do: Allocations, Entitlements and Value," in I. Tinker (ed.), *Persistent Inequalities: Women and World Development*, Oxford: Oxford University Press.

Pessar, P.R. (1999) "The Role of Gender, Households, and Social Networks in the Migration Process," in C. Hirschman, P. Kasinitz and J. DeWind (eds), *The Handbook of International Migration: The American Experience*, New York: Russell Sage Foundation.

Portes, A. (ed.) (1995) *The Economic Sociology of Immigration: Essays on Networks, Ethnicity, and Entrepreneurship*, New York: Russell Sage Foundation.

PRR *See* World Bank (2001)

Punch, S. (2001) "Household Division of Labor: Generation, Gender, Age, Birth Order and Sibling Composition," *Work, Employment and Society*, 15(4): 803–23.

Pyle, J. (2001) "Sex, Maids, and Export Processing: Risks and Reasons for Gendered

Global Production Networks," *International Journal of Politics, Culture, and Society*, 15(1): 55–76.

Reese, L. (2001) "Morality and Identity in Mexican Immigrant Parents' Visions of the Future," *Journal of Ethnic and Migration Studies*, 27(3): 455–72.

Rahman, M. Md. (2000) "Emigration and Development: The Case of a Bangladeshi Village," *International Migration*, 38(4): 109–28.

Sen, A. (1990) "Gender and cooperative conflicts," in I. Tinker (ed.), *Persistent Inequalities: Women and World Development*, Oxford: Oxford University Press.

Sen, A. (1995) "Agency and Well-being: The Development Agenda," in N. Heyzer (ed.), *A Commitment to the World's Women*, New York: UNIFEM.

Sen, A. (1999) *Development as Freedom*, New York: Knopf.

Song, H. (2001) "The Mother–Daughter Relationship as a Resource for Korean Women's Career Aspirations," *Sex Roles*, 44(1–2): 79–97.

Summerfield, G. (1998) "Allocation of Labor and Income in the Family," in N. Stromquist (ed.), *Women in the Third World: An Encyclopedia of Contemporary Issues*, New York and London: Garland Publishing.

Tinker, I. (1999) "Women's Empowerment Through Rights to House and Land," in I. Tinker and G. Summerfield (eds), *Women's Rights to House and Land: China, Laos, Vietnam*, Boulder, CO: Lynne Rienner Publishers.

Woolley, F. (1999) "Family, Economics of," in J. Peterson and M. Lewis (eds), *The Elgar Companion to Feminist Economics*, Cheltenham: Edward Elgar.

World Bank (2001) *Engendering Development: Through Gender Equality in Rights, Resources, and Voice*, Washington, DC and New York: World Bank and Oxford University Press.

World Bank (2002) *Education and HIV/AIDS: A Window of Hope*, Washington, DC: World Bank.

12 Engendering development or gender main-streaming?

A critical assessment from the Commonwealth Caribbean

Violet Eudine Barriteau

> In this report we define gender equality in terms of equality under the law, equality of opportunity – including equality in access to human capital and other productive resources and equality for rewards for work – and equality of voice. We stop short of defining gender equality in terms of equality of outcomes, however for two reasons. One is that different societies can follow different paths in their pursuit of gender equality. The second is that an intrinsic aspect of equality is letting women and men choosing different (or similar) roles and different (or similar) outcomes according to their preferences and goals.
>
> (World Bank 2001: 35)

> The issue, therefore, is whether the economic empowerment of poor women in CARICOM is increasing, or that any such claim is smoke and mirrors. The economic empowerment of women would require changes both in the power relations between North and South, and in the power relations of gender.
>
> (Andaiye 2003a: 101)

Introduction

The World Bank's policy research report, *Engendering Development* is a worthwhile and timely study for developing countries. Not only because it is written by a powerful international development institution that with this report attempts to grapple with the intersection of gender issues and development concerns, but more so because of the multiplier or demonstration effect of this premier Western, development institution devoting time and resources to gender analysis. Governments and other institutions in developing countries may be more willing to engage with the ideas in the World Bank's publication if only because of moral suasion and their dependence on this institution for long-term development financing and the Bank's ongoing involvement in influencing subsequent development planning. Similarly, governments may be more inclined to ignore academic or feminist analyses of the same concerns if only because of the absence of the political will to engage with more progressive or alternative discussions, and the absence of a critical mass of feminist thinkers within government bureaucracies. It is precisely because of these considerations that the publication has to be scrutinized and critiqued. It has the potential to be cited as an authoritative source of information on engendering the development agenda in regions such as the Commonwealth or Anglophone Caribbean.

In this chapter I offer a critique of the Bank's latest policy report on gender. I undertake this assessment by arguing that the Bank's stated objective to engender development through introducing a prescribed set of measures to attain gender equality is instead identical to the promotion of gender main-streaming strategies currently being offered as a panacea for all gender trouble in developing countries. Instead of engendering development, the sum effect of these policies would be the promotion of gender main-streaming.

A genealogy of gender main-streaming

Gender main-streaming first gained international attention in the gender and development discourse by its emergence in the Platform for Action and Beijing Declaration (United Nations 1996). The Platform for Action advocated twelve strategic objectives and corresponding plans of action to achieve them. A common theme running throughout the strategic objectives and the proposed actions is the recommendation that gender analysis and gender planning be incorporated into all aspects of government, private sector and NGO policies and programmes (United Nations 1996; Sen 1999: 9; Andaiye 2003b).

The 1995 Commonwealth Plan of Action on Gender and Development is a good example. Endorsed by the Commonwealth heads of Government in Auckland in 1995, the Commonwealth Plan "gave the Commonwealth Secretariat a mandate to advise and assist governments in mainstreaming gender in all their policies, programmes and activities" (Sen 1999: 11). The Commonwealth Secretariat defines gender main-streaming as, "the central strategy of the Plan of Action for advancing gender equality and equity. It refers to the consistent use of a gender perspective at all stages of the development and implementation of polices, plans, programmes, and projects" (Commonwealth Secretariat 1999a: 6). The Commonwealth Plan traces its emphasis on gender main-streaming to the policy approach, Gender and Development (GAD). Its Plan of Action states:

> GAD tries to integrate gender awareness and competence into mainstream development to account for the different life courses and different impact of development policies on women and men. It emphasises that all development activities affect women and men differently and calls for appropriate "gender planning" to address them. It also calls attention to "outcomes" and the need to take the necessary steps to ensure that the resulting conditions and outcomes are equitable, rather than being preoccupied with giving only identical treatment . . . This new perspective forms the basis upon which the Plan of Action has been developed
>
> (Commonwealth Secretariat n.d.: 14)

The discussion of gender main-streaming moves from gender main-streaming being the central strategy to promote gender equality and equity to gender main-streaming being a consistent use of a gender perspective. The Commonwealth Plan defines a gender perspective without, however, challenging unequal power relations in gender:

> A gendered perspective looks not at women alone but at the relationship between women and men and how societies are structured along gendered lines. It is concerned with:
>
> • Women's involvement, concerns, needs, aspirations as well as those of men;
> • The outcomes of policies, plans and projects on women, men and children;
> • Assessing to whom the benefits accrue and in what ways. Financial and other quantitative and qualitative benefits may be assessed;
> • The whole process of gender planning.
>
> (Commonwealth Secretariat n.d.: 14)

In practice the development and incorporation of a gender perspective have been approached through rounds of workshops on gender training, gender sensitization, and gender analysis, with many of them discussing gender as divorced from feminist inquiries into women's persistent experiences of adverse power relations and conditions of subordination.

The Commonwealth Secretariat produced elaborate, well-written manuals to guide the process of gender main-streaming and in 1999 introduced the first national-level gender main-streaming and gender management system exercise in the Commonwealth Caribbean. Like the World Bank's strategies these focus on inputs, in this case the structures, processes and mechanisms necessary to facilitate the introduction of gender main-streaming, There is an over-emphasis on what goes into creating an enabling environment for gender main-streaming without a corresponding focus on what emerges from the process. It could be that because the planners were creating a new and "comprehensive network of structures, mechanisms and processes for bringing a gender perspective to bear in the mainstream of all government policies" (Commonwealth Secretariat 1999a: 5), they concentrated on the inputs of this new structure. However, the demonstration effect in developing countries could prove disastrous if new layers of bureaucracies are created without a clear emphasis on what should be achieved or on the mechanisms for gauging these achievements. Gender main-streaming strategies will not engender development and as currently conceived will produce very few meaningful changes to challenge institutionalized unequal relations of gender. I argue that the engendering of development promised by the World Bank collapses into gender main-streaming and inherits its limitations.

The three-pronged strategy of rights, resources and voice the report promotes is identical to the measures recommended to achieve gender main-streaming in the public sector in developing countries. However, the latter are problematic for several reasons. To date gender main-streaming is the most sophisticated and systematic attempt to implement a Gender and Development (GAD) strategy (Barriteau 2001: 86) and has become the key mechanism advocated to promote gender equality. However both its conceptualization and the experiences with its introduction in the Caribbean indicate that gender main-streaming results in a shift away from dealing with inequalities affecting women and men and instead produce a concentration on methodologies. The residual effect is that gender relations that maintain and reinforce hierarchies and inequalities are left intact.

In a study of gender main-streaming in five Commonwealth Caribbean countries Sonja Harris found there was great conceptual confusion on gender main-streaming. Only in Jamaica did the Planning Institute come closest to the definition the study used, of "ensuring that gender considerations are taken in the development of policies, plans and programmes" (Harris 1999: 6). She observed that, "all other countries interpreted the concept as involving men in services and programmes so as to create balance in the relationship between men and women" (ibid.: 6).

I suggest that gender main-streaming and gender management systems pose even greater problems for states in their attempts to address the inequalities women experience. This is so because these strategies are "conceptually unclear, structurally unsound, and create fragmentary programs that sidestep the real issues in women's lives – ongoing attempts by institutions and individuals to maintain conditions of inequality for women" (Barriteau 2001: xiii). The core of any programme or strategy to achieve gender equality should address relations and practices that actively seek to maintain women or men as subordinate, second-class citizens.

Engendering development

By stating it is "engendering development," I expect the Bank to expose the gendered character of the inequities in how women and men experience contemporary development policies and practices. In engendering development the Bank should actively promote strategies that seek to alter these. I expect the Bank to be aware of how developments in globalization generally, and specifically trade liberalization, and its effects on regional economies exacerbate gender-based inequalities. As Ann Denis argues, these "inequalities remain evident, reinforced, often implicitly, by the neoliberal policies and pressures in the public and private sectors. These pressures in fact constitute a backlash against gains that women had gradually, if unevenly, been making" (Denis 2003: 506). In other words, to engender development the Bank has to target and seek to effect particular outcomes. Instead it resorts to strategies that mirror the problematic gender main-streaming practices that do not destabilize entrenched inequalities.

As a result, in spite of its stated objectives, the Bank's measures constitute a reductionist package of measures and approaches that are proving counter-productive to promoting the goals of gender equality and justice in the

Commonwealth Caribbean. This slippage from the stated objectives to what is actually designed occurs because of three reasons. The first is that the conceptualization of gender and gender equality is deficient, thus providing a false set of assumptions to guide the measures introduced around the goal of gender equality. Second, the World Bank authors avoid examining power relations in relations of gender. A focus on the power relations of gender would move the analysis toward seeking to change the ideological and institutional foundation that supports gender inequality. Third, the World Bank refuses to engage with gender equality in terms of outcomes. By doing this, it abandons the most important set of measures that could indicate whether societies were serious about pursuing policies that would attempt to remove structural and ideological conditions that perpetuate gender inequalities.

I comment on the experiences of the Commonwealth Caribbean with gender main-streaming strategies to illustrate the inherent difficulties with the World Bank's prescriptions for achieving gender equality. Many of the measures the World Bank holds as desirable for achieving gender equality in developing countries already exist in the Commonwealth Caribbean. Yet gender relations are at their most contested and hostile (Vassell 2003; Bailey 2003; Pargass and Clarke 2003; Noel-Debique 2003; Andaiye 2003a; Bailey 2003a; Barriteau 2003; Harris 2003). Additionally, instead of tackling existing inequalities the new measures being introduced result in a shift away from them. This happens because

> gender main-streaming strategies are approached as if they are bundles of value-free methodologies that can be applied with the right mix of funding, personnel and training . . . We know and those committed to patriarchal practices understand, that what we are addressing or sidestepping is power relations feminist and other investigations have revealed. We should never undertake work on gender unless we are willing to address this.
>
> (Barriteau 2001: 175)

The socioeconomic, cultural and political expressions and experiences of relations of gender in the Commonwealth Caribbean[1] provide a sound body of quantitative and qualitative empirical evidence to challenge the certainty with which the World Bank offers its assessments and predictions for achieving gender equality in the developing world. Conditions in the Commonwealth Caribbean constitute a litmus test on whether development can in fact be engendered by promoting gender equality with the specific mix of strategies identified by the Bank.

In the Report, socioeconomic data on the Commonwealth Caribbean is merged with that of Latin America. This is unfortunate. Because of this, the uniqueness and dynamic character of gender relations and gender systems in the region is lost. It is subsumed in trends that reflect developments primarily in Latin America. The grouping of the data does not capture and address the compelling changes in material and ideological relations of gender in the Caribbean that began in the last twenty-five years of the twentieth century and continues into the twenty-first (Tang-Nain and Bailey 2003; Denis 2003; Barriteau 2001, 1998a; Barrow 1998b; Freeman 2000; Kempadoo 1999; Leo-Rhynie *et al.* 1997; Social and Economic Studies 1986; Mohammed and Shepherd 1988; Albuquerque and Ruark 1998; Mohammed 1998b, 2002).

I use occurrences in the social relations of gender in the Anglophone Commonwealth Caribbean to illustrate my analysis. The countries comprising this geopolitical grouping are largely missing from the World Bank's study, even though the region is perhaps one of the best models of developing countries/ regions undergoing rapid changes in relations of gender. In some global studies, especially those given to socioeconomic analyses, there is an unfortunate tendency to link Latin America and the Caribbean and then be satisfied that the latter region has been adequately investigated. This is inaccurate. This approach uses the bulk of data from Latin America with some statistical flavoring added by the inclusion of the Hispanic Caribbean countries of Cuba, Puerto Rico or the Dominican Republic. These countries are very much a part of the geographic Caribbean. However because of the comparatively greater size of their populations and national territories, and the sharply divergent patterns within their history, political institutions, culture and economic activities, the particular features that define the Anglophone Caribbean are submerged in these globalizing analyses.

The problem of definition: discussing gender/avoiding power

The first difficulty with the policies and strategies recommended by the Bank begins with its definition of gender and gender equality. The Report starts its analysis by locating, "gender equality as a core development issue – a development objective in its own right" (World Bank 2001: 12), and then defines gender equality in terms of inputs, or conditions necessary for its attainment. The Bank is not interested in assessing whether or not gender equality has actually been achieved or even approached. The Report states, "[g]ender equality is equality under the law, equality of opportunity (including equality of rewards for work and equality in access to human capital and other productive resources that enable opportunity), and equality of voice" defined as the ability to influence and contribute to the development process (ibid.: 2–3). The World Bank's definition and discussion of the core concept of gender emphasizes social expectations arising from the biological differences between male and female bodies without emphasizing the power relations that constrain the gender identities women and men acquire as part of prevailing gender ideologies (ibid.: 34). The discussion avoids the considerable feminist investigations of the concept of gender (for example, Scott 1986; Flax 1990; Chodorow 1995; Nicholson 1994; Hawkesworth 1997). Instead *Engendering Development* relies extensively on discussions produced by international development institutions and agencies. Many of these studies refrained from engaging in feminist theorizing of gender. They minimize the feminist genealogy of the concept and emphasize its utility to formulating policy on gender but without the conceptual rigor and analytical strengths feminist analysis offers. When one considers the intense negotiations, debates and challenges that are intrinsic to producing international policy statements to satisfy all the contending constituencies, reliance on these processes and subsequent documents to support a particular definition does not do justice to the analytical worth of the concept. This reliance enables diplomatically defined language to neutralize and define conditions that are about inequalities of power and justice.

What is required in terms of the World Bank's work on gender is not the need (as it states) to collect more and better data to be disaggregated by gender analysis (World Bank 2001: 27). Instead it is the need to revisit and rethink the conceptual analysis of gender. The Report approaches gender inequalities as merely a problem of inadequate resource allocation. Therefore it concludes that what is required are measures to reassign and reallocate resources.

It identifies the factors standing in the way of gender equality as institutions, households and the economy as if these are value-free institutions whose operations are not driven by relations of power to operate in distinct ways to serve specific, hierarchical and patriarchal interests. But it offers no discussion of the idea that built into norms and practices is a recurring inferior ranking of women and women's roles that arise in ideological relations of gender.

The second difficulty I want to mention here is that the World Bank is not addressing the social relations of power that coalesce in the concept of gender. It speaks about rights, resources and voice but avoids speaking about power. This is exactly what gender main-streaming turns out to be in practice. The net result is a further packaging and marketing of the gender product without tracking what its implementation is supposed to achieve.

Material and ideological relations of gender are relations of power. They make up the two dimensions of a gender system which comprise a network of power relations. The material dimensions of gender reveal how women and men gain access to or are allocated the material and non-material resources in a state and society (Barriteau 2001: 30). I define ideological dimensions of gender as

> involving the construct of masculinity and femininity. It indicates how a society's notion of masculinity and femininity are constructed and maintained. The ways in which [they] are constructed reveal the gender ideologies operating in a state and society . . . Gender ideologies reveal what is appropriate or expected of the socially constituted beings, "women" and "men". They also expose how individuals create gender identities. The social expectations and the personal constructions of gender identities form the core of gender ideologies within a particular society.
>
> (Barriteau 2001: 30)

Built into the construct of masculinity and femininity are hierarchies of gender, so that what it means to be a man is ranked and valued more by societies than what it means to be a woman. Because of these hierarchies and inequalities built into and continuously reinforced in gender relations, gender systems are unjust.

The third difficulty I want to stress is that the World Bank definition of gender emphasizes equality of access but does not say anything about distribution nor existing prejudices after access has been formally attained. If the existence of those conditions mean gender equality then in the Commonwealth Caribbean we would have to conclude that we are very advanced in achieving gender equality. In fact the Men's movement in Barbados concludes there is now widespread gender inequality for men because governments, universities and states have gone too far in ensuring women have gender equality under the law, and in access to and distribution of resources.

> The university [of the West Indies] is not saying how it will help men, head of the Men's Educational Support Association, MESA, said last Monday night during the organisation's's general meeting. Boyce said men were driving women to the Cave Hill Campus and other institutions of higher learning and paying school fees for them while not concentrating on their own educational advancement.
>
> (*Weekend Nation* 2000: 33)

> Barbadian men are being "unfaired" by local legislation and are justified in believing they are getting a raw deal. The legal inability of men to seek maintenance and adopt or foster children with the ease that women do, and the proposed amendment to the Family Law Act, are both examples of this discrimination, says chairman of the Men's Educational Support Association, Ralph Boyce.
>
> (Bennett 2002: 1)

Other news items by the Men's Association protesting perceived gender inequalities for men include, "Help Men too" (Ejimofor 2002: 1B); "Fair Treatment for all Men Needed" (Millington 2003: 3); and "Boys Losing their Way?" (Niles 2000: 14A).[2]

The analysis of gender systems in the Caribbean shows that ideological relations of gender are embedded within patriarchal relations that are very resistant to change (Barriteau 2001: 20–71). By ignoring the contents of the construct of masculinity and femininity, that is the gender identities that societies and individuals hold as appropriate for men and women, it also ignores the hierarchies built into these identities and their attendant complications (ibid.: 30–4).

The Caribbean experience

The Report does not investigate conditions in the Anglophone Caribbean. Yet Barbados, which has consistently ranked first in the Caribbean measured by the UNDP's gender development indices (see Table 12.1), provides an excellent example of ideological relations of gender, constraining women's capacity

Table 12.1 World rank of Caribbean countries on Human Development Index, 1995–2001

Country	1995		1996		1997		1998		1999[1]		2000[2]		2001	
	Rank	Value	Rank	Value	Rank	Value	Rank	Value	Rank	Value	Rank	Value	Rank	Value
Antigua/Barbuda	55	.84	40	.86	29	.89	29	.89	38	.82	37	.83	–	–
Bahamas	26	.89	26	.89	28	.89	32	.89	31	.85	33	.84	42	.82
Barbados	25	.90	25	.90	25	.90	24	.90	29	.85	30	.85	31	.86
Belize	29	.88	67	.75	63	.80	63	.80	83	.73	58	.77	54	.77
Cuba	72	.76	79	.72	86	.72	85	.72	58	.76	56	.78	–	–
D'can Republic	69	.77	87	.70	41	.87	41	.82	53	.77	51	.79	86	.72
Dominica	96	.70	65	.76	87	.71	88	.72	88	.72	87	.72	–	–
Grenada	67	.78	77	.72	54	.84	51	.85	52	.77	54	.78	–	–
Guyana	105	.62	103	.63	104	.64	100	.67	99	.70	96	.70	93	.70
Haiti	148	.36	145	.35	156	.33	159	.34	152	.43	150	.44	134	.46
Jamaica	88	.72	86	.70	83	.73	84	.73	82	.73	83	.73	78	.73
St Kitts/Nevis	37	.87	45	.85	49	.85	50	.85	51	.78	83	.73	–	–
St Lucia	84	.73	76	.73	56	.83	58	.83	81	.73	47	.79	–	–
St Vincent	79	.76	73	.73	57	.83	55	.84	75	.74	79	.73	–	–
Suriname	77	.76	75	.73	66	.79	65	.79	64	.75	67	.76	64	–
T'dad & T'bgo	39	.87	38	.87	40	.88	40	.88	46	.79	50	.79	49	–

Notes
1 See page 160 and TN1, Report 1999.
  Measure of development based on indicators of longevity, education, income per head.
  See UNDP 1999: 23.
2 Can be compared with 1999.

to participate fully in politics. The CEDAW's committee reaction to the presentation of the Barbados Country Report to the United Nations in 2002 exemplifies this. The Barbados report stated that there are no legal nor institutional barriers to women's full political participation and that Barbadian women had the right to vote since 1943.[3] The Country Report explained women's comparatively lower participation in elective politics as due to cultural barriers. In response to this report, the CEDAW committee, referring to the facts that the government had identified cultural barriers as an impediment to women's full participation and that Barbados was a signatory of CEDAW since 1980, asked what the government was planning to do to dismantle these barriers? CEDAW stressed that these barriers were not natural and unchangeable and requested that the Barbados government address gender stereotyping and state the identification of measures to combat these as a priority (*Daily Nation* 2002b; CEDAW 2002; Barriteau 2003: 224).

The Caribbean experience shows that what is crucial is for the authors of the Report to recognize the power relations inhering in gender. They need to spell out the specific interests that are served by gender hierarchies and examine who benefits and who is harmed by these. Gender inequalities are not a benign manifestation of inefficient resource distribution. They are symptomatic of deliberate attempts to deny women's full economic, political and cultural citizenship. The collective work of Andaiye (2003a, b), Ann Denis (2003) and Barbara Bailey (2003) demonstrates that changes in the Caribbean's political economy, even when punitive to some men, have not meant that women have gained. Barbara Bailey emphasizes that the focus on quantitative gains made by women in education distorts the reality of where women are located in the educational system and how this translates into less of a comparative advantage in labour markets (Barriteau 2003: 217).

When this point is not fully grasped in terms of its implications for policy, very poor strategies are put forward. When policy-makers conclude that there are only benign gender biases within a set of social interactions or policy, they assume what is needed are new strategies of socialization. This misunderstanding has created an industry on gender that is productive and lucrative but it leaves the character of unequal gender relations unchanged. It is unable to alter unequal gender relations because the analysis and the prescriptions are uninformed by feminist investigations that contributed the analytical strength of the concept and revealed the character of power relations within it.

Avoiding outcomes or denying persistent inequalities?

At the core of my critique of the World Bank's approach is the exposing of the flawed assumption made by the authors that they can concentrate on various dimensions of material resource allocation as inputs and have those inputs produce (as outcomes) sex equity (or parity).[4] This bifurcation of analysis and subsequent policy has two major implications. It predisposes the Bank's strategies to mimic the gender main-streaming strategies, a tendency which promises much but delivers little in relation to challenging gender inequalities. More significantly this focus on inputs is unable to make sense of the experiences in the Caribbean that demonstrate, for example, that it is possible for boys and girls to have equal access to education (the input) and to have relatively similar completion rates (the output), but that boys and men continue to maintain economic, social and political power or dominance, since the gender hierarchies were not fundamentally challenged in the first place. Instead these sex equity policies are embedded in the existing gender hierarchies and do not destabilize them.[5]

The World Bank deliberately avoids addressing any conditions that could indicate some measure of outcomes on gender equality. It is as if the authors of the Report are saying "we are advocating the adoption of certain strategies as inputs but we are not interested in what emerges. We will make no predictions or offer any advice on what should be the end product of these various mixes of policies since all societies and cultures have specific understandings of how they want relations between women and men to be." It thus limits the effectiveness of the measures it advocates for developing countries. Measures of equality that address changes in women's and men's lives on the basis of changes in their experiences of relations of gender provide a better assessment of whether the package of measures actually do produce gender equality.

Instead the World Bank chooses to hide behind what is really a diplomatic disclaimer that each culture and society can follow different paths to gender equality differently so that the pursuit of measuring gender equality as seeking changes in outcomes is meaningless (World Bank 2001: 35). This may buy the World Bank space or peace with its member countries which still cling to rigid and hierarchical gender roles and identities for women, but it is unacceptable. It is precisely because some countries argue that their pursuit of gender equality is unique to their culture that we have so many women in different regions of the world experiencing inhumane, unjust conditions in their daily lives.

The Report speaks to the universality of roles and responsibilities for women and girls around reproductive and unpaid work. It notes that this work is time-consuming and seriously constrains their capacity and ability to benefit from resources where these exist. The Report notes that irrespective of culture and society women bear a disproportionate share of work in the reproductive and care economy. Yet after identifying a universal, asymmetrical, feature of relations of gender, it tries unsuccessfully to make an argument for particularity. It does this as a means of avoiding the admittedly difficult task of holding countries accountable to some measure of gender equality in outcomes. Not having the mechanisms or political authority to insist on certain measures does not mean these mechanisms cannot be developed. Neither does it remove the moral responsibility to insist, or at the least provide, some guidelines on what attaining gender equality could look like. The World Bank and the IMF are well known for insisting on adherence to fiscal and financial rules even when countries claim that culturally adhering to these prescriptions would provide social and cultural upheavals.

Caribbean realities

At approximately 6 million, the population of the Commonwealth or Anglo-phone Caribbean is less than half of the population of the Hispanic Caribbean country of Cuba (UNDP 1999). Until three years ago the Commonwealth or Anglophone Caribbean and CARICOM[6] were synonymous. With the admission of Suriname followed by Haiti to CARICOM, the latter now includes non-Anglophone Caribbean countries. Many of the conditions the Report discusses and advocates as evidence of gender equality currently exist in the region. For example, life expectancies and gross primary and secondary school enrollment ratios are both relatively high and significant for both women and men.

In 1995 the United Nations Development Programme (UNDP) intro-duced two indices, the Gender Development Index (GDI) and the Gender Empowerment Measure (GEM) to capture gender disparities and their adverse effects on social progress in the policies, programmes and practices of countries (UNDP 1995: 72).[7] For the period 1995–2001 all the independent CARICOM countries receive a Human Development Index (HDI) ranking as shown in Table 12.1.[8] In 1995 Barbados, the Bahamas, Belize, St Kitts-Nevis, Trinidad and Tobago, and Antigua-Barbuda were ranked as high-income developing countries (ibid.: 52). By 2001 only Barbados and the Bahamas received that listing in the geographic and Commonwealth Caribbean (UNDP 2001: 141). Table 12.2 shows the comparative rank of Caribbean countries on the GDI between 1995 and 2001. Why is there this reporting gap on the GDI for the countries com-prising the Organisation of Eastern Caribbean States (OECS)? These countries, Antigua-Barbuda, Dominica, Grenada, St Lucia, St Kitts-Nevis and St Vincent have state machineries focusing on gender issues and have signed the Beijing Platform of Action. The omission is even more puzzling since the annual Human Development Reports display the statistics on the HDI for OECS countries and input the same data that is used to calculate the HDI to calculate the GDI.[9]

Evidence from the Caribbean contradicts some of the assumptions about the positive changes likely to occur because of women's access to material resources. The evidence also indicates why an exclusive focus on inputs, whether as resource allocation as advocated by the Bank, or on structures, as an enabling environment as stressed by gender main-streaming strategies, is insufficient. With all the widespread concern that men are being marginalized in labour markets and women are becoming dominant in traditional male occupations, men's economic advantage over women, as expressed in the earned-income differential remains consistently higher throughout the Caribbean and in fact in all 162 countries reporting on the Gender-Related Development Index. This is the economic evidence for the arguments made by Barbara Bailey (2003) questioning the alleged shift in a balance of power among women and men because of women's higher educational enrolment ratios. The estimated earned income for women and men underscore the disparity between inputs (material resource allocation) and outcomes around achieving gender equality.

Table 12.2 Comparative rank of Caribbean countries on the Gender Development Index, 1995–2001

Country	1995 Rank in Caribbean	World	1996 Rank in Caribbean	World	1997 Rank in Caribbean	World	1998 Rank in Caribbean	World	1999 Rank in Caribbean	World	2000 Rank in Caribbean	World	2001 Rank in Caribbean	World	Change in World Rank on GDI 1999–2001
Barbados	1	11	1	16	1	17	1	16	1	27	–	–	–	–	–
Bahamas	2	26	2	18	2	18	2	21	2	29	1	32	1	38	↗
T'dad & T'bgo	3	36	3	34	3	32	3	38	3	44	2	48	2	47	↗
Jamaica	5	52	4	60	4	63	6	65	5	69	4	67	4	68	↗ ↗
Guyana	8	70	7	78	7	91	9	95	7	83	6	80	6	88	↗ ↗
Cuba	4	47	–	–	5	68	7	69	4	53	–	–	–	–	–
Suriname	6	54	–	–	–	–	5	63	–	–	–	–	–	–	–
Belize	–	–	5	75	–	–	4	56	–	–	3	60	3	59	↖
D'can Republic	7	69	6	71	6	75	8	81	6	75	5	73	5	78	↗ ↖
Haiti	9	105	8	112	8	130	10	144	8	124	7	123	7	118	↗ ↖
Antigua/Barbuda	–	–	–	–	–	–	–	–	–	–	–	–	–	–	–
Dominica	–	–	–	–	–	–	–	–	–	–	–	–	–	–	–
Grenada	–	–	–	–	–	–	–	–	–	–	–	–	–	–	–
St Kitts/Nevis	–	–	–	–	–	–	–	–	–	–	–	–	–	–	–
St Lucia	–	–	–	–	–	–	–	–	–	–	–	–	–	–	–
St Vincent	–	–	–	–	–	–	–	–	–	–	–	–	–	–	–

Source: UNDP Human Development Reports 1995, 1996, 1997, 1998, 1999, 2000, 2001.

Notes
HDI: Human Development Index.
GDI: Gender Development Index, introduced for the first time in 1995. The GDI concentrates on the same variables the UNDP used to create its HDI, but compares and takes note of differences in the achievement of women and men to determine a country's progress on efforts to attain gender equity.

Tables 12.3 and 12.4 present a statistical sketch of this economic reality. Table 12.3 discloses that from 1995 to 1998 earned-income differentials for women and men in the Caribbean were reported as a percentage of total income earned. These tables enable a serious reexamination and contextualization of the arguments about achieving gender equality by following the prescribed set of measures. They are also relevant to the debate about gender and poverty (Andaiye 2003a). One fact is indisputable in these ratios. Women consistently earn considerable less than men in all Caribbean countries. In 1995 only in Barbados and Jamaica did women's earned-income share of all income earned exceed 30 percent. However, for most countries reporting these figures increased for women, albeit incrementally. Table 12.4 depicts these gender differentials in earned income as real GDP per capita for 1999 to 2001. These differences in earned income are even sharper, with the exception of Haiti where in 2001 women earned 54 percent of real GDP per capita as compared to Belize where women's earnings were 23 percent.

To promote gender equality the issues surrounding women and work should engage the attention and energies of the World Bank policy-makers and practitioners working in the field. Deep-seated ideological tensions about material relations of gender are embedded in discussions of women and work that remain unexamined, thus making it very difficult to unravel the policy and practical implications of these challenges (Denis 2001: 31). Yet with its exclusive

Table 12.3 Earned income share, 1995–1998

Country	1995		1996		1997		1998	
	Female	*Male*	*Female*	*Male*	*Female*	*Male*	*Female*	*Male*
Barbados	39.4	60.6	39.1	60.9	39.5	60.5	39.6	60.4
Bahamas	28.3	71.7	39.4	60.6	39.5	60.5	39.5	60.5
T'dad & T'bgo	24.7	75.3	28.5	71.5	29.7	70.3	26.8	73.2
Jamaica	38.6	61.4	39.2	60.8	39.2	60.8	39.2	60.8
Guyana	21.2	78.8	25.4	74.6	26.4	73.6	26.9	73.1
Cuba	27.2	72.8	29.7	70.3	31.1	68.9	31.5	68.5
Suriname	–	–	–	–	–	–	26.1	73.9
Belize	–	–	–	–	–	–	18.5	81.5
D'can Republic	12.1	87.9	22.4	77.6	23.1	76.9	24.0	76.0
Haiti	34.2	65.8	36.1	63.9	36.2	63.8	36.0	64.0
Antigua/ Barbuda	–	–	–	–	–	–	–	–
Dominica	–	–	–	–	–	–	–	–
Grenada	–	–	–	–	–	–	–	–
St Kitts/ Nevis	–	–	–	–	–	–	–	–
St Lucia	–	–	–	–	–	–	–	–
St Vincent	–	–	–	–	–	–	–	–

Table 12.4 Real GDP per capita (US$), 1999–2001[1]

Country	1999		2000		2001	
	Female	*Male*	*Female*	*Male*	*Female*	*Male*
Barbados	9,252	14,496	–	–	–	–
Bahamas	13,296	20,238	11,577	15,153	12,138	18,457
T'dad & T'bgo	4,101	9,600	4,131	10,868	4,510	11,878
Jamaica	2,756	4,138	2,629	4,163	2,746	4,400
Guyana	1,760	4,696	1,852	4,994	1,949	5,435
Cuba	2,013	4,181	4,973	7,839	–	–
Suriname	2,794	7,569	–	–	–	–
Belize	1,617	6,928	1,704	7,368	1,858	7,972
D'can Republic	2,374	7,186	2,333	6,787	2,794	8,133
Haiti	928	1,624	976	1,805	1,030	1,916
Antigua/ Barbuda	–	–	–	–	–	–
Dominica	–	–	–	–	–	–
Grenada	–	–	–	–	–	–
St Kitts/ Nevis	–	–	–	–	–	–
St Lucia	–	–	–	–	–	–
St Vincent	–	–	–	–	–	–

1 Estimated Earned Income (ppp US$) 1999.

Source: UNDP *Human Development Report* 2001.

focus on the material relations of gender, that is access to and distribution of resources, the factors that influence who benefits are unexamined. There are both micro and macro dimensions to material and ideological relations of gender, especially as these relate to women and economic autonomy.

At the level of aggregates, Caribbean states have amended or removed most discriminatory legislation and facilitated women's access to public resources through expanded access to tertiary education and comparatively better health care. At the micro level, gender ideologies have disrupted or influenced material relations of gender, specifically the relationship between the woman worker and her employer. For example a decision to use women as piece-workers in manufacturing not only denies women more prestigious work, it also guarantees lower wages, affects income levels, spending power and accumulation of wealth.

Given the emphasis the Bank places on enhancing women's political voice the data on women and political participation indicates what happens when there is a concentration on equality of inputs without paying attention to outcomes. Table 12.5 discloses the extent of women's political participation in Caribbean countries in 2001. Between 1980 and 1995 the percentage of women participating in parliamentary assemblies in sixteen Caribbean countries averaged 9.6

Table 12.5 Women's political participation in Caribbean countries, 2001

Country	HDI rank	GDI rank	Yr of right to vote	Yr of right to stand for election	Yr first elected or appointed to parliament	% in gov't at ministerial level	% seats held in lower or single house	% of seats in upper house or senate
Barbados	31	–	1950	1950	1950	14.3	10.7	33.3
Bahamas	42	38	1961	1961	1977	16.7	15.0	–
T'dad & T'bgo	49	47	1946	1946	1962	8.7	11.1	32.3
Belize	54	51	1954	1954	1984	11.1	6.9	37.5
Suriname	64	–	1948	1948	1975	–	17.6	–
Jamaica	78	68	1932	1932	1962	–	6.0	–
Guyana	93	88	1953	1945	1968	–	18.5	–
Haiti	134	118	1950	1950	1965	–	12.5	8.0
D'can Republic	86	78	1942	1942	1942	–	16.1	6.7

Source: UNDP *Human Development Report* 2001.

percent in 1980, with a high of 14.3 percent in Guyana and a low of 4.6 percent in the Bahamas. In 1985 the regional average was incrementally higher at 11.0 percent with a high of 28.6 percent in Grenada (two seats out of seven), and lows of 0 percent in Antigua-Barbuda, St Vincent and the Grenadines, and the British Virgin Islands (Mondesire and Dunn 1995: 102).

By 1992 the regional average of women's participation in parliamentary assemblies was 12.6 percent, with a high of 30.8 percent in Montserrat (4/13 seats) and lows of 0 percent in Anguilla and Antigua-Barbuda (Mondesire and Dunn 1995: 102). As Table 12.5 shows, in 2001 the average number of seats held by women elected to a lower or single house stood at 11.6 percent. Even though women have been able to vote and stand for elections for over fifty years, at the beginning of the twenty-first century the region still lacks a critical mass of women as key political leaders.

Women's participation at the highest level of political decision-making fluctuated in most dependent territories and independent countries between 1980 and 1992. Women's overall political representation as a result of national competitive politics grew by 3 percent. In contrast men's successful participation in national competitive politics never dropped below 70 percent in any Caribbean independent or dependent country. Between 1980 and 1992 in fifteen out of sixteen Caribbean countries men held 81 percent or more of the seats in parliament (Barriteau 1998b: 20; Mondesire and Dunn 1995: 102). As Table 12.5 shows, in 2001 in all the countries reporting, men held 81.5 percent or more of all elected seats. This statistical description of political participation in the region offers a different reading and runs counter to the popular arguments of the take-over by women of traditional sites of male power.

There is simultaneously a widespread belief in and about the region that women have overtaken men educationally and financially. Sonja Harris reported that there was confusion in the region as to the legitimacy of continuing to focus on women given male "underachievement" in education (Harris 1999: 3). The thesis of the marginalization of the Caribbean male is so pervasive that in New Delhi in 2000 it was the action of Indian feminists who managed to stop the sixth annual meeting of Commonwealth Ministers of Women's Affairs from adopting that theme as a priority area for the Caribbean (Chadha 2000). Caribbean women have attained comparatively higher levels of education: in fact the ratio of female to male enrolment at the university of the West Indies is 70/30. Yet female unemployment in the region is higher and Tables 12.3 and 12.4 substantiate the fact that the wage differential is still wide.

In a study of three economies in the Commonwealth Caribbean Stephanie Seguino found that women are much more likely than men to be unemployed and on average men earn 20 percent more than similarly qualified women. Her study reveals that in an economic upturn men are more likely to find employment than women. She concludes that her results imply that relying on economic growth to reduce gender equality in job access will not suffice and more targeted efforts are needed to ensure that women stand a fair chance of being hired (Seguino 2002).

Some of the strategies the World Bank recommends concentrate on reducing time spent on housework through introducing or enhancing time-saving infrastructure. The strategies do not attempt to unravel the fundamental ideology that housework is the responsibility of women. By focusing almost exclusively on material conditions through altering resource allocation, the Bank's report creates the assumption that such changes will produce gender equality. Caribbean women's alleged comparatively better use of educational resources have unleashed many misogynous statements and practices, and there are ongoing demands to curtail this access or introduce new restrictions (*Trinidad Guardian* 2000; Taitt 2000; *Barbados Advocate* 2000, 1993; *Daily Nation* 1993).

The following statement from the Report is not accurate for the Caribbean, as it relates to man as the sole or traditional breadwinner: "Women command fewer resources with which to cushion shocks – while men, as the traditional breadwinner, are particular vulnerable to stress associated with large changes in or uncertain employment" (World Bank 2001: 25). While the ideology certainly exists, in practice men have not been the traditional breadwinners for several reasons.

Historically Caribbean women have played and continue to play a major role in contributing to the financial upkeep of families. The high percentage of female-headed households, at a regional average of about 44 percent, remains a significant and contributory factor. Caribbean men have migrated in search of work, leaving women to run households and families sometimes with or without remittances (Newton 1984; Momsen 1987; Mondesire and Dunn 1995). In the Caribbean as elsewhere there is the ideology of Man the Breadwinner. Helen Safa analyzed this as *The Myth of the Male Breadwinner* rather than seeing it as the reality (Safa 1995).

It is precisely because women theoretically can have equality before the law (inputs) and still experience serious institutionalized inequalities in the application of the law (outcomes) (World Bank 2001: 37) that a measurement of gender equality as equality before the law or access to the law is inadequate.

When the Report concludes that men now experience gender inequalities in Latin America and Eastern Europe it needs to examine the conditions that give rise to what is being described as gender inequalities for men. Do these inequalities arise from societally or individually held beliefs in men's inferiority as citizens? Do these conditions arise out of policies of the state and society to deny men access to resources? Are they due to changes that arise when developments in the global political economy intersect with how men construct their gender identities? Are there institutionalized practices in customary and civil law that deny men access to rights, resources and voice?[10]

Conclusion

A commitment to removing the foundational ideological and material conditions that sustain gender inequalities would move the analysis and subsequent policies away from notions of more or less equality. It would avoid conclusions such as one sex enjoying more gender equality than the other in having access to a given resource because the other is not benefitting from that resource to the same degree.

The World Bank's analysis requires some means of assessing attempts to remove ingrained gender inequalities. Since women historically have been denied autonomy, I suggest that a useful measure for women would be to pay attention to the degree of autonomy they can exercise over their lives. To what extent do they have a voice in matters concerning themselves and their families? I find it useful to begin to think of an outcome of gender equality as the capacity of an individual to have autonomy to influence decisions and choices about one's life without restrictions or limitations being imposed because of one's sex.

When states exist with hierarchies and injustices embedded in their gender systems they cannot produce or implement gender-neutral policies. Gender-based power relations permeate all social relations (Barriteau 2001: 33). This is perhaps *the* major weakness of the World Bank study. This is also the flaw it shares with gender main-streaming strategies. As currently conceived, they both attempt to construct and offer a set of gender-neutral practices or policies on a foundation of deeply entrenched, gendered structures and behaviours. The policies may be designed to apply to men and women equally, but women and men will not be equal beneficiaries. The ideological relations of gender that actively seek to maintain conditions of inferiority or lack of civil relevance has to be dismantled. This is where Commonwealth Caribbean countries are now located, at the crossroads of transforming or reifying unequal relations of gender. Material relations of gender have been radically reconfigured. Ideological relations of gender remain anchored precariously to some mythical notion of appropriate gender identities. The product is tension, hostility and resentment. No amount of well-intentioned policy prescriptions that ignore the brittle character of ideological gender relations will alter that. No set of policy prescriptions that seek to end conditions of inequalities can afford to ignore women's and men's dissimilar experiences of contemporary gender relations.

Notes

1 By Commonwealth Caribbean and Caribbean I refer to the independent, Anglophone island states (Antigua-Barbuda, Barbados, Bahamas, St Christopher-Nevis (St Kitts-Nevis), Dominica, Grenada, Jamaica, St Lucia, Trinidad and Tobago, St Vincent and the Grenadines), and British Dependencies within the Caribbean Sea, (Anguilla, British Virgin Islands, Cayman Islands, Montserrat and Turks and Caicos), the Central American country of Belize, and the South American country of Guyana. These countries have a similar historical, political, social and cultural legacy. They are former colonies of Britain and in the case of a few, British Protectorates.

2 This is only a representative sample. The Association has a weekly column in the leading daily newspaper and uses that medium to undertake advocacy on behalf of men that is often very critical of feminists and feminism.

3 With property restrictions, universal adult suffrage was achieved in 1951.

4 I thank Drucilla Barker for making this very clear to me.

5 Again I thank Drucilla Barker for helping me to clarify these points.

6 CARICOM refers to the Caribbean Community established in 1973 by the independent Anglophone Caribbean countries who are also members of the British Commonwealth. The three objectives are economic integration, coordination of foreign policy and functional cooperation. Before the admission of Suriname and Haiti to full membership, CARICOM, Commonwealth Caribbean and Anglophone Caribbean were interchangeable terms. However it is still common practice for researchers and lay persons to use the terms interchangeably even though CARICOM is now the larger grouping.

7 The UNDP employs the same variables it used to construct the HDI but uses them to focus on the inequality between women and men as well as the average achievement of all people taken together (UNDP 1995: 72). The GDI measures achievement on the same basic capabilities as the HDI but takes note of inequality in achievement between women and men. The methodology used imposes a penalty for inequality such that the GDI falls when the achievement levels of both women and men go down or when the disparity between their achievement increases. The greater the gender disparity in basic capabilities the lower a country's GDI compared with its HDI. The GDI is simply the HDI discounted or adjusted downwards for gender inequality (ibid.: 73).

8 Yet since the UNDP began publishing the GDI and GEM indices in 1995, not once have these statistics ever included data on the eight independent countries comprising the Organisation of Eastern Caribbean States, OECS; see Table 12.2.

9 The GDI is the HDI discounted or adjusted downwards for gender inequality (UNDP 1995: 73). This enables the UNDP to assign a ranking for the countries' efforts to prioritize a human-centered development approach. Countries may have a high HDI ranking and fall in ranking on the GDI. This indicates that improvements in society have not benefited women as much as men (Barriteau 1998b: 447).

10 For a framework for assessing whether men are being marginalized, see Barriteau 2000, 2001C.

References

Albuquerque, K. and S. Ruark (1998) "'Men Day Done': Are Women Really Ascendant in the Caribbean?", in Christine Barrow (ed.), *Caribbean Portraits: Essays on Gender Ideologies and Identities*, Kingston: Ian Randle Publishers: 1–13.

Andaiye (2003a) "Smoke and Mirrors: The Illusion of Women's Growing Economic Empowerment in the CARICOM Region, Post-Beijing," in Gemma Tang Nain and Barbara Bailey (eds), *Gender Equality in the Caribbean: Reality or Illusion?*, Kingston: Ian Randle Publishers: 73–108.

—— (2003b) "Plan of Action to 2005: Framework for Mainstreaming Gender into Key CARICOM Programmes," Caribbean Community Secretariat, Georgetown, Guyana.

Bailey, B. (2003) "The Search for Gender Equity and Empowerment of Caribbean Women: The Role of Education," in Gemma Tang Nain and Barbara Bailey (eds), *Gender Equality in the Caribbean: Reality or Illusion?* Kingston: Ian Randle Publishers: 108–145.

Barbados Advocate (1993) "Will Girls Continue Dominance? Co-Education and Scholarship Performance," September 23: 32.

—— (2000) "No Girls Will Get On Board: Forde Strictly for Boys," March 2: 2.

Barriteau, E. (1998a) "Theorizing Gender Systems and the Project of Modernity in the

Twentieth Century Caribbean," *Feminist Review*, 59(Summer), Rethinking Caribbean Difference: 187–210.

—— (1998b) "Liberal Ideologies and Contradictions in Caribbean Gender Systems." Christine Barrow (ed.) *Caribbean Portraits: Essays on Gender Ideologies and Identities*, Kingston and Cave Hill: Ian Randle Publishers in Association with the Centre for Gender and Development Studies: 436–57.

—— (2000) "Examining the Issues of Men, Male Marginalisation and Masculinity in the Caribbean: Policy Implications", Working Paper No. 4, Cave Hill, Barbados: Center for Gender and Development Studies, University of the West Indies.

—— (2001) *The Political Economy of Gender in the Twentieth Century Caribbean*. London and New York: Palgrave International.

—— (2003) "Beyond a Backlash: The Frontal Assault on Containing Caribbean Women in the Decade of the 1990s," in Gemma Tang Nain and Barbara Bailey (eds), *Gender Equality in the Caribbean: Reality or Illusion?*, Kingston: Ian Randle Publishers: 201–32.

Barrow, C. (ed.) (1998) *Caribbean Portraits: Essays on Gender Ideologies and Gender Identities*, Kingston: Ian Randle Publishers and Centre for Gender and Development Studies.

Bennett, D. (2002) "Men 'Unfaired'", *Sunday Advocate*, March 24: 1.

Braidotti, R., E. Charkiewicz, S. Hausler and S. Wieringa (1994) *Women, the Environment and Sustainable Development: Towards a Theoretical Synthesis*, London: Zed Books in association with INSTRAW.

CEDAW (Committee on Elimination of Discrimination Against Women) (2002) "Equality in Barbados: 'Committee Points out Gap Between Aspirations, Achievements'," Press Release, WOM/1357, CEDAW 579th meeting, United Nations, August 13.

Chadha, K. (2000) "Male Marginalisation Clause Dropped," *The Hindustani Times Online*, Friday, April 21, New Delhi.

Chodorow, Nancy J. (1995) "Gender as a Personal and Cultural Construction", *Signs: Journal of Women in Culure and Society*, 20(3): 516–44.

Commonwealth Secretariat (n.d.) [1995?] *A Commonwealth Vision for Women Towards the Year 2000: The 1995 Commonwealth Plan of Action on Gender and Development*, London: Commonwealth Secretariat.

—— (1999a) *Gender Mainstreaming in the Public Service: A Reference Manual for Governments and Other Stakeholders*, London: Commonwealth Secretariat.

—— (1999b) *A Quick Guide to the Gender Management System*, London: Commonwealth Secretariat.

Commonwealth Secretariat/ECLAC-CDCC (2000) "Summary Report of the Regional Workshop on Gender Mainstreaming", Antigua and Barbuda, 2–4 May.

Daily Nation (1993) "Co-Ed Classes May Not be Best for Boys," July 16: 32.

—— (2002a) "Male Input Vital, Too," October 16: 30A.

—— (2002b) "Fall-Out from Report: UN Chides Barbados on Women's Progress," August 20: 5.

Denis, A.B. (2001) "Whither Work? A Comparative Analysis of Women and Work in the Commonwealth Caribbean and Canada", Working Paper No. 6, September, Cave Hill: Centre for Gender and Development Studies, University of the West Indies.

—— (2003) "Globalization, Women and (In)equity in the South: Constraint and Resistance in Barbados," *International Sociology*, 18(3): 491–512.

Ejimofor, P. (2002) "Help Men Too," *Daily Nation*, October 24: 1B.

Flax, Jane (1990) "Post Modernism and Gender Relations in Feminist Theory", in Linda J. Nicholson (ed.), *Feminism/Postmodernism*, New York: Routledge: 39–62.

Freeman, C. (2000) *High Tech and High Heels: Women, Work, and Pink Collar Identities in the Caribbean*, Durham, NC and London: Duke University Press.

Harris, S. (1999) "Study on Gender Main Streaming in Caribbean Sub Regional Countries," ECLAC-CDCC Third Caribbean Ministerial Conference on Women, Port of Spain, October.

Harris, Sonja (2003) "Review of Institutional Mechanisms for the Advancement of Women and for Achieving Gender Equality 1995–2000," in Gemma Tang Nain and Barbara Bailey (eds), *Gender Equality in the Caribbean: Reality or Illusion?*, Kingston: Ian Randle Publishers: 178–200.

Hawkesworth, Mary (1997) "Confounding Gender", *Signs: Journal of Women in Culture and Society*, 22(3): 649–85.

Kempadoo, K. (ed.) (1999) *Sun, Sex, and Gold: Tourism and Sex Work in the Caribbean*, London: Rowman & Littlefield.

Leo-Rhynie, E.B. Bailey and C. Barrow (eds) (1997) *Gender: A Caribbean Multi-disciplinary Perspective*, Kingston: Ian Randle Publishers.

Millington, J. (2003) "Fair Treatment for All Men Needed," *Barbados Advocate*, March 4: 3.

Mohammed, P. (1998a) "Editorial," *Feminist Review*, 59 (Summer), Rethinking Caribbean Difference: 1–4.

—— (1998b) "Towards Indigenous Feminist Theorizing in the Caribbean," *Feminist Review*, 59 (Summer), Rethinking Caribbean Difference: 6–33.

—— (2002) "Introduction: The Material of Gender," in Patricia Mohammed (ed.) *Gendered Realities Essays in Caribbean Feminist Thought*, Jamaica: University of the West Indies Press: xiv–xxiii.

Mohammed, P. and C. Shepherd (eds) (1988) *Gender in Caribbean Development*, Kingston: Women and Development Studies Project, University of the West Indies.

Momsen, J. (1987) "The Feminisation of Agriculture in the Caribbean," in J.H. Momsen and J. Townsend (eds), *Geography of Gender in the Third World*, New York: State University of New York Press: 344–7.

Mondesire, A. and L. Dunn (1995) *Toward Equity in Development. A Report on the Status of Women in Sixteen Caribbean Countries*, Guyana: Caribbean Community Secretariat.

Newton, V. (1984) *The Silver Men: West Indian Labour Migration to Panama 1850–1914*, Kingston: Institute of Social and Economic Research.

Nicholson, L. (1994) "Interpreting Gender", *Signs: Journal of Women in Culture and Society*, 22(3): 649–85.

Niles, B. (2000) "Boys Losing Their Way?" *Sunday Sun*, December 10: 14A.

Noel-Debique D. (2003) "Gender Equality and Women's Health in the Caribbean," in Gemma Tang Nain and Barbara Bailey (eds), *Gender Equality in the Caribbean: Reality or Illusion?*, Kingston: Ian Randle Publishers: 146–77.

Pargass, G. and R. Clarke (2003) "Violence Against Women: A Human Rights Issue," in Gemma Tang Nain and Barbara Bailey (eds), *Gender Equality in the Caribbean: Reality or Illusion?*, Kingston: Ian Randle Publishers: 39–72.

Safa, H. (1995) *The Myth of the Male Bread Winner: Women and Industrialization in the Caribbean*, Boulder, CO: Westview Press.

Scott, Joan W. (1986). "Gender: A Useful Category of Historical Analysis", *American Historical Review*, 91(5): 1053–75.

Seguino, S. (2002) "Why Are Women in the Caribbean so Much More Likely than Men to be Unemployed?" paper prepared for presentation at the Caribbean Studies Association Meeting, Nassau, Bahamas, May 27–June 1.

Sen, G. (1999) *Gender Mainstreaming in Finance: A Reference Manual for Governments and Other Stakeholders*, London: Commonwealth Secretariat.

Social and Economics Studies (1986) "Special Issues: Women in the Caribbean Project," *Social and Economics Studies*, 35(2–3).

Taitt, R. (2000) "Women Dominance Posing Serious Challenge Says PM," *Trinidad Express*, March 21, reported in *Gender Dialogue* (July 2000), ECLAC/CDCC, Port of Spain: 5.

Tang-Nain, G. and B. Bailey (eds) (2003) *Gender Equality in the Caribbean: Reality or Illusion*, Kingston: Ian Randle Publishers.

Trinidad Guardian (2000) "Men Belittled in Dominica – Minister," March 18: 7.

United Nations Development Program (1995) *Human Development Report 1995*, New York: Oxford University Press.

—— (1996) *Human Development Report 1996*, New York: Oxford University Press.

—— (1997) *Human Development Report 1997*, New York: Oxford University Press.

—— (1998) *Human Development Report 1998*, New York: Oxford University Press.

—— (1999) *Human Development Report 1999*, New York: Oxford University Press.

—— (2000) *Human Development Report 2000*, New York: Oxford University Press.

—— (2001) *Human Development Report 2001*, New York: Oxford University Press.

Vassell, L. (2003) "Women, Power and Decision-Making in CARICOM Countries: Moving Forward from a Post-Beijing Assessment," in Gemma Tang Nain and Barbara Bailey (eds), *Gender Equality in the Caribbean: Reality or Illusion?*, Kingston: Ian Randle Publishers: 1–38.

Weekend Nation (2000) "What Help for Men?" November 3: 33.

World Bank (2001) *Engendering Development: Through Gender Equality in Rights, Resources, and Voice*. World Bank Policy Research Report, New York: Oxford University Press.

13 "Disciplining" and "engendering" the World Bank

A comment[1]

Laura Parisi

There is considerable debate these days across and within many academic disciplines about what constitutes inter-, trans-, and multidisciplinary work and the value of such work. Although the authors of the chapters in this section, Disciplinary Paradigms/Development Paradigms, are loosely united in their viewpoint about the positive value and necessity of interdisciplinary work and perspectives, they also have rather different entry points into their evaluations of the World Bank's *Engendering Development* report. This comes as no surprise given the many feminist perspectives on scholarship, policy-making, and activism, and the authors' theoretical and methodological pluralism serves to underscore the importance and richness of such perspectives. Yet, as I suggest below, there are several discernible areas of agreement among the four authors with regards to the World Bank's approaches to gender and development. This analysis will highlight those connections, as well as raise additional questions for further consideration.

What does it mean to examine the World Bank's *Engendering Development* report as both an interdisciplinary project and as, to use its term, an "engender-ing" one? Although disciplines are usually thought of as knowledge organization systems, it is also the process of this knowledge organization that is of interest here, given the enormous impact the World Bank's systems of ordering have on inequalities in terms of causation, perpetration, and problem solving. The process by which the World Bank understands gender (in)equalities, for example, is deeply implicated in its primary discipline of economics, to the exclusion of many other disciplines. However, following Linda Tuhiwai Smith (1999: 67), the World Bank's relatively insulated disciplinary approach to development does not mean it is not deeply implicated in other disciplines (and vice versa), particularly those that share neo-liberal philosophic foundations. By way of analogy, one might think of the World Bank as a branch connected to the trunk of the Enlightenment tree whose roots are sustained by western philosophical traditions of liberal individualism, rights, and democracy.

Indeed, in the forward to *Engendering Development*, James Wolfensohn, the President of the World Bank, explains that the World Bank is concerned with two main issue areas with regards to gender and development: (1) Poverty, which perpetuates gender inequalities; and, (2) The extent to which these resultant gender inequalities undermine or slow down development (Wolfensohn 2001: xi). In his stated goal to promote gender equality in development, Wolfensohn does not question the current neo-liberal conceptualization of development itself nor its presumed "benefits." The authors of the subsequent preface also assume this stance, and commend the World Bank for taking on the difficult questions of gendered, religious, and cultural norms and moving these issues to the center of the policy dialogue (King and Mason 2001: xiii). They further map out the research methodology of the report, suggesting that it is multidisciplinary (not inter- or transdisciplinary, as is most feminist research), and "rigorous" (read: reliant on econometric studies to the exclusion of qualitative research). Both of these methodological claims, as we shall see below, extend the neo-classical/liberal project of the World Bank.

Disciplining knowledge

In their chapters, Suzanne Bergeron, Cynthia Wood, Violet Eudine Barriteau and Aida Orgocka and Gale Summerfield consider the World Bank's record with regards to multi- and interdisciplinary research. Bergeron does this through an analysis of the *Engendering Development* report more generally, Wood examines the World Bank's Structural Adjustment Policies (SAPs), Barriteau explores the limitations of gender mainstreaming in the Commonwealth Caribbean, and Orgocka and Summerfield focus specifically on chapter 4 ("Power, incentives, and resources in the household") of the report.

Suzanne Bergeron's chapter, "Colonizing knowledge", suggests that the World Bank's supposed paradigm shift from traditional neo-classical economic models of analysis to more inclusive, multidisciplinary approaches is limited at best. While it is true that the World Bank has begun to take gender (women? more on this question below) more seriously, she suggests that there has not been a fundamental theoretical or ideological transformation in the World Bank's perspectives on development. The title of Bergeron's chapter, "Colonizing knowledge," sums up the issue succinctly in that the World Bank extracts insights and ideas from other disciplines, such as anthropology, sociology, and political science, in so far as those disciplines help maintain and legitimize its central project of neo-liberal economic and political development. Thus, the central core around which development economics is founded is not fundamentally altered but repackaged and maintained. This process of knowledge extraction greatly mirrors colonization processes of states and institutions that seek to maintain their power, and subsequently, their legitimacy.

Wood's chapter on SAPs, Barriteau's chapter on gender mainstreaming in the Commonwealth Caribbean, and Orgocka and Summerfield's chapter on gender and intrahousehold decision-making make a similar claim to Bergeron's, although in slightly different ways. The authors suggest that the World Bank is also purposely ignoring whole sets of knowledge within the discipline of economics itself. In her examination of the World Bank's response to gender issues and SAPs, Wood uncovers a World Bank willing to engage with only those discourses and criticisms of SAPs that do not challenge the basic premise of the neo-classical paradigm that undergirds SAPs. As is well known, there is no dearth of research on gender and structural adjustment by feminist scholars, but because this research by and large challenges the neo-classical paradigm, it has generally been marginalized by the World Bank and other international financial institutions, as evidenced by the lack of public dialogue on the topic, as well the World Bank's conclusion in *Engendering Development* that women's equality has improved under SAPs . Instead, as Wood points out, the World Bank has engaged with other critiques, such as *Adjustment with a Human Face*, that are easily defined, contained, or incorporated within the neo-classical economic frame. Similarly, Orgocka and Summerfield argue that while the World Bank has shifted to incorporate some critiques on the unitary household model which originally served as a foundation of its development programs, it ignores relevant research from both economics (the capabilities approach) and other disciplines that would challenge the assumption that gender inequality in the household is really just a problem of resource allocation. Finally, Barriteau suggests that although the World Bank does incorporate some research from feminist economics and the gender and development literature, it does so in a selective way that excludes a sustained analysis of gendered ideologies, structures, and institutions that go beyond the simple positivist biological sex binary which frames the report. This results in oversimplified prescriptions that serve to promote sex equity in the existing neo-classical framework rather than strategies to dismantle the gendered hierarchies that are deeply embedded in and sustained by neo-classical economic theory and practice. All of these chapters reveal that this strategy of selective inclusion/exclusion around gender issues gives the World Bank the appearance of having taken feminist and other critical perspectives seriously without having redrawn the disciplinary borders of economics.

These authors' observation is an important one because it allows us to consider the extent to which the World Bank's (in)attention to gender, social, and cultural norms as well as to "multidisciplinarity" is politically motivated. For as Bessis (2003: 647–8) notes, the World Bank's focus on these issues may "serve goals other than that of women's emancipation" and it is important to take this idea seriously, as the World Bank's report is likely to viewed as an authoritative source on gender and development issues (Barriteau, this volume). It is no secret that World Bank policies, particularly structural adjustment policies, have been heavily criticized by many both within and outside the institution.[2] The discursive move of the World Bank to publicly proclaim its "paradigmatic shift" bears scrutiny, and commands our attention to the process by which the World Bank re-orders, reifies, and disperses understandings of gender, development, and structural adjustment. Bergeron's and Wood's reading of the World Bank's script on these issues reveals that in fact the World Bank has added additional acts to its development play but has not altered the neo-classical economic story line in any substantive way.

By identifying "appropriate" disciplines from which to draw upon, the World Bank has engaged in an ordering process of knowledge that has considerable consequences for both feminist research on gender and development issues as well as the recipients of such programs. As Bergeron notes, the World Bank has been willing and able to engage with disciplines that seem to further its goals and aims. The result of this disciplinary navigation is that the World Bank has decided which knowledge counts and is worthy of engagement, and which does not. By selectively incorporating research from the mainstream sectors of disciplines such as political science and sociology which have considerable investments of their own in upholding the neo-liberal paradigm, the World Bank avoids having to engage in a self-reflective process that would be required of it if it identified and took seriously the notion of "feminist studies" as a discipline, or at the very least, as an interdisciplinary or transdisciplinary process that by definition entails transformation of ordering systems.[3] At a minimum this would require the World Bank to question the neo-classical paradigm and acknowledge that this paradigm is fundamentally gendered in terms of its assumptions and outcomes (Barriteau, this volume). As all of the authors suggest, the retention of the neo-classical paradigm of economic development does not allow for a more revolutionary engagement with gender issues, one that would go far beyond the simple question posed by Wolfensohn (how should the World Bank rectify women's inequality so as to remove the barrier to economic development?) and the simple solution (by defining gender equality as "equality under the law, equality of opportunity, and equality of voice", page 35). The solution itself is deeply embedded in neo-liberal ideology with emphasis on equality under largely western androcentric notions of the law, opportunity structures, and political participation, all of which are not problematized by the World Bank's report, but have been critiqued at length by feminist scholars[4] in many of the other disciplines from which the World Bank extrapolates.

The World Bank's theoretical perspective on gender and development is also deeply intertwined with its methodological approaches, and it is to this topic I now turn.

Disciplining methodology

Smith (1999: 68) suggests that "the concept of a discipline is even more interesting when we think about it not simply as a way of organizing knowledge but also as a way of organizing people or bodies." By what method(s) does the World Bank organize people, especially women, in development theory and practice? The answer to this question requires an analysis of what the World Bank "sees" through its neo-classical, econometric, positivist lens. While all four authors have numerous points to make about the World Bank's epistemological and methodological approaches, I will discuss two major concerns here that reinforce the World Bank's neo-liberal, Enlightenment-derived paradigm – dualisms and over-reliance on econometric models.

The World Bank's implicit emphasis on positivism and explicit focus on econometric models locate women in very specific ways. Bergeron's analysis identifies a number of gendered dualisms in the World Bank's *Engendering Development* such as economic sphere–socio-cultural sphere, North–South, productive–reproductive labor, and so forth. In conjunction with essentialist assumptions about men and women, these dualisms privilege the male-identified spheres over the female-identified ones, thus rendering many women's bodies and activities marginal or invisible. This is no small implication given that the model of liberal individualism and agency is inextricable from masculinist ideology that underpins neo-classical economic understandings of both the public and private spheres.

For example, both Wood and Orgocka and Summerfield focus their discussions on the household and the private sphere to illustrate this point. From their point of view, the World Bank's neo-classical lens simply does not allow for a more complex reading and recognition of gender roles because of its privileging of formal economic activity over reproductive or domestic labor. Wood notes that the neo-classical economic paradigm constrains the World Bank to locating and defining women's activities purely in economic and market terms, with no recognition that unpaid domestic labor is in fact affected by SAPs. Thus, this framing upholds the artificial and gendered hierarchy of the public–private, and identifies women as economic actors only in accordance with a masculinist conception of labor. As such, this does not bring gender issues to the center of the discussion as the World Bank claims, rather it seeks to integrate women into a very limited set of theoretical parameters that rests heavily on gendered dualisms. In this way, the World Bank's lens on the development is still market-based, not gender-based because as Wood suggests, this would entail the recognition that unpaid domestic labor is "central to understanding gender bias in adjustment" in the first place.

Orgocka and Summerfield's discussion of intrahousehold bargaining highlights a similar concern to Wood's in that they suggest that even when the World Bank does look at women's agency in households, it overemphasizes both micro-credit and education as the solutions to empowerment. Micro-credit and education are economic growth and market strategies to move women out of households into the paid labor force, which can be counted in terms of assessing a country's level of development. Orgocka and Summerfield argue that the World Bank's insistence on using econometric models to study gender, household, and development distort and confine its analysis to the parameters of neo-classical economics. Therefore, both the ideological and methodological approach of neo-classical economics defines and promotes policies within this narrow framework, which misses many important gendered dynamics of households. Orgocka and Summerfield offer an alternative interdisciplinary qualitative methodology grounded in the capacities approach that ruptures the traditional positivist binary subject–object assumptions of econometric modeling. Their case study of negotiations between immigrant Muslim mothers and daughters (rather than between husband and wives which would be the typical World Bank approach to the study of gender and households) living in the United States about sex education programs reminds us of the necessity of building inclusive knowledges that are truly gender-focused and "countertopographic" in analytically tying together different places and spaces in way that econometric models cannot capture (McIlwaine and Datta 2003: 373).

Barriteau also uses her case study of the Caribbean as a tool for critiquing the World Bank's epistemological assumptions and methodological approaches. Barriteau rightly contests the World Bank's disciplinary grouping of the Commonwealth Caribbean with Latin America, as this has important implications for how gender relations are understood in the Commonwealth Caribbean. Barriteau's analysis of gender mainstreaming in the Commonwealth Caribbean reveals that the World Bank's methodological emphasis on inputs, such as resource allocation, to the exclusion of outputs does little to alter structural and systemic gendered hierarchies. She uses the UNDP data (the UNDP in turn often uses data produced by the World Bank) to illustrate her point about how although numerically there appears to be little sex inequity in terms of "rights, opportunities, and voice," this binary juxtaposition of men vs. women tells us little about how gendered ideologies play out in the Commonwealth Caribbean context. Rather, Barriteau's analysis points to the importance of framing the study and practice of gender and development as an issue of oppression, rather than as an issue of sex discrimination which permeates the World Bank's report. Indeed, as Iris Marion Young (1992: 177) reminds us, "oppression often exists in the absence of overt discrimination."

Like Orgocka and Summerfield, Barriteau suggests that a more holistic approach to challenging the ideological and material systems that produced gendered inequalities in the first place would be to take seriously women's autonomy and capacity to lead the kind of lives they want to lead. That is, a gendered lens focused on agency would allow us to attend to the all important aspect of power, which cannot be captured in the World Bank's emphasis on gender mainstreaming.

Conclusion

Ultimately, as Barriteau points out, the World Bank's neo-classical/liberal ideology and methods cannot address in a serious way questions about power which is central to exploding and transforming gendered binaries. The World Bank's approach serves to reify masculinist neo-classical/liberal ideology under the guise of promoting gender equality and as a result, the World Bank's approach can tell us little about gender oppression in development.

Indeed, in my view, even the term "Engendering" in the title of the report diverts attention away from truly centralizing the intersections of gender, race/ethnicity, class, and sexuality in the development dialogue, since engendering also means "facilitating" or "enabling." The World Bank's report, as all of the authors in this section note, is focused on the notion of facilitating and promoting neo-classical economic development rather than actually gendering development. By confusing biological sex with gender, the process by which the World Bank constructs and locates women in terms of a (multi)disciplinary project harks back to the era of Women in Development frameworks, which sought to include women in existing development projects without fundamentally challenging the notion of development itself.

In addition, attaching the development discourse to a notion of gender equality that is rights-based frames inequality as a question of sex discrimination rather than gender oppression. Yet, this also serves to show how deeply implicated neo-classical economics is in other disciplines informed by western neo-liberalism to promote and sell a view of the world that normalizes hegemonic masculinity and its attendant structural inequalities. Thus, for the World Bank to seriously address the issue of gender inequalities, it must be willing to challenge not only the neo-classical economic assumptions of development but also its theoretical linkages to neo-liberal democracy, which also exacerbates gender inequalities.[5] As all of the authors of this section suggest, the only way to engage in this challenge as a transformative process is to truly move the analytic and relational concepts of gender, race/ethnicity, class, and sexuality to the center of analysis, rather than just adding the variable of women to the neo-classical/liberal pot of development and stirring. Only then will the disciplinary boundaries of "development" be redrawn.

Notes

1 I would like to thank the editors, Drucilla Barker and Edith Kuiper, for inviting me to comment on the chapters for this section, "Disciplinary Paradigms/Development Paradigms," and for their helpful suggestions on an earlier draft of my comment. Any remaining errors, of course, are attributable solely to me.
2 Yet, interestingly enough, Joseph Stiglitz's scathing indictment of structural adjustment in his book, *Globalization and its Discontents* (2003), mentions women only once – in the preface.
3 This is not to say that the World Bank ignores all feminist scholarship. However, it tends to be highly selective in its application of feminist scholarship, leaning towards those studies that employ the use of econometrics, thereby limiting the scope of feminist scholarship it considers.
4 See, for example, essays in Cook (1994), Peters and Wolpers (1995).
5 For an excellent discussion of the "immunity" of the concept of neo-liberal democracy from critical scrutiny in the social sciences, see Hawkesworth (2001).

References

Bessis, S. (2003) "International Organizations and Gender: New Paradigms and Old Habits," *Signs*, 29: 633–47.

Cook, R. (ed.) (1994) *Human Rights of Women: National and International Perspectives*, Philadelphia, PA: University of Pennsylvania Press.

Hawkesworth, M. E. (2001) "Democratization: Reflections on Gendered Dislocations in the Public Sphere," in R.M. Kelly, J.H. Bayes, M.E. Hawkesworth and B. Young (eds), *Gender, Globalization, and Democratization*, Lanham and Oxford: Rowman & Littlefield.

King, E.M. and A.D. Mason (2001) "Preface," in World Bank, *Engendering Development: Through Gender Equality in Rights, Resources, and Voice*, Washington, DC and New York: World Bank and Oxford University Press.

McIlwaine, C. and K. Datta (2003) "From Feminising to Engendering Development," *Gender, Place, and Culture*, 10: 369–82.

Peters, J. and A. Wolper (eds) (1995) *Women's Rights, Human Rights: International Feminist Perspectives*, New York and London: Routledge.

Smith, L.T. (1999) *Decolonizing Methodologies: Research and Indigenous Peoples*, London and New York: Zed Books.

Stiglitz, J.E. (2003) *Globalization and Its Discontents*, New York: W.W. Norton & Company.

Wolfensohn, J. (2001) "Foreword," in World Bank, *Engendering Development: Through Gender Equality in Rights, Resources, and Voice*, Washington, DC and New York: World Bank and Oxford University Press.

World Bank (2001) *Engendering Development: Through Gender Equality in Rights, Resources, and Voice*, Washington, DC: World Bank.

Young, I.M. (1992) "Five Faces of Oppression," in T.E. Wartenberg (ed.), *Rethinking Power*, New York: SUNY Press.

Part IV

Explorations

Future directions of feminist
economic research

14 A seat at the table

Feminist economists negotiate development[1]

Drucilla K. Barker

From its inception economic development has affected women and men differently. The pernicious effects of economic development strategies, and of the structural adjustment policies (SAPs) that followed them, on poor women have been well documented (Benería and Feldman 1992; Sen and Grown 1987; Elson 1991). So it is curious that the World Bank report, *Engendering Development: Through Equality in Rights, Resources, and Voice* (World Bank 2001), advocates the empowerment of women as necessary for economic development and the eradication of poverty. "Poverty exacerbates gender disparities" and "gender inequalities hinder development" (ibid.: xi). The message to the development community is to find the types of strategies that promote gender equity and hence foster more effective development.

In many ways *Engendering Development* should be good news for feminist economists since it creates a space for feminist economists to constructively engage with the World Bank and other national and international development institutions. Yet, as many of the chapters in this volume show, when the goals of feminist progress are seemingly commensurable with the goals of an international institution such as the World Bank we must cast a critical eye on such engagements. This critical gaze, must, of course, include an exploration of our own intentions and goals, positions and interests.[2] In this short comment, I will examine the ways in which feminist economists and other social researchers have engaged with development institutions and the methodological challenges this entails.

Feminist economic interventions

Feminist economists were examining the differential effects of poverty, development, international trade, and international finance even before the field "feminist economics" was named. The 1970 publication of Ester Boserup's monumental work, *Women's Roles in Economic Development*, marked the beginning of academic interest in these issues. The United Nations became involved as a result of the convergence of interests of two different groups of women, the UN Commission on the Status of Women and the women's movement in the US (Tinker 1990). The UN group was primarily interested in legal and educational equality for women, while feminists in the US women's movement were primarily interested in equal pay and equal employment. As their interests converged, the UN declared 1975 the Year of the Woman, and marked this with a world conference in Mexico City. Subsequently, 1976 to 1985 was designated by the UN as the Decade for Women with two more conferences, one in Copenhagen in 1980 and one in Nairobi in 1985. (A decade later the Fourth World Conference was held in Beijing and in 2000 Beijing Plus Five was held in New York City.) The theme for the decade was Equality-Development-Peace.[3]

This theme reflected a commitment to promoting equality between women and men, to fully integrating women into development efforts, and to strengthening women's contributions to world peace. The importance of women's participation in the development process as both agents and beneficiaries was stressed during the 1980 mid-decade Copenhagen conference, and again in the 1986 Nairobi conference. During this period the emphasis on women and development was firmly established. As Lucille Mathurin Mair, secretary-general of the Copenhagen conference, writes, "'Women in Development' became the Decade's catchphrase, a seductive one, which for a time at least, could evade the question of what kind of development women were to be drawn into" (quoted in Tinker 1990: 31).

It was not long before the answer to this question become painfully clear. The progressive strategies advocated by the UN, to fight inequalities, economic exploitation, and women's oppression, were accompanied by another set of policy changes taking place at the World Bank. Beginning in 1981, the Bank replaced its focus on basic infrastructure and human resource development with an emphasis on structural adjustment policies (Tzannatos, this volume). Whereas early development theorists saw tradition as the principal impediment to economic development, the proponents of structural adjustment viewed governments as the main problem. SAPs were premised on the notion that countries could return to economic health and repair their economies only if they reduced the size and influence of government on economic activity and opened their markets to international trade and finance (Kukreja 2001). The effects on the poor, and especially on poor women, were predictably egregious: massive impoverishment, food insecurity, financial crises, and environmental degradation.

These policies were introduced with the cooperation and assent of the neo-classical economics community, a community that reveres mathematics as its methodological foundation and neoliberalism as its ethical and philosophical cornerstone. SAPs reflected neoclassical thinking, particularly its emphasis on the notion of economic efficiency, or Pareto optimality, as the central evaluative criterion for judging economic policies. Economic efficiency implicitly assumes that measures of economic well-being can be collapsed into a single metric, that all values are commensurable, and that all human needs can be met through a type of market exchange. These assumptions privilege market activities and obscure the significance of unpaid reproductive labor/caring labor activities

(Barker 1995). Feminist economists were quick to demonstrate that such activities need to be valued appropriately or economics models will be misleading (Elson 1991; Benería 1999).

Diane Elson demonstrated that the implicit assumption behind many structural adjustment models was that the reproductive labor necessary to maintain and reproduce the labor force would be provided independently of its valuation and compensation. Without feminist analysis the full economic costs of structural adjustment were seriously underestimated. Structural adjustment required government spending cutbacks on health, education, and other social services. As public provisioning was reduced, families had to provide these services for themselves or go without them altogether. Costs were shifted from the monetized public sector to the non-monetized household sector. Policy-makers apparently assumed that there was an unlimited supply of women's labor available to compensate for the reduction in public sector social services. Since the value of household labor was not officially accounted for (and still isn't), these costs were hidden (Elson 1991). The bulk of these costs fall mainly on women and girls, as they increase their paid and unpaid working hours. As Cynthia Wood demonstrates, the Bank continues to marginalize women's unpaid household labor (Wood, this volume).

The end of the UN Decade for Women also saw the first publication of the classic monograph, *Development, Crisis, and Alternative Visions,* by Gita Sen and Caren Grown. Sen and Grown argued that since women's contributions as workers and managers of human welfare were central to the ability of households, communities, and nations to survive, national and international economic policies needed to start from the perspective of poor, Third World women (Sen and Grown 1987). They were absolutely correct, and their prescription is no less necessary now. The question is, how are scholars and policy-makers, located as they are in the elite reaches of the academy, governments, NGOs, and international organizations like the World Bank, to discern what this perspective is.

For Sen and Grown the answer lies in an examination of economic development strategies in terms of their effects on the abilities of the poor to meet their basic needs and on the abilities of poor women to gain access to economic resources and political power. This work was informed by at least a year of debates and discussions with scholars, activists, and policy-makers all over the world. Recognizing the diversity of women in terms of their social positions in terms of ethnicity, class, and nation, they posited a vision of diverse feminism that could respond to the needs and concerns of different women, as "*defined by them for themselves*" (ibid.: 19, emphasis in the original). The unity of diverse groups of women was to be built on women's common gender oppression that follows from the sexual division of labor.

Fight to Δ Patriarchal Institutions

Feminist dilemmas

The notion that women's labor constitutes a common gender oppression has been widely criticized (Hirshman 1995; Barker 1998; Mohanty 1991, 2003; Charusheela 2003). But of course, Sen and Grown were confronting the perennial feminist dilemma, which is to reconcile the supposed universal nature of gender subordination and the oppression of women by patriarchal systems and masculinist ideology with the diversity of women's social positions and attendant oppressions. For poor women in the global South this dilemma takes a particular form. Women are either accused of not being feminist enough because they are unwilling to separate struggles against gender subordination from struggles against other oppressions, or they are accused of being too feminist and dividing class struggles or nationalist struggles by following the dictates of Western feminism (Sen and Grown 1987). Is there any other way of theorizing this dilemma?

Considering gender as an ideological as well as an empirical category provides an important starting point. Using gender as an empirical category enables researchers to examine and measure the gender division of labor (which jobs are done by women and which ones are done by men); the gendered distribution of resources (to what extent do women have access to existing resources); and the gendered impact of new resources coming into the system (to what extent do women have access to new resources) (Cloud 2003). Considering the ideological dimensions of gender allows different questions to be asked and relations of power to be examined. As Violet Eudine Barriteau has pointed out, the ideological dimensions of gender entail power relations that privilege masculinity and uphold unjust political/economic hierarchies (Barriteau, this volume). Or as V. Spike Peterson puts it, feminism is not only about empowering women, but also a "transformative critique of hierarchies that are linked and ideologically 'naturalized' by denigration of the feminine" (Peterson 2003: 28). Gender casts the subordinate – women as well as economically, racially, and culturally marginalized men – as "other" and naturalizes hierarchy and domination. The denigration of the feminine naturalizes domination and "*produces even as it obscures* vast inequalities of power, authority and resource distribution" (ibid.: 28, emphasis in the original).

Cynthia Enloe similarly argues that struggles against oppressions based on class, race, ethnicity, and nation must begin with dismantling patriarchal norms (Enloe 2000). Women's cooperation with other systems of oppression is enhanced by their conformity to local gender norms. For example, women are the preferred labor force in export processing zones because they are perceived to be docile, obedient, compliant and have "nimble fingers." Local patriarchal norms enforce/ encourage these traits in women. Resistance, organizing, alliances, and so forth require acting against gender norms. These sorts of analyses show that feminism, understood as the dismantling of gender norms and gender privilege, is a necessary part of any struggle for social and economic justice.

The feminist theorist Chandra Mohanty provides another entry point for theorizing feminist tensions. Like Sen and Grown, she advocates anchoring feminist analyses in "the place of the most marginalized communities of women

– poor women of all colors in the affluent and neocolonial nations; women of the Third World/South or Two Thirds World" (Mohanty 2003: 510). Her position is based on feminist standpoint theory and explicitly assumes causal links between marginalized social locations and the ability to explain and analyze features of capitalist societies. This epistemological commitment is not, however, necessary for my purposes here. It is only necessary to notice that privilege nurtures indifference to those without the same privileges.[4] Beginning from the lives of poor and marginalized communities of women reads "*up the ladder of privilege*" (ibid.: 511, emphasis added) and reveals the politics of knowledge and the power investments that accompany it. The idea of reading up, of theorizing the embeddedness of the local and particular within the global and universal is the crucial point here.

A recent essay by Christine Koggel provides an example of this approach in feminist economics. She weaves together analyses by Chandra Mohanty, Maria Mies, Elisabeth Fussell, Ruth Pearson, Diane Elson, and Linda Lim, to concretely demonstrate the ways in which local sites of power and oppression are shaped by the global forces of capitalism (Koggel 2003).[5] Building on the well-established fact that the high degree of mobility enjoyed by transnational corporations enables them to quickly move their production operations to countries characterized by low wages and business-friendly political regimes, she shows that economic dominance in local labor markets gives multinational corporations the power to determine both who gets to work and *the social norms and perceptions of the work itself*. While social norms and perceptions are specific to local contexts, they are shaped by global forces. Examining the specific characteristics of the global/local linkages makes visible the economic, political, and cultural spaces in which women (and, I would add, men) can negotiate and implement policies that mitigate the power of global capital. Revealing and dismantling gender hierarchies is integral to this project.

Power and privilege in feminist economics

Power, as Foucault has argued, is both a condition of subjection and the field through which subjectivity is constituted. Individuals are not only the subjects of power, but also its articulation (Foucault 1980). Power in this sense is diffuse, omnipresent, and manifested through social practices and institutions. Thus, the modernist position in which the intellectual – embedded within social institutions of power and control – could still step outside of power and find a neutral vantage point from which to take an ethical, oppositional stand will no longer suffice (Sandoval 2000).

Feminist economists are embedded in a network of power relations by virtue of their connection to economics, a discipline that calls itself the "queen of the social sciences." The power and prestige of economics is not to be underestimated. Economics, particularly neoclassical economics (the type of analyses taught in most undergraduate economics courses, extolled in publications such as the *New York Times* and the *Wall Street Journal*, and lauded by national and international politicians and policy-makers) is widely considered to be objective, gender-neutral, and value-free. Its pronouncements are couched in the same terms as natural laws, and the "laws of supply and demand" are accorded the same status as the law of gravity. The scientific status of economics depends crucially on its methods of inquiry: methodological individualism, rational choice theory, and mathematical modeling.

Although feminist economists contest the notion that explanations based on methodological individualism and rational choice theory are the best way to achieve scientific rigor and objectivity, most are committed to the notion of scientific inquiry. That is, they are committed to transforming economics by including gender, race, ethnicity, and nation as categories of analysis, while at the same time retaining the scientific character and status of economics. This commitment is motivated not only by self-interest – becoming established in the profession, attaining tenure, and publishing in top journals – but also a genuine desire to pursue knowledge that will materially help the lives of women, especially poor women. Feminist economists want a seat at the table – at the IMF, the World Bank, the WTO, the United Nations, and the academy. They want to challenge the hegemony of neoclassical economics by demonstrating that economic models that do not account for gender are biased and incomplete.

Feminist economists have had only limited success in challenging the hegemony and prestige of neoclassical economics. We are not alone here. Marxists, institutionalists, post-Keynesians, and other heterodox schools have likewise had little success in this endeavor. And it is most likely the case that no amount of "better" science and analysis will ever replace the pseudo scientism that characterizes neoclassical economics. This is because neoclassical economics does one thing very, very well – it articulates the ideology of contemporary capitalism in a manner that makes it seem natural, inevitable, and beneficent. Neoclassical economics does not "speak truth to power," but on the contrary, accommodates and naturalizes it. This raises the question of whether it is possible to articulate analyses that reveal, resist, and transform power while at the same time working within those very structures of power – the academy, governments, and transnational organizations like the World Bank.

This question can be framed in terms of Audre Lorde's famous metaphor: can we use the master's tools to dismantle the master's house?[6] Or put another way, can we transform the master's house while simultaneously living in it? The political scientist Kathleen Staudt notes that though World Bank is surely one of the master's houses, there are many other institutions designed and sustained by the masters such as "families, workplaces, universities . . . and NGOs" where feminists live, work, and exercise some degree of agency (Staudt 2002: 57). These are the places to work for change and transformation. Staudt argues that engagement in the master's house, or the politics of the inside, complements strategies that place on the outside. The challenge is for insiders and outsiders to work together. Professionals, busy at work on computers in air-conditioned offices, can not effect change unless they form relationships with people involved in alliances and coalitions that produce material results.

These relationships, Staudt argues, may be murky and compromised and require multiple discourses and languages to forge collaborations that move policies, institutions, and budgets (ibid.). Likewise, feminist economics requires a pluralistic approach to methodology that facilitates critical evaluations of the dialectic between power and knowledge, between the effects of social, cultural, and political values on knowledge production and between the material and the symbolic. This does not mean that feminist economists should give up either the tools or prestige of economics. To resist and transform power and work for social change, we need to speak the language of power, in this case the language of neoclassical economics as well as the language of feminism.

The lack of time and resources as well as the marginalization and degradation of feminist economic views and arguments is a significant problem here. As Staudt notes, concerns about women and gender are rarely central even in relatively progressive organizations (ibid.). Feminist economists suffer from a lack of professional recognition and funding for feminist research. Since they are vastly underrepresented in academic departments and other professional venues, they pursue their work in relative isolation. This makes it extraordinary difficult to find the voice and courage necessary to advance alternative feminist visions. Moreover, it is not enough just to produce better work, because the elite status and hegemonic influence of mainstream economics stems not from its superior fidelity to the real, but rather from its connection to power. It is this connection that makes feminist struggle so difficult.

Concluding remarks

The question remains as to whether the instrumental vision of gender equality put forth by a transnational institution such as the World Bank can ever really be commensurable with feminist goals and aspirations. Author Andrew Mason's press conference remarks shortly after the publication of *Engendering Development* are telling here. He responded to feminist criticism that the Bank does not go far enough in criticizing specific cultural practices that oppress women by saying that the Bank is working toward building a policy dialog at the highest levels of government with the most repressive attitudes toward women (Moline 2002). In other words, it is the best they could do. Unfortunately, the best is not good enough. As the other chapters in this volume have amply demonstrated, the World Bank's commitment to gender equity is tenuous at best. SAPs, which are arguably the biggest impediment to the well-being of poor girls and women in the developing world, are barely mentioned. It is clear, however, that the gender policies advocated by the Bank amply serve the needs of transnational capital and have the blessing of the international financial community. It remains to the feminist community to build alliances between women in the North and women in the South, between women in the cities and women in the countryside, and between women who enjoy the privileges of education and wealth, and women not so fortunate, so that we may continue to work in effective ways for gender equity and social justice.

Notes

1   I would like to thank Edith Kuiper, Laura Parisi, and the Faculty Writing Workshop at Hollins University for their help comments and suggestion on earlier drafts.
2   As the feminist philosopher Lorraine Code puts it, self-critique reveals the ways in which an author's position and interests contributes to the production of knowledge and hence challenges the notion of "timeless, placeless universality"(Code 1995: 2).
3   The terms were in the Forward-looking Strategies for the Advancement of Women at the 1985 Nairobi conference. See the "Report of the World Conference to Review and Appraise the Achievements of the United Nations Decade for Women: Equality, Development and Peace" (United Nations 1986).
4   Mohanty's exact statement is that "privilege nurtures blindness to those without the same privilege" (Mohanty 2002: 510). I have chosen to paraphrase Mohanty's comments for two reasons. First, in respect for my friend and colleague Darla Schumm, I try not to privilege sight as a metaphor for sympathy and empathy. Second, I wanted to escape the epistemological commitment entailed by the metaphor of blindness.
5   Koggel's purpose in this essay is to provide a critique of Sen's empiricist account of women's empowerment through paid work (Koggel 2003).
6   The exact quote is "The master's tools will never dismantle the master's house" (Lorde 1984: 112).

References

Barker, Drucilla K. (1995) "Economists, Social Reformers and Prophets: A Feminist Critique of Economic Efficiency," *Feminist Economics*, 1(3): 26–39.
—— (1998) "Dualisms, Discourse, and Development," *Hypatia*, 13(3): 83–94.
Benería, Lourdes (1999) "Structural Adjustment Policies," in Janice Peterson and Margaret Lewis (eds), *The Elgar Companion to Feminist Economics*, Cheltenham and Northampton, MA: Edward Elgar: 687–95.
Benería, Lourdes and Shelley Feldman (eds) (1992) *Unequal Burden: Economic Crises, Persistent Poverty, and Women's Work*, Boulder, CO, San Francisco CA, and Oxford: Westview Press.
Boserup, Esther (1970) *Women's Roles in Economic Development*, London: George Allen and Unwin.
Charusheela, S. (2003) "Empowering Work? Bargaining Models Reconsidered," in Drucilla K. Barker and Edith Kuiper (eds), *Toward a Feminist Philosophy of Economics*, London and New York: Routledge: 287–303.
Cloud, Kathleen (2003) "Modeling Gender," iaffe-l. Online posting, available e-mail: http://www.carleton.ca/lists (13 September).
Code, Lorraine (1995) *Rhetorical Spaces: Essays on Gendered Locations*, New York and London: Routledge: Chapter 1.
Elson, Diane (1991) "Male Bias in Macro-economics: The Case of Structural Adjustment," in Diane Elson (ed.), *Male Bias in the Development Process*, Manchester and New York: Manchester University Press: 164–90.
Enloe, Cynthia (2000) *Bananas, Beaches and Bases: Making Sense of International Politics*, 2nd edn, Berkeley, CA, Los Angeles, CA and London: University of California Press.
Foucault, Michel (1980) "Truth and Power," in Colin Gordon (ed.), Colin Gordon, Leo Marshall, John Mepham, Kate Solper (trans.), *Power/Knowledge: Selected Interviews*

and Other Writings 1972–1977 by Michel Foucault, New York: Pantheon Books: 78–108.

Hirschman, Mitu (1995) "Women and Development: A Critique," in Jane L. Parpart and Marianne H. Marchand (eds), *Feminism/Postmodernism/Development*, London and New York: Routledge: 42–55.

Koggel, Christine M. (2003) "Globalization and Women's Paid Work: Expanding Freedom?" *Feminist Economics*, 9(2 and 3): 163–84.

Kukreja, Sunil (2001) "The Two Faces of Development," in David N. Balaam and Michael Veseth (eds), *Introduction to International Political Economy*, second edition, Upper Saddle River, NJ: Prentice Hall: 320–45.

Lorde, Audre (1984) *Sister Outsider*, Berkeley, CA: Crossing Press.

Mohanty, Chandra Talpade (1991) "Under Western Eyes: Feminist Scholarship and Colonial Discourses," in Chandra Talpade Mohanty, Ann Russo and Lourdes Torres (eds), *Third World Women and the Politics of Feminism*, Bloomington and Indianapolis, IN: Indiana University Press: 51–80.

—— (2003) "'Under Western Eyes' Revisited: Feminist Solidarity Through Anticapitalist Struggles," *Signs*, 28(2): 499–536.

Moline, Ann (2002) "World Bank to Rate All Projects for Gender Impact," *WEnews*, April 4. Available http://www.womensenews.org/article.cfm/dyn/aid/866/context/archive (accessed 26 April 2004).

Peterson, Spike V. (2003) *A Critical Rewriting of Global Political Economy: Integrating Reproductive, Productive and Virtual Economies*, London and New York: Routledge.

Sandoval, Chela (2000) *Methodology of the Oppressed*, Minneapolis, MN and London: University of Minneapolis Press.

Sen, Gita and Caren Grown (1987) *Development, Crises, and Alternative Visions: Third World Women's Perspectives*, New York: Monthly Review Press.

Staudt, Kathleen (2002) "Dismantling the Master's House with the Master's Tools? Gender Work in and with Powerful Bureaucracies," in Kriemild Saunders (ed.), *Feminist Post-Development Thought: Rethinking Modernity, Postcolonialism, and Representation*, London and New York: Zed Books: 57–68.

Tinker, Irene (1990) "The Making of a Field: Advocates, Scholars and Practitioners," in Irene Tinker (ed.), *Persistent Inequalities: Women and World Development*, New York and Oxford: Oxford University Press: 27–53.

United Nations (1986) "Report of the World Conference to Review and Appraise the Achievements of the United Nations Decade For Women: Equality, Development and Peace," Nairobi, 15–26 July 1985, United Nations, New York. Available http://www.un.org/womenwatch/confer/nfls/Nairobi1985report.txt (accessed 1 July 2004).

World Bank (2001) *Engendering Development: Through Gender Equality in Rights, Resources, and Voice*, Washington, DC: World Bank; Oxford: Oxford University Press.

15 Why feminist economists should pay more attention to the coherence between the World Bank and the WTO[1]

Mariama Williams

Over the years feminist economists have devoted considerable time and resources in exploring the relationship between gender and macroeconomic theory and policy. This work has extended to areas of fiscal policy (for example, gender budgets), monetary and financial policy, and, lately, trade policy and trade agreements. In the former cases, the institutional focus of attention has been national governments, regional development banks, the International Monetary Fund (IMF or the Fund), and the World Bank (or the Bank), given their critical role in the design, formulation, and implementation of these policy areas. In the area of trade, attention has focused on the World Trade Organization (WTO) as well as regional trade arrangements.

However, while the attention of feminist economic theoretical and policy-oriented analyses has been focused on the policies of the International Financial Institutions (IFIs) and, more recently, the WTO, individually, there has not been much critical analysis, diagnosis, and prescriptions focused on the joint interaction of these two set of institutions who are increasingly coordinating their activities towards ensuring consistency and complementarity in international economic policy-making.

This interaction is occurring under a formal framework of "coherence," underpinned by a set of coherence agreements (CA) between the WTO, the Fund and the Bank. While the coherence framework (CF) involves both informal and formal mechanisms as well as other parties[2] such as the International Trade Center, UNCTAD and UNDP, the coherence agreement refers to sets of co-operation agreements and memorandum of understanding signed between the IMF and the WTO, on the one hand, and the WTO and the Bank, on the other. Under the coherence framework trade liberalization is now becoming the foundation underpinning the determination of the substantive issues of the development cooperation, trade, and macroeconomic policy agendas, as well as in helping to shape the contours of such policy shifts.

While the promotion of trade liberalization has been a key aspect of World Bank- and IMF-inspired Structural Adjustment Programs implemented in the developing countries, especially since the 1980s, it has mainly occurred in the form of policy prescriptions and as part of loan conditionalities. However, trade liberalization under the WTO is legally binding and subject to a powerful dispute settlement mechanism. Furthermore, because of the legalistic nature of the WTO agreements they are not easily reversible and therefore act as significant constraints on national policy flexibility. WTO agreements are also increasingly reaching "behind the borders" into areas of domestic regulations and policy concerns. Thus, trade agreements of the WTO and the trade liberalization agenda it is pursuing are spreading beyond the traditional confines of the foreign policy domain and intruding more directly in areas of national macroeconomic and social policy.

On its own trade liberalization has specific economic, political, and social effects, which would pose particular problems for the men and women located in the export and import sensitive sectors of developing and developed countries' economies. And, so trade liberalization, *per se*, would be a cause for looking at how female and male economic actors in these spheres are faring *vis-à-vis* changes in trade policy regimes oriented towards the reduction and elimination of import barriers (import liberalization). But today, trade liberalization also engenders a wide range of changes in domestic regulatory processes and industrial and social policies.

At the sectoral level, agricultural liberalization has implication for men's and women's access to food and sustainable livelihoods. Services liberalization impacts access to water, health care, and electricity, which are essential for social reproduction. Intellectual property rights agreements such as the trade-related intellectual property rights agreement (TRIPS) impact access to affordable medicines, which are critical for men's and women's health and morbidity. Through its potentially adverse implications on technological transfer, TRIPS also poses serious problems for long-term economic development.

These actual and potential impacts of trade policy and trade agreements on all areas of men's and women's daily lives raise a number of critical questions, concerns, and serious reservations by some governments, civil society, and some international institutions on the nature of this coherence, which appears to be biased towards implementing WTO rules and ensuring that countries promote trade liberalization. What is the nature and impact of coherence on economic and social development? What is the impact and implications for gender equality objectives of these policies? What is the operating principle behind coherence – is it in alignment with international human rights documents such as the Convention on Economic, Social and Cultural rights, the Convention on the Elimination of Discrimination Against Women (CEDAW), the Convention on the Rights of the Child, etc.? How will it foster the achievement of inter-nationally agreed goals and targets such as the Millennium Development Goals and International Development targets,[3] especially around gender equality, women's empowerment, and poverty eradication?

These issues pose at least two sets of challenges to the future development of feminist economics analysis, policy prescriptions, and research as they relate to the international political economy. The first set of challenges, which has already been taken on by existing feminist research and activists agenda, revolves around the validity and necessity of incorporating critical gender perspective and analysis as a cross-cutting issue both in the substantive areas of trade agreement as well as in the general area of the governance of the multilateral trading system. The second set of challenges, which has not yet been incorporated in feminist work programs, has to do with critical gender-sensitive analysis and policy prescriptions around the coherence agenda. These concern the impact of market access[4] and trade liberalization on critical areas that in the trade debate are identified as "non-trade concerns": food security, public health, rural livelihood and development, environment, and labor conditions. Gender and trade advocates are working to integrate gender as one of the cross-cutting issues within this debate.

The nature and dynamics of IMF–WB–WTO coherence

The Uruguay Round of Trade agreements which concluded in 1994 transformed the limited General Agreement on Tariffs and Trade (GATT 1947), which was the set of rules that governed the multilateral trading system since the 1940s, into a more comprehensive, legalistic, and binding framework (GATT 1994).[5] It also extended multilateral trade rules into the areas of services (the General Agreement on Trade in Service, GATS), intellectual property rights (the trade-related intellectual property rights agreement, TRIPs), as well as incorporating agricultural trade (the agreement on agriculture, AOA) under multilateral trade rules. The Uruguay Round culminated in the coming into force, in 1995, of the World Trade Organization. The WTO was established[6] as a permanent negotiation forum and to supervise the implementation of the Uruguay Round and subsequent rounds of trade agreements. Its rules are legally binding and underpinned by a powerful dispute settlement process.

The emergence of a coherence framework and subsequent coherence agreement, hereafter, CF&A, can also be traced to the Uruguay Round of trade negotiations. The Punte del Este Mandate of September 20, 1986, which launched the Uruguay Round of trade negotiations, called for "concerted co-operative action at the national and international level to strengthen the international coordination between trade policies and other economic policies affecting growth and development." The final Uruguay Round document called for greater coherence in global economic policy and recommended that this may be achieved by strengthening the relationship between the 'other' international organizations (IMF and World Bank) responsible for monetary and financial matters.

The Marrakech Agreement, article III and the Marrakech Ministerial Declaration on Coherence (Annex 1, 1994) first outlined the coherence mandate. The 1994 WTO Ministerial Summit, Marrakech, argued for the WTO, IMF, and the Bank to collectively review the issue of coherence in global economic policy-making. To this end, the WTO–World Bank agreement noted: "Such coherence maybe viewed as efforts by the three institutions, individually and collectively, to work towards harmonious implementation of common and complimentary objectives" (IBRD 1998).[7]

According to the WTO, "(t) he IMF and the World Bank have the means to support an ambitious and successful conclusion to the Doha market access negotiations in a variety of ways" (WTO 2003). These ways include IMF and World Bank undertaking trade policy surveillance and advocacy directed at political resistance to trade liberalization. The IMF and the World Bank were also expected to give assurance to developing and less developing countries. This was to be achieved by providing technical assistance and financial support for balance of payment and revenue loss to accommodate trade liberalization reforms as well as investments in trade-related institutions and infrastructure.

Trade liberalization and trade reform have consistently been important aspects of World Bank programs. From the point of view of the Bank, "trade is an essential ingredient for development" (OED 2003: 5). Thus 85 percent of Structural Adjustment Loans (SALs) in the 1980s had trade-related conditions (ibid.: 5). As "SALs could only be adopted with an IMF stabilisation program in place" this tended to foster cooperation between the Bank and the Fund (ibid.: 5). In the 1990s, however, there appeared to be lull in the trade-related activities of the Bank. According to an OED review of Bank trade practises, trade issues were "crowded out" by other issues such as gender, environment . . . " (ibid.: 6). This lull in trade activities was somewhat compensated for by the activities of the Fund, which began to introduce trade conditionalities in standby programs (ibid.: 6).

Since 2000, there has been an expansion of role of the World Bank into trade lending at country level. This was in part due to the Bank's new strategy of "leveraging trade for development," which is being administered through the poverty reduction strategy paper (PRSP) and country assistance strategy (CAS). It may also be a reflection of the Bank's increased collaboration with the WTO process. Thus for example, the World Bank created a new Trade Department, which reviews all bank lending operations involving trade and new CAS. The focus is on addressing "weak trade facilitation institutions," "weak governance," and "poor infrastructure." From this purview, the World Bank has shifted away from adjustment lending and support for general liberalization of border measures to a wider array of instruments for addressing trade issues: technical assistance, support for public sector, public-private sector initiatives, and programs that facilitate private sector activity to generate export supply capacity (ibid.). The Bank is also focusing on lending for trade facilitation activities such as institution-building, physical infrastructure, and trade finance. This amounted to 80 percent of total trade lending over the period 2001–2003 (WTO 2003). Increasingly the Bank is also involved in trade issues such as behind-the-border protection, services, administered protection (anti-dumping, countervailing duties, and use of safeguards), and technical standards. It also played a very high-profile role in the Doha Development Agenda, for which it takes a significant amount of credit (OED 2003: 31).

The Bank and the WTO have evolved many processes and mechanisms for facilitating the coherence of many of their different work areas. This cooperation on trade also include the deepening of trade in Poverty Reduction Strategy Papers (PRSPs) and Country Assistance Strategies (CASs) as well as under the Integrated Framework and capacity-building loans. Ultimately, as noted by Caliari, the "mainstreaming of trade" in development strategies is to take place within the framework of PRSP (Caliari 2002a).

Other less formalized ways of operating the coherence framework are through policy advice coordination, joint research and analysis, and the cross-sharing of macroeconomic, trade, and social information. However, how this coherence on trade will impact long-term development remains an open question that will require serious examination by all groups who are concerned with issues of poverty and social equity

Trade agreements, coherence, and development

There are many negative and many positive synergies between trade liberalization, trade reform, and economic development in developing countries. Theoretically, trade liberalization could create a more competitive environment including price competition and greater efficiency in production by reducing artificial obstacles to the entry and exit of goods and services. Such an environment, it is argued, would lead to rising export shares, an expansion of employment and growth in business activity in the domestic economy. Thus the net results are expected to be rapid economic growth, favorable change in the demand for factors of production involved in the production of export-oriented goods and services, and the availability of a wide assortment of consumer goods at relatively low prices.

However, there are also likely to be quite significant negative synergies between trade liberalization and economic development. Trade liberalization may simply result in more imports that may increase the trade deficit and exert more pressure on the balance of payments leading to worsening external debt which further constrains growth. Trade liberalization could also lead to declining market shares of domestically produced goods and hence loss of employment and livelihoods for some sectors of the domestic farming and commercial sector. Thus unbridled trade liberalization is not wise. Other factors that must be considered include timing, sequencing and scope of trade liberalization, strengthening local enterprises and farming, and building human capital, technology and export capacity (UNCTAD 1998; Rodrik 1999, 2001; UNDP 2003).

The WTO Doha Ministerial (2001) aimed to set the multilateral trading system on the path to resolving these problems. By proclaiming the Doha Development Agenda (DDA) and Work Plan, the Doha Ministerial re-affirmed the rights of states to over-ride patent protection for public health reasons and mandated the WTO General Council to address the issue of special and differential treatment (S&DT)[8] and over fifty other implementation issues of the developing countries. The DDA therefore attempted to put economic development concerns at the center of the WTO trade liberalization agenda. But after two years of mostly deadlocked negotiations on the key issues of the DDA and Work Plan, most especially the agricultural negotiations, the impasses at the Cancun Ministerial (September 2003) over a set of new issues such as competition policy, transparency in government procurement, investment, and trade facilitations does not bode well for the future.

From the point of focus of this chapter, two important questions arise: (1) Can the Coherence Framework and Agreements (hereafter, CF&A) make trade work for sustainable development? And, (2) What does this mean for gender equality and women's economic and social empowerment? The answer to the first question is not very clear-cut and thus presents cause for concern with regard to the second question.

There are at least four broad reasons to be doubtful that CF&A are likely to promote sustainable development. First, the WTO principle of "Single Undertaking" imposes the same obligations on all members without regard to their level of development. Allowances are only made for a transition period, in which developing and least-developing countries are given a five-to-ten year lag in implementing the agreements. Thus, for all practical purpose the developmental needs of individual countries are assumed away. This compounds the already negative effects of the over 100 implementation issues arising from the developing countries implementation of the Uruguay Round Agreement. The implementation issues[9] are due to imbalances in the agreements, and the reduced importance of the principle of S&DT[10] for developing countries.

Second, the CF&A are premised on achieving uniformity in the implementation of trade liberalization across developing and less developing countries in all aspects of international economic policy. But with regard to the developed countries there are no effective tools for implementation, monitoring, and ensuring compliance. See, for example, the continue debacle in agricultural subsidies and problems with the developed countries commitment on clothing and textiles. In the context of developing countries, especially those dependent on concessional lending, the main tool that Coherence is relying on are the Enhanced Heavily Indebted Poor Country Initiative-Poverty Reduction Strategy Papers (HIPC-PRSPs), and PRSP-based poverty reduction support credit and the poverty reduction growth framework. But as will be discussed below, these tools thus far have not yielded the expected results.

Third, CF&A are premised on the ability of the IFIs (especially the World Bank) to have a proactive development agenda that works to reduce or eliminate the negative effects of trade liberalization. The reality is that both the World Bank and the IMF have not been successful in helping developing countries to shift from a debt, dependency, and persistent under-development trajectory to a sustainable development path. There is ample evidence of the contrary in the failure of SAPs to generate sustained growth, and in the East Asian Crisis and the challenges of the HIPC/PRSP process.

Between 1980 and 1989 there were a total of 241 World Bank/IMF Structural Adjustment Programs implemented in Africa (Jespersen 1992; Bangura 1994). Yet recent evidence show that, at best, only a modest growth of about 2.5 percent occurred between 1980 and 1991 and that no significant difference exist between the growth rates of 1980–1985, when the programs were in their infancy, and 1985–1991, the periods when the reforms were expected to yield greater positive results (Bangura 1994). Other than ensuring the continued flow of the debt services to foreign creditors, the other major thrusts of SAPs (especially in Latin America and the Caribbean) has been to further re-orient the economies of heavily indebted economies towards the global market and to create the conditions for further penetration of core parts of the economy by foreign capital.

To date, SAP-induced trade liberalization has not generated significant improvement in developing countries' trade profiles. SAPs aimed at generating budget surpluses by forcing substantial reduction in domestic absorption through reducing government spending and increasing revenues, primarily via cutbacks in personnel and services; privatization initiatives and indirect taxes. While SAPs addressed the budgetary problem it was not able to correct the foreign exchange or the market access problem. There is not much that is really new in today's new generation of SAP-type programs – the Poverty Reduction Growth Framework (PRGF), the Policy Framework Paper (PFP), the Poverty Resource Support Credit (PRSC) – and the PRSP to which they are ostensibly to be aligned, that will necessarily make them any more successful than their predecessors.

Above all, the East Asian crisis of 1997 raised serious questions about the efficacy of the IMF and the World Bank (Walters 2000). Specifically, it raised serious questions about the model underpinning IMF and World Bank analysis, policy prescriptions, and monitoring of developing countries. These models continue to be the foundation for the CF&A. It is therefore important to more closely examine the implications of these models for growth and poverty, inflation, and public expenditure (Singh and Zammit 2000). The outcomes of these models as demonstrated by the crisis had significant distributional consequences including a high interest rate effect on real incomes, lack of a safety net, and lack of effective stabilizers in developing countries for poor women and men (Bakker 2000). A brief scan of the PRSP process and outcomes over the last three years shows that while PRSPs have led to increased scrutiny and actions around some of the previously neglected social dimensions of past Bank and Fund programs, the results are not always as expected, not deeply rooted, and vulnerable to trade and other shocks. Pervasive threats to the social sector are endemic features of PRSPs. Many of these threats are linked to the macroeconomic policies content, which have contradictory effects for poverty reduction, as well as are constraints on PRSP implementation. Some macroeconomic content identified in this regard include the findings that in many PRSP programs there are over one hundred trade measures, most of which focus on tariff and non-tariff reduction (Oxfam 2001) as well as IMF Article IV consultations which privileges the restoration of macroeconomic stability over poverty reduction. (See, for example, the experience of Uganda – a successful PRSP country where poverty has increased with increased growth, Oxfam 2001.)

Fourth, CF&As are premised on the gender and other social equity neutrality of trade liberalization. This in a context in which trade liberalization and WTO rules tend to define most social and environmental regulation as "trade barriers."

Therefore, trade liberalization and WTO rules may engender changes in domestic labor legislation, social insurance programs and policies as well as new forms of regulations. There is bound to be a certain amount of coordination and economic management which will directly impact the duties and obligations of states to their citizens. Such changes will not simply be confined to the business sector but will have important impacts on community and social institutions at the meso and micro levels.

The World Bank, coherence and gender

Because the CF&A assumes gender neutrality and does not seem to recognize or align itself with gender equality goals, as articulated by the Beijing Platform of Action or the Millennium Development Goals or even in the World Bank's *Engendering Development*, there must be serious doubts about the beneficial outcome of coherence for women and other groups that are marginal in the local economies. Even though the Bank has done quite significant work in the area of identifying women's contribution to the economy, as is discussed in *Engendering Development*, this has not carried over into its trade policy work. Gender does not appear to be a critical variable either in the work of its new trade department or in the broader macroeconomic framework undergirding its new flagship program, the PRSP. Gender also does not play a significant role in the trade-related technical assistance or capacity building frameworks.

In *Engendering Development* as well as in chapter 10 on "Gender" in the PRSP Sourcebook, gender has been identified as "a key developmental issue" (Klugman 2002: 335). Gender equality has also been flagged as "a core developmental issue – a development objective in its own right" (World Bank 2000: 1). In addition, gender is supposed to be one of the critical cross-cutting themes in the thematic areas of PRSP. However, the work of "engendering development" falls short in macroeconomic models, policy formulation, and hence policy prescriptions of the Bank. The work of broadening and deepening gender within the Bank's programs also falls short, due in part to under-funding of financing of gender mainstreaming strategy and lack of systematization of gender across all departments and subject areas (Zuckerman and Qing 2003). Zuckerman and Garrett, in a gender audit of 13 PRSPs completed in 2002, found that while some PRSPs examined the impact of changes in social services etc. on women, few extended the gender lens into the hard areas of structural adjustment or trade liberalization. Even more disturbing, Zuckerman and Garrett argued that "the majority of Joint Staff Assessments that accompany PRSPs to the Bank and Fund Boards only contained superficial gender analyses" (Zuckerman and Garrett 2003: 1).

Given these shortfalls in integrating gender analyses and perspectives in the Bank core programs it is doubtful that gender considerations will have significant impact on the Coherence process. But gender biases and constraints play a significant role in the formulation of trade agreements, trade policy, and the coherence framework. Trade expansion and trade intensification rely on the incorporation of women's labor both in the formal and informal sectors of the economy. In addition, the cost of adjusting to the consequences of trade liberalization (such as cuts in public services due to budget shortfall from the reduction of trade tariffs) is disproportionately borne by women. Ultimately, trade liberalization and the economic adjustment it engenders or which accompanies it often leads to the intensification of women's care activities.

From the above discussion it is clear that gender concerns and issues must be integral to international economic policy coordination including international trade. Configuring gender concerns into trade agreements and trade policy, feminist economists must develop and shape analysis and research around the critical role and inter-link between social reproduction (the care of human beings) and production and how these are shaped and reshaped by trade agreement and the changes it engenders in trade policy and programs.

The reality is that trade policy forges the link between the micro (household), meso (labor and credit markets and other institutions), and the macro level (fiscal, monetary, and exchange rate policy). Trade liberalization is an inherently political process that generates winners and losers internationally and nationally and as such would engender significant changes (imbalances and disturbances) in access to economic and social resources and income. Trade agreements and trade policies are also inherently economic, political, and social processes grounded in gender asymmetries at the local and national level, and power asymmetries between men and women and among different groups of countries at the regional and multilateral levels.

Coherence between the Bank and the WTO and the future direction in feminist economic research and advocacy in international development and economic policy

A feminist economist approach to developing a framework for analysing trade policy and trade agreements in the context of the Coherence Framework, in the first instance, should have a critical stance towards international economic policy coordination at the global and regional levels. Within this framework it must develop analysis, research, and methodologies around critical issues such as social reproduction and globalization, reform of the international trade and financial system, privatization, rights, and economics. In addition, there is need for more focused attention on influencing the economic analysis underlying the on-going discussion on global economic governance.

However, feminist economists must recognize the current imbalance and power asymmetries between developing countries, as a group, and developed countries within international financial and trade institutions. From the vantage point of a feminist understanding of power, marginalization, and empowerment, future directions for feminist economic research must be grounded in a commitment to ensuring the full and effective participation of developing countries in the governance of the multilateral trade and financial systems.

Ultimately, any framework that seeks to promote coherence in international economic policies at the global level should be grounded in a commitment to international human rights norms and the sets of agreements and commitments to poverty eradication and human development that have been agreed to in the major UN conferences over the past twenty years. It should also be accountable to the UN system. Some suggestion for how this might be achieved already exist in the Monterrey Consensus (para 6, 2002), the idea of an Economic and Social Security Council in the UN floated by the Commission on Global Governance, and in a variety of civil society proposals submitted within the context of the Financing for Development Conference 2002 and its continuing follow-up processes (see Adaba *et al.* 2003 and Caliari 2003).

In the final analysis, the dynamics between women's location in and identification with social reproduction, and critical gaps between men and women regarding access and ownership of resources are impacted by changes in trade policy and trade agreements. Since women in most economies generally have less access than men to tangible and intangible economic and social resources – land, credit, training – gender concerns are generally overlaid with gender inequality. Inequality in the present system of allocation means that women have greater need for specific types of goods and services (Longwe 2002). This need is not counterbalanced by women's contribution to economic activity in their multiple roles as care-givers in the household and community sectors and workers, knowledge-providers, and entrepreneurs in the formal and informal sectors of the market economy.

Coherence in macroeconomic policy centered on trade liberalization would seem to be a critical element either for mitigating or exacerbating this trend. This points to future work for researchers on gender and trade, fiscal, and monetary areas to pinpoint and highlight the nature of on-going social reproduction in country analysis, how and in what directions changes in trade, fiscal and monetary instruments, projects, and programs are impacting social reproduction and how this is influencing the underlying gender and social relations between men and women as well as among different social and ethnic classes in society. Thus feminist economists must necessarily focus their analytical lens and policy-oriented research on the emerging coherence between international trade and financial institutions.

Notes

1 Many thanks to the Steering Committee of IGTN and DAWN for their contribution to the political and economic analysis in the evolution of the work on gender and trade. Thank you also to Aldo Caliari of the Center of Concern, whose immensely useful work on Coherence between IFIs and Trade Institutions provided the grounding for this chapter.

2 The integrated framework was initiated by the WTO Singapore Ministerial Declaration, which called for a plan of action for less developing countries. It was initiated in 1997 and has two official objectives: (1) to enable least developed countries to use trade as an effective vehicle for development and (2) to effectively advance

their interest through the WTO. Specific mechanisms include: trade-related technical assistance, pilot testing of diagnostic "trade integration studies" for analyzing trade obstacles and prioritizing technical assistance requirements, and capacity-building loans (within the framework of the PRSP).

3 Explicit commitment to gender equality (goal 3: Promoting gender equality/ empowerment of women), the Millennium Declaration of the Millennium Summit, September 2000: "No individual and no nation must be denied the opportunity to benefit from development. The equality rights and opportunity of women and men must be ensured." The other remaining goals are: eradication of poverty/hunger (goal 1), achieving universal primary education (goal 2), a decrease in child mortality (goal 4), improved maternal health (goal 5), control of HIV/AIDs, malaria, and other diseases (goal 6), ensuring environmental sustainability (goal 7) and developing a global partnership for development (goal 8).

4 Market access refers to provisions for expanded market for goods and services produced by a member country into another member's economy. Generally market access is blocked by government-imposed conditions (ranging from health regulations, distribution channels, documentation to tariffs, and the nature and extent of domestic support (subsidies)).

5 GATT 1994 is quite extensive and includes understandings in six areas: other duties and charges, state trading enterprises, balance of payment provision, custom union and free trade areas, waivers of obligations and modification, tariff schedules (and the manner of implementation of these schedules); other agreements are in the areas of goods, specifically, twelve agreements covering: agriculture (AOA), sanitary and phytosanitary measures (SPS), agreement in textile and clothing (ATC), technical barriers to trade (TBT), trade-related investment measures (TRIMs), anti-dumping, customs valuations, pre-shipment inspection, rules of origin, import licensing, subsidies and safeguards. (Market access commitments in financial services, basic telecommunications, and maritime transport are under GATS while information technology is under GATT 1994.)

6 The Marrakech Declaration (1994) established the World Trade Organization to oversee and implement the set of new trade agreements as well as to enforce the dispute settlement process regarding members' rights and obligations.

7 According to OED 2003, the World Bank and the IMF have been working on trade since 1986, starting with the production of a joint staff paper for the development committee on the linkage between trade and development. The report also noted that the World Bank was very active in the promoting the launch of the Uruguay Round in terms of giving input to *Trade Policies for a Better Future*, hereafter the Leutwiler Report (also known as the "Report of the Wise Men on Trade Issues") (GATT 1985). The Bank also organized a symposium on trade and produced special issues of the *World Economic Review* in 1986 and *World Development Report on Trade and Industry* in 1987. The Bank was also very proactive in the Uruguay Round especially in the areas of the phase-out of the Multifiber Agreement, agricultural policies of the OECD, and liberalization of agriculture (OED 2003).

8 See note 9.

9 Implementation issues refers to the set of systemic issues including structural imbalances and weaknesses that work to the disadvantage of the South in the WTO Agreements. The more protracted battle areas are anti-dumping rules, exemption from TRIPS, and the extension of transition periods under TRIPS, TRIMS, removal of restrictions on textile trade and subsidies and custom valuation.

10 Special and differential treatment refers to provisions and measures in trade agreements that attempt to take account of and adjust for economic disparities between states. The conceptualization of S&DT has a long history going back to the Havana Conference of 1947–8 that laid the foundations for the GATT. It was set in place in response to the developing countries' argument that trade liberalization

based on most-favored nation (MFN) status would not necessarily respond to the structural features of their economies. A pervasive feature of this distortion was the historical trade relations and structural dependency in the world economy. Developing countries argued that they needed other measures rather than simply MFN in order to benefit from trade liberalization. These included: improved terms of trade, reduction of dependence on exports of primary commodities, correcting balance of payments (BOP) volatility, and the promotion of industrialization through the use of protection (for infant industry) and export subsidies.

References

Adaba, G., A. Caliari, F. Foster and E. Hanfstaengl (2003) "A Political Agenda for the Reform of Global Governance," Background Policy Paper (draft), Washington, DC: The Center of Concern.

Alexander, N. (2002) "Coherent Policies to Phase Out Universal Access to Services: Privatization in World Bank-IMF Programs and Issues in Negotiations on Trade in Services at the WTO," in A. Calieri (ed.), "Report on the Meeting on Coherence," Washington, DC: Center of Concern.

Bakker, I. (2000) "Gender and the New International Financial Architecture," Background Paper for Gender Equality Briefing Note, Office of the Special Adviser on Gender Issues and the Advancement of Women, United Nations, New York.

Bangura, Y. (1994) "Economic Restructuring, Coping Strategies and Social Change: Implications for Institutional Development in Africa," UNRISD Discussion Paper No. 52, Geneva: UNRISD. Available online http://www.unrisd.org/engindex/publ/list/dp/dp/52/toc.htm (accessed December 2000).

Caliari, A. (2002a) "Coherence in Global Economic Policymaking and Cooperation between the WTO, the IMF and the World Bank, An NGO response," Washington, DC: The Center of Concern.

—— (2002b) "Coherence Between Trade and Finance Policies: Summary of Current Issues and Possible Research and Advocacy Agenda," Washington, DC: The Center of Concern.

—— (2002c) "Report on the Meeting on Coherence," Washington, DC: The Center of Concern.

—— (2003) "Some Selected Issues in the Coherence Agenda of the WTO and Bretton Woods Institutions, Center of Concern." Available online http://www.coc.org/pdfs/coc/cancoherence.pdf.

GATT (1985) *Trade Policies for a Better Future*, Geneva: GATT.

Hall, D. (2001) "Water in Public Hands: Public Sector Water Management – a Necessary Option," Public Services International. Available online www.org/reportsindex.asp (accessed March 2003).

IBRD (1998) "Report of the Managing Director of the International Monetary Fund, President of the World Bank and Director General of the World Trade Organization on Coherence," Washington, DC: World Bank.

IMF and World Bank (2002) *External Comments and Contribution on Joint Bank/Fund Staff Reviews of the PRSP Approach, Vol. II, Civil Society Organisations and Individual Contributions*, New York: Washington, DC.

Jespersen, E. (1992) "External Shocks, Adjustment Policies and Economic and Social Performance," in A.G. Cornia, R. Van der Hoeven and T. Makandwire (eds), *Africa's Recovery in the 1990s*, Basingstoke: UNICEF/Macmillan.

Klugman, Jeni (2002) *A Sourcebook for Poverty Reduction Strategies*, Vol. 12, Washington, DC: World Bank.

Longwe, S.H. (2002) "Assessment of the Gender Orientation of NEPAD," Zambia: Longwe & Associates.

OED (2003) "World Bank's Advocacy Role in Trade vis-à-vis OECD Countries: An Evaluation". Operations Evaluation Department (OED), Review of World Bank Assistance on Trade Entry Workshop, Dar es Salaam, Tanzania, December 11–12, OED Country Evaluation and Regional Relations.

Oxfam (2001) "Are PRSPs Working?" in IMF and World Bank (2002) *External Comments and Contribution on Joint Bank/Fund Staff Reviews of the PRSP Approach, Vol. II, Civil Society Organisations and Individual Contributions*, Washington, DC.

—— (2002) *Rigged Rules and Double Standards*, Oxfam International.

Rodrik, D. (1999) *The New Global Economy and the Developing Countries: Making Openness Work*, Washington, DC: Overseas Development Council.

—— (2001) "The Global Governance of Trade As If Development Really Mattered," Background Paper for Trade and Sustainable Human Development Project, New York: UNDP.

Singh, A. and A. Zammit. (2000) "International Capital Flows: Identifying the Gender Dimension," in *World Development 2000*, Special Issue on Growth, Trade, Finance and Gender Inequality, 28(7).

Spieldoch, A. (2001) "GATS and Health Care – Why Do Women Care?" Economic Literacy Series: GATS #3. Washington, DC: International Gender and Trade Network. Available online www.igtn.org (accessed March 2002).

UNCTAD (1998) *Trade and Development Report, 1998*, New York/Geneva: United Nations Publication.

UNDP (2003) *Making Global Trade Work for People*, UNDP/Heinrich Boell Foundation/ Rockefeller Brothers Fund/Wallace Global Fund, London and Sterling, VA: Earthscan Publications.

Walters, B. (2000) "The East Asian Crisis," Background Paper for Gender Equality Briefing Note, Gender Equality Briefing Note, Office of the Special Adviser on Gender Issues and the Advancement of Women, United Nations, New York.

Williams, Mariama. (2002) "IMF-World Bank-WTO Coherence: The Implications for Water Privatisation," paper presented at the Forum, "Is Your Water Safe?: The World Bank, the WTO and Our Social and Economic Future," Accra, Ghana: Gender and Economic Reform in Africa (GERA)/Third World Network-Africa (TWN) Public Forum. Folks Place, National Theatre, Accra, November 27.

—— (2003) *Gender Mainstreaming in the Multilateral Trading System*, London: Commonwealth Secretariat.

World Bank (2000) *Engendering Development* (Consultative Draft), Washington, DC: World Bank.

—— (2002) "Roadmap of World Bank Adjustment and Lending Assistance on Trade, 1981–2001," Draft, Washington, DC: World Bank.

—— (2003) "World Bank's Advocacy Role in Trade vis-à-vis OECD Countries: An Evaluation," OED Review of World Bank Assistance on Trade Entry Workshop, Dar es Salaam, Tanzania, December 11–12, Operations Evaluations Department, Country Evaluation and Regional Relations.

World Trade Organization (2003) "Coherence in Global Economic Policymaking and Cooperation between the WTO, the IMF and the World Bank," Note by the Secretariat (prepared in consultation with the Staff of the World Bank and the IMF,

Geneva. Available online, http://docsonline.wto.org/DDFDocuments/t/wt/tf/cohs7.doc (accessed January 2004).

Zuckerman, E. and A. Garrett (2003) "Do Poverty Reduction Strategy Papers Address Gender? A Gender Audit of 2002 PRSPs," Washington, DC: Gender Action. Available online www.genderaction.org (accessed January 2004).

Zuckerman, E. and Wu Qing (2003) *Reforming the World Bank: Will the New Gender Strategy Make a Difference? A Study with China Case Examples*, Washington, DC: Heinrich Böll Foundation.

16 Engendering the German Parliamentary Commission Report on "Globalization of the World Economy"

Brigitte Young

Many political conflicts of our age, positively or negatively, are linked to globalization. As a result, globalization is one of the most overused and undertheorized concepts. Some suggest that liberalization and privatization of the goods, service and financial markets, and the flexibilization of the labour markets will lead to more global economic growth and hence lower poverty. Others warn about a new trend toward higher levels of poverty and inequality in the developing, but increasingly also in the developed, countries. Virtually all the debates have as a starting point "globalization." Whether the disputed issue is about the best strategy for achieving sustainable economic growth and employment, dealing with the indebtedness of developing countries, formulating the best tax policy, or protecting the climate (or even the controversial debate over importing embryonic stem cells, seemingly a purely ethical issue), deliberations in Germany have been conducted around the importance of a globalized research landscape. So it is no wonder that globalization has become a buzzword that can stir up strong emotions in those who see free trade as expanding global wealth and lifting people out of poverty, and others who argue that free trade may have adverse effects, including an increase in poverty (Deutscher Bundestag 2002a, 2002b).

In response to the increasing controversy regarding the political, social, and economic effects of globalization, the German Parliament decided – as the first parliament in the world – to set up an Enquete-Commission to systematically investigate issues relating to globalization and develop recommendations to shape the globalization process in a responsible manner. The mandate of the German Parliament was to study the economic, social, and political impacts of globalization at the German and European levels, as well as its impacts on developing countries and to propose options for action by the national and international communities to influence such development. Most importantly, the Parliament mandated the gender-mainstreaming of the topics analyzed by the Commission.

This chapter will provide insights into the process of engendering the Enquete-Report on "Globalization of the World Economy" over the two-and-half-year period of the Commission's existence. Describing this process is also a personal account, since I was the only female expert member among 13 outside experts specifically nominated by the SPD to include a gender-economic perspective.

The mandate of the German Parliament

In December 1999, the parliamentary groups in the Deutscher Bundestag (SPD, CDU/CSU, Alliance 90/The Greens, and the FDP) introduced a motion to appoint an Enquete-Commission on "Globalization of the World Economy – Challenges and Responses." The Commission met from March 2000 and submitted its 620-page Final Report with 200 recommendations to the full Parliament on 28 June 2002.[1]

The purpose in setting up the Commission was to acknowledge the growing importance of globalization for economic and social development. The Commission was called upon to develop possible political responses and measures relating to globalization at German, European, and international levels. The central task of the Commission was to carry out preparatory work in respect to decisions that the German Parliament is increasingly required to make in the context of the de-territorialization of economic, environmental, cultural, political, and social issues. The mandate of the Bundestag for the Commission was to:

- investigate the factors that have led to globalization of the world economy;
- describe its economic, social and political impacts; and
- propose political strategies for national and international communities to intervene and shape its further development (Deutscher Bundestag 1999).

To ensure that the complex issues relating to globalization would be dealt with across a wide area of topics, the Commission divided the Final Report into nine issue areas:

1　Financial markets
2　Goods and services markets
3　Labour markets
4　Global information society
5　Gender equality
6　Natural resources
7　Sustainable development
8　Development of the world population
9　Global governance.[2]

The full Enquete-Commission held both public and non-public hearings.[3] It solicited opinions and research documents from experts. Most importantly, it invited the written advice on gender from four German feminist scholars. This greatly facilitated the discussion of gender in the various working groups and the eventual inclusion of gender issues in the Final Report.

Make-up of the Commission and its gender dimension

The Enquete-Commission comprised 13 members of Parliament from the parliamentary groups represented in the Bundestag (detailed above) and their 13 deputies.[4] In addition, 13 experts (non-parliamentary members) from academia, business, labour unions, and NGOs were chosen by the respective parliamentary groups depending on the proportional representation of the political parties in the Parliament. Of the 13 members of Parliament, six were women. In addition, the chairs of the respective parliamentary groups were all women, except for that of the CDU/CSU. Despite this rather strong gender representation among the members of the parliamentary groups, the situation was very different among the expert advisors. Of the 13 members selected from academia, business, labour unions, and NGOs, I was the only women expert nominated by the SPD. However, the mere fact of having women as members or chairs of the various parliamentary groups does not mean that women will necessarily identify with gender issues. For example, one female member of the parliamentary group had no interest in gender issues and strongly disclaimed any relationship between gender and globalization. To the contrary, she believed that liberalization and privatization of the world's market was essential for reducing global poverty and that economic activities are essentially gender-neutral.

Although the presence of women does not guarantee attention to gender, it is certainly necessary to include gender experts for that to happen. That gender was discussed in the Commission at all had to do with the strong representation of German women in the Parliament. In the 14th electoral term of the Bundestag, women represented 36 percent of the total membership of the German Parliament. When the motion by the parliamentary groups was submitted to the Parliament to set up a Commission on Globalization of the World Economy, the women parliamentarians of the SPD and Alliance 90/The Greens made sure that the Commission's work would also focus on issue areas from a gender perspective.

The inclusion of "women and globalization" under the heading of "Globalization also demands international responses and approaches" in the original motion to the full Parliament was a sufficient mandate to persuade the Commission that "gender" had to be mainstreamed throughout the various policy areas. The Final Report went far beyond the original task of studying the impact of globalization on women stipulated by the Parliament in its motion to set up the Commission. This shows that although one woman cannot move a mountain, nevertheless, building coalitions with women members of Parliament (and some men), with sympathetic (male) experts and with staff members including the head of the Secretariat made it possible to integrate gender across a wide spectrum of issues.

Gender mainstreaming in the Enquete-Commission

We can differentiate four phases in how gender was dealt with in the Commission:

- Phase I: "**No Gender**" (March 2000–early 2001)
  Gender did not play a role at all. The Interim Report, published July 2001, made no reference to gender (Deutscher Bundestag 2001). In hindsight, I realize that the strategy of not raising gender in the Commission had to do with the vulnerable position I was in as the only female expert advisor. First I had to gain the trust of the parliamentary colleagues and the other advisors. Even more importantly, I had to show my willingness to work on economic issues such as shareholder value, a topic that was vital to the work of the Financial Working Group. Only after I had shown my expertise in many other areas was it possible to authoritatively demand that gender be included in the Commission's work.

- Phase II: **Sensibility Phase** (early 2001–July 2001)
  Increasingly, I started to ask gender questions at the public hearings. The fact that international experts from UNDP, UNCTAD, UNEP, the EU-Commission, ILO, FAO, World Bank, IMF, leaders from academia, labour unions, financial institutions, and NGOs responded very positively to gender questions did much to sensitize the members of the Commission to the topic. Noticeably, the chair of the Commission, Ernst-Ulrich von Weizsaecker (MP-SPD), the chairs of the parliamentary groups of the SPD, Alliance 90/The Greens, the PDS, and individual members of the parliamentary groups started to pay more attention to gender and increasingly their statements acknowledged that globalization had different effects on women and men. After months of laying the ground-work in the Commission, gender was slowly accepted as a legitimate topic.

- Phase III: **Integrating Gender** (autumn 2001–spring 2002)
  By the end of the summer, the chairs of the parliamentary groups agreed that written expert opinions on various aspects of gender and globalization must be obtained. Surprisingly, even the conservative CDU/CSU asked for written expert advice on "Gender and Globalization," entrusting me, an SPD advisor, with the task of formulating the questions given to the experts. As a result, four gender expert opinions were authorized from Ilse Lenz (University of Bochum); Monika Goldmann (Social Science Institute – Dortmund); Uta Ruppert (University of Frankfurt); Jutta Allmendinger (University of Munich). The questions that were addressed dealt with globalization and its different impact on women and men in industrial, developing, and newly industrial countries; the role played by the spread of the informal labour markets; education, skills, and the need for new qualifications for the information society; empowering social and women's movements at the national and international level; global governance and global gender equality; environment and gender; new frameworks for gender

and economics; the need to create reliable gender statistics at the national, regional and international level; and women in the sciences and education.[5] No expert could be found for gender and international financial markets. As a result, I decided to undertake this task, since I was a member of the Working Group on Financial Markets.

At this point, the gender issue also gained added ground through a change in the Secretariat. The Commission was supported by a secretariat with five researchers selected in accordance with the proportional representation of the parliamentary groups in the Parliament. When one of the positions became vacant, the chair of the parliamentary group of the SPD, Dr Sigrid Skarpelis-Sperk, adamantly pushed to fill the vacancy with Dr Hella Hoppe, a feminist economist. This addition to gender experience in the Secretariat made it possible to expand the gender agenda and plan a public hearing on "Globalization and Gender" on 18 February 2002.

- Phase IV: **Taking Gender Seriously** (February 2002–June 2002)
  The first-ever public hearing on "Globalization and Gender" in the German Parliament attracted an audience of over 240 women and men. Women came from as far as Israel to listen to the international feminist experts who offered analyses and recommendations on what could be done to counter the negative effects of globalization.

  Diane Elson provided the background on macroeconomic theory and liberalization of the finance markets. Mariama Williams discussed the WTO and the impact of the free trade policy on developing countries. Achola Pala Okeyo provided insights into the increasing food insecurity in Africa. Friederike Maier turned to the transformation of the German and East German labour markets after 1989. Financing for development was discussed by Maria Floro, and Caroline Moser drew on her experience in the World Bank. She discussed gender mainstreaming and stressed the gendered nature of terror and violence. Finally, Pawan Surana spoke about the effects of globalization on human trafficking and forced prostitution in India, and the importance of education and economic independence to counter women's vulnerability.[6]

  Due to the positive response of the audience and the members of the Commission, the chair of the Commission, Ernst-Ulrich von Weizsaecker (MP-SPD), announced at the end of the public gender hearing that a separate gender chapter on "Gender Equality" should be prepared and included in the Final Report and that gender had to be horizontally and vertically mainstreamed throughout the Report. The acknowledgment that gender issues were seen by the Commission as an integral part of globalization was truly a moment of great victory.

Substantive gender topics covered in the report

Gender specific themes were integrated in virtually all the chapters. However, there were marked differences as to the coverage, differences that are strongly correlated with the presence of a gender expert in the working group. I was a member in the working groups on Financial Markets, Labour Markets, and Global Information Society. Hella Hoppe was responsible for preparing the drafts for the Working Group on Labour Markets. As a result of the gender reports written by German feminists, we could channel the necessary gender information to the staff members working in the groups on Natural Resources and Global Governance. Two additional women staff members guided these two working groups who were sensitive to gender issues although they did not regard themselves as feminist researchers. Nevertheless, finding a point of intervention through sympathetic staff members was essential to include gender in working groups where there was no official representation of gender experts.

The working groups on Financial Markets and Labour Markets have the most gender coverage. The chapter on Goods and Service Markets contains the least attention to gender issues. The absence of gender in this chapter is particularly problematic, since this chapter discussed the WTO focusing particularly on the General Agreement on Trade in Services (GATS), issues that are vitally important for women and their future access to public goods. Unfortunately, given the small number of gender experts in the Commission, not all the working groups could adequately address gender issues. As a result, the coverage of gender in the Report is highly uneven.

In addition to the inclusion of gender aspects across the topics in the working groups, a separate chapter on Gender Equality was included. This chapter starts with the assumption that globalization processes are rather contradictory and contain both opportunities and risks for women. The risks specifically affect the marginalized who have only restrictive access to economic and natural resources, to education and skills, and have little power to influence decision-making structures.

The interdependence between globalization and gender relations were analyzed from three different focus points:

1   Globalization has different impacts on the concrete life and work experiences of women and men. As a result, many poor women in developing countries may in the short term, but also in the long term, be the "losers of globalization."
2   Globalization builds on existing social inequalities which precede globalization.
3   Globalization changes existing gender relations, which creates both opportunities and risks for women.

The issues included in the Final Report and recommendations to the German Government ranged across a wide variety of topics. The necessity for gender budgets at various levels of local, regional, national, and international levels are discussed in the chapter on financial markets, an issue which drew the most criticism from the FDP, which argue that this would lead to bureaucratic nightmares and lead to "absurd results" (Deutscher Bundestag 2002a: 514). The gender chapter entitled Gender Equality has a section on feminist economics pointing out that economic theories and data are mostly gender-blind and thus systematically undervalue the contribution women make to the economy. In particular, we argued that the insights of feminist economics show that production is not just an activity confined to the private sector, it includes production by a domestic sector, a largely voluntary-based work sector in NGOs as well as the public sector (UNIFEM 2000). We also made recommendations against human/women trafficking and violence against women, and demanded human security particularly for the most vulnerable around the globe. In the section on the social, economic and political costs of financial crises, we focused on the vicious circle between financial crises and the debt burden in those same economies, the rise in unemployment, and the growing presence of women from developing countries in the illicit/shadow economy of the global economy. Much attention was also given to the UN Conference on Financing for Development in Monterrey in March 2002 and support was given to the demand for equity, participation, ownership, transparency, and accountability as an overarching guide for the implementation of development measures.

The role of *Engendering Development*

The Commission relied very much on the information and data provided by the World Bank Report, *Engendering Development: Through Gender Equality in Rights, Resources, and Voice*. In order to show the inequalities between women and men, and between developing and developed countries, we used the Gender Development Index and compared it to the Gender Empowerment Measure. Reliable quantitative data demonstrating the discrimination and inequalities women suffer in virtually all countries of the globe was a highly effective instrument to convince many members of the Commission that globalization is a highly gendered process. The Commission's Report differs from *Engendering Development* in that its mandate was not to "engender" the Final Report on "Globalization of the World Economy." The final outcome depended very largely on the personal make-up of the Commission and the skill to present the gender dimension in such a way that it was accessible and easily grasped even by those members who had never encountered a gender argument previously. In contrast, the World Bank Report had the specific goal of engendering development.

On the positive side, the Commission's Report differs from *Engendering Development* in that we focus on fewer issues, but in greater depth, between globalization and gender within a national and local context. For example, we were able to focus on German discriminatory labour market practices, relate this to the existing gendered tax structure and social systems, and came up with specific recommendations to change labour markets and tax policies. We also recommended gender budget at various levels of governments (national, state, city, county) to make the budgetary allocations more transparent. In addition, we were able to show that the absence of child-care places in Germany is strongly correlated with the high proportion of women who have to accept part-time work and/or are not employed at all. In addition, we recommended that the German Government should ensure that the various ministries gather gender-specific indicators and statistics, and also take action that more gender-sensitive data is collected at the EU and global level. Some of the specific recommendations in the Gender Equality chapter are to:

- Expand on the Definition of Human Trafficking in Para. 180, 181b of the German Criminal Code. We criticized the fact that the Convention on the Suppression of Human Trafficking from 1949 covers only human trafficking in regard to prostitution, but neglects other forms of exploitation and slavery;
- Promote equal access to education and professional qualifications in international labour markets and in cooperative developing work;
- Demand and provide protection for the rights of women workers in accordance with the demands as set out in the Resolution of the UN Special Conference "Beijing + 5";
- Implement the human right demands for "equal wages for equal work." The Commission called for improving social protection and safeguards for those working in the informal sector of the global economy, many of whom are women. In this context, the Commission stressed the important connection between equality of the sexes and sustainable economic growth in a globalized world;
- Demand that international treaties on human rights, women's rights, bio-diversity, environment, and many other are not subordinated to the free trade objective of the World Trade Organisation;
- Provide specific support for women in developing countries by including women in decision-making structures; providing access to education and qualifications; giving equal access to economic and natural resources; supporting women in gaining political offices (Deutscher Bundestag 2002a: 322–4).

In contrast to the World Bank Report, the Final Report of the Commission was targeted at the German Government and the recommendations were within the perimeter of German power at the national level – on changing discriminatory gender policies – and at the international level – on influencing decisions in international organizations. Altogether, the Final Report contained about 20 gender recommendations out of a total of 200.

The public impact of the Report and its duplication in other countries

On the negative side, the Report with its 200 recommendations was largely ignored by the SPD/Alliance 90/The Greens Government when it was submitted to the Parliament in 2002. However, such parliamentary reports are developed as a long-term "road-map" and not a short-term guidance for particular parties or governments in power. Given the slowness of the legislation process it cannot be expected that very controversial recommendations would pass the Parliament in a short time. There have been some political successes (although not specifically concerning gender issues). The Financial Markets Group worked on a recommendation for stricter German money-laundering guidelines prior to the 9/11 attack on the World Trade Center. In response to the attacks, the German Parliament was eager to tighten the restrictions on money-laundering and our preparatory work was introduced in the Parliament and became law on 1 January 2002.[7]

In the public and scientific community, however, there has been an overwhelmingly positive response to the systematic study of globalization in the areas of financial markets, markets for goods and services, natural resources, global governance, labour markets, the global information society, demography, sustainable development, and gender equality. The Report is cited positively in virtually every study on globalization in Germany and increasingly also in European countries, and is widely used as an academic resource in many university courses. In particular, the inclusion of gender is praised even by non-gender experts. The Report provides an in-depth analysis of the impact of globalization and suggests responsible political strategies to shape global developments. For this reason alone, other parliaments should be encouraged to follow the German example and provide reliable studies that could stimulate a systematic and comparative public discussion on globalization and its economic, political, cultural, social, and gendered impacts (negative as well as positive) in various regions and countries of the world.

Most importantly, such reports would give gender and policy experts a reliable research document that could be used to systematically compare other countries and regions in terms of gender discriminatory practices and the strategies that have been used to combat such practices. One of the great problems in analyzing the link between gender and globalization is the rather unsystematic empirical research base. This makes it difficult to arrive at generalizable hypotheses across political and economic systems, cultural traditions, and geographic and temporal spaces. Initiating parliamentary commissions in various countries to study the interdependence of globalization and gender could do much to arrive at common strategies in how best to counter the negative aspects of globalization and further strategies that have been successful in providing opportunities for women and the marginalized around the globe.

Acknowledgments

I want to thank, in particular, all the women who made the Parliamentary Commission's Report, "Globalization of the World Economy" a gender success story. Foremost, Dr Sigrid Skarpelis-Sperk (spokesperson SPD); Annelie Buntenbach (spokesperson Alliance 90/The Greens); Ursula Lötzer (spokesperson PDS); and Ruth Moeller (advisor SPD). A special thanks also to my German feminist colleagues for writing the excellent reports: Uta Ruppert

(University of Frankfurt); Ilse Lenz (University of Bochum); Monika Goldmann (Social Science Institute – Dortmund); Jutta Allmendinger (University of Munich). For the persuasive arguments presented at the public hearing on "Globalization and Gender," my gratitude goes to Diane Elson, Mariama Williams, Achola Pala Okeya, Friederike Maier, Maria Floro, Pawan Surana and Caroline Moser. Last but not least, to the staff members of the Secretariat, particularly Hella Hoppe, Doerte Bernhardt, and Marianne Beisheim.

Notes

1   Summaries of the findings are also available in English, French and Spanish on the Webpage of the German Parliament (www.bundestag.de/parlament/Kom missionen/archiv/welt/index.html).
2   Six working groups on: the Stabilization of the Global Financial Markets; Global Goods and Service Markets; Global Labour Markets; Global Information Society; Protection of Natural Resources; and Shaping Globalization through Global Governance were created. Each group assigned a chairperson, according to the proportional representation of the parliamentary groups, and was responsible for drafting the chapter for the Final Report. Three topics were added: Gender Equality, Development of World Population, and Sustainable Development. These issues were written by individual members of the Commission and then introduced and discussed before the full Commission prior to being included in the Final Report.
3   The Full Commission met 32 times, of which there were 13 public hearings with national and international experts. A public hearing on "Gender and Globalization" took place on 18 February 2002. Most of the work was done in the non-public working groups, organized by the respective chairs. In addition, 40 written expert opinions were sought on particular topics, four from gender experts.
4   The SPD parliamentary group nominated six Members of Parliament and six experts, the CDU/CSU parliamentary group four Members of Parliament and four experts. The Alliance 90/The Greens parliamentary group, the FDP parliamentary group and the PDS parliamentary group nominated each one Member of Parliament and one expert.
5   The very informative expert reports are available on www.bundestag.de/parlament/ Kommissionen/archiv/welt/index.html under "Gutachten" (in German).
6   Audio files of the presentations and discussion papers are available at http://e-education.uni-muenster.de/enquete (the texts are in English except for the introductory speech by the Chair, Ernst-Ulrich von Weizsaecker and the paper by Friederike Maier).
7   In addition, we recommended that the European Central Bank (ECB) not only pursue the objective of maintaining price stability, but also support the objectives of the Community in regard to employment policy. Chancellor Schroeder has now (beginning of 2004) taken up this position and has increasingly voiced his dissatisfaction with the restrictive monetary policy of the ECB.

References

Deutscher Bundestag (1999) Motion submitted by the Parliamentary Groups of the SPD, CDU/CSU, Alliance 90/The Greens and FDP, setting up of an Enquete-Commission on "Globalization of the World Economy – Challenges and Responses," (Printed Matter 14/2350), Berlin: Deutscher Bundestag.
—— (2001) Interim Report of the Enquete-Commission on "Globalization of the World

Economy – Challenges and Responses," (Printed Matter 14/6910), Berlin: Deutscher Bundestag.

—— (2002a) Final Report of the Enquete-Commission on "Globalization of the World Economy – Challenges and Responses," 14th Legislative Period (Printed Matter 14/9200), Berlin: Deutscher Bundestag.

—— (2002b) Short Version of the Final Report, Enquete-Commission on "Globalization of the World Economy – Challenges and Responses," 14th Legislative Period, Berlin: Deutscher Bundestag.

UNIFEM (2000) *Progress of the World's Women 2000*, New York: United Nations Fund for Women.

17 Women's rights and *Engendering Development*

Diane Elson

[handwritten margin notes: W.B.'s "E.D. says → ↓♀ ≠ → ↑econ. growth + ↑econ growth → ↓♀ ≠]

Introduction

Pragmatic neo-liberal economists are becoming more aware of the importance of gender, as demonstrated in the World Bank report, *Engendering Development* (World Bank 2001). However, as Suzanne Bergeron (this volume) has shown, they do so in a way that preserves the key features of the neo-liberal paradigm. *Engendering Development* focuses mainly on charting the relationship between gender inequality and economic development, arguing that reducing gender inequality promotes economic growth, and promoting economic growth promotes gender equality. It devotes only a few pages to considering the implications of neo-liberal policies for women, focusing on the impact of structural adjustment policies in sub-Saharan Africa and Latin America and the Caribbean. It reviews some arguments and evidence on how these policies harm gender equality and also some arguments and evidence on how adjustment promotes gender equality. It concludes "While there is evidence to support both sides of the debate about the impact of structural adjustment, on balance the evidence suggest that females' absolute status and gender equality improved, not deteriorated over the adjustment period" (ibid.: 215). *[handwritten: (WB)]*

[handwritten margin note: p. 215 WB]

This conclusion is based on the argument that, over the adjusting period, girls' enrolment in school generally rose relative to boys' enrolment; that female life expectancy continued to rise, with the exception of sub-Saharan Africa; and that the gender gap in wages has decreased in Latin America and sub-Saharan Africa over the adjustment period. It also claims that in sub-Saharan Africa and Latin America and the Caribbean gender equality in the enjoyment of rights either stayed the same or improved between 1985 and 1990.

In this chapter, I take up the issue of the treatment of women's rights in *Engendering Development* and offer an alternative account, focusing both on the conceptualization of women's rights, and on the empirical investigations of enjoyment of those rights. I also comment on the claims made in the report on the impact of structural adjustment measures on women.

Conceptualization of women's rights in
Engendering Development

It is to the credit of the report that it does raise the issue of links between economic policies and women's rights, but it does so in a very cursory way. As Bergeron points out, it takes an instrumental view of rights, as important legal tools which provide an enabling environment for participation in development. It is important to note that the report does not take as the point of departure the articulation of women's rights in the human rights Declarations and Treaties that have been created through the UN system since 1945, including the Convention on the Elimination of All Forms of Discrimination Against Women (1979). The key feature of human rights in this context is that they are ends in themselves, a moral entitlement to which economic policy must be subordinate.

The articulation of women's rights in the human rights system has been the focus of a huge amount of feminist scholarship and of activism by women's organizations, nationally, regionally, and internationally (Bunch 1990; Cook (ed.) 1994; Fraser 1999; Peterson and Parisi 1998; Shuler (ed.) 1995). This has succeeded in making the human rights system more sensitive to gender, as exemplified in the Vienna Declaration (1993) that "women's rights are human rights"; recognition of domestic violence as a human rights issue in the UN Declaration on Violence Against Women; and the articulation of "reproductive rights". Women's struggle within the human rights system still continues, for instance to ensure that the interpretation of economic and social rights in the International Covenant on Economic, Social and Cultural Rights incorporates an understanding that women must be treated as autonomous beings, not dependants of men (Elson and Gideon 2004). And of course there is an ongoing struggle to use the system of monitoring compliance with human rights treaties to press for the realization of women's human rights (Landsberg-Lewis 1998). None of this is mentioned in *Engendering Development*.

Instead, the economist authors of the report reach for an "expert" from another discipline to give them some concepts and data. The "expert" they reach for is Charles Humana, author of a series of world human rights guides, which addressed gender equality in the 1986 and 1992 editions. Humana identifies three categories of rights which are important to looking at gender equality: political and legal, social and economic, and marriage and divorce. (It is not made clear exactly how these are related to UN human rights instruments.) He then constructs indicators of political and legal equality for women; social and economic equality for women; and equality of men and women in marriage and divorce proceedings. This is reportedly done by collecting information from the United Nations and other international institutions, governments, NGOs, research institutions and the media. Humana then assigns a grade to each country, constructed on a 0–3 scale, on the basis of this evidence: 0 represents a constant pattern of violation of rights; while 3 represents unqualified respect for rights.

Engendering Development uses these indicators to look at gender equality in rights on a regional basis, comparing gender equality in rights in 1985 and 1990, using data from the World Human Rights Guide (Humana 1986, 1992). The regions are East Asia and Pacific; Eastern Europe and Central Asia; Latin America and the Caribbean; the Middle East and North Africa; South Asia; sub-Saharan Africa and the OECD countries. As well as aggregating Humana's country grades to get regional grades, the grading scale is changed from 0–3 to 1–4.

Gender equality in rights, according to *Engendering Development*

With respect to gender equality in political and legal rights, the report finds that gender equality is highest in the OECD countries and has not changed in the period 1985–1990. Next highest is Europe and Central Asia (formerly centrally planned economies) – but in this region there was a deterioration over the period to levels comparable with South Asia. Latin America and the Caribbean, in contrast, have enjoyed an increase over the period to almost the same level as the OECD. South Asia has seen virtually no change. After South Asia in terms of levels of rights, as measured by Humana, comes sub-Saharan Africa, where there has been an increase in gender equality. Middle East and North Africa come next, and are judged to have experienced a deterioration. Last in the ranking is East Asia and the Pacific, where gender equality is judged to have improved somewhat over the period. So the picture is mixed, with two regions staying the same, three regions improving, and two regions deteriorating in the period 1985–90.

Turning to gender equality in social and economic rights, the indicators show a different pattern, both in terms of rankings and changes over time. The OECD again ranks highest and has not experienced any change. Next in order are East Asia and the Pacific, which has shown a small increase. The formerly centrally planned economies of Eastern Europe and Central Asia have fallen from second place to more or less the same level as Latin America and the Caribbean, where there has been only a slight increase. Middle East and North Africa is judged to come next and to have experienced deterioration. Next in order are sub-Saharan Africa, with no change, and finally South Asia, with a small increase. The World Bank report sums this up by saying "there was little, if any, improvement in gender equality in these rights between 1985 and 1990" (World Bank 2001: 38).

Since these are the rights most directly linked with neo-liberal economic polices, one might have expected more attention to be paid in *Engendering Development* to the deterioration of these rights in two regions which have introduced neo-liberal policies: Eastern Europe and Central Asia, and Middle East and North Africa. But the assessment of the impact of neo-liberal policies is limited to structural adjustment policies in Latin America and the Caribbean, and sub-Saharan Africa.

Equality in marriage and divorce rights appears to vary across the regions more than gender equality in the other two categories of rights. There are judged to have been improvements in the OECD (which has the highest ranking); a deterioration in Europe and Central Asia, which nevertheless still ranks second; a big increase in Latin America and the Caribbean, which ranks third; and no change in East Asia and the Pacific, which ranks fourth. There have been improvements in the other regions, which in 1990 ranked as follows, fifth, sub-Saharan Africa, sixth Middle East and North Africa and seventh, South Asia. So in relation to marriage and divorce rights, most regions have apparently seen an improvement in the period 1985–1990.

Overall, the most striking change in the second half of the 1980s has been in the formerly centrally planned economies, where gender equality is indicated to have fallen from its previously high level on all the three indicators. The second significant pattern shown by the indicators is that gender equality in economic and social rights is lower than for the other two type of rights and has shown only slight improvements in only two regions.

Problems with the indicators

There are, however, many problems in using Humana's indicators in this way. As is apparent from a glance at Humana's Guides, his indicators are composite indicators that reduce complex and multidimensional social practices to a single scale, on the basis of subjective judgments, using information which is not specifically identified. In his Guides, Humana does not discuss exactly what statistics and other evidence he uses; nor how he weights different aspects of the rights he considers. For instance in his comments on the grades assigned to countries for equality in economic and social rights, he sporadically mentions education, employment, earnings and female circumcision. But no indication is given of how he weights these components; or how reliable the evidence about them is; or what thresholds he uses to transform continuous measures of variables into ordinal scales. Nor is there any mention of why female circumcision is singled out when other forms of gender-based violence (which are more prevalent in OECD countries than is female circumcision) are not mentioned.

In addition, composite indicators of gender equality do not reveal whether an improvement in gender equality has been achieved as a result of equalizing up, so that women's position comes closer to that of men; or equalizing down, so that men's position comes closer to that of women. There have been concerns expressed that neo-liberal economic policies can lead to harmonizing down, especially in the labor market.

Nor is it clear how Humana deals with the problem of how far a legal right is actually enjoyed in practice by the majority of people in a country. Many countries have laws protecting labor rights. The problem is enforcing them. Moreover the realization of many economic and social rights is more difficult in poor countries than in rich countries. This is recognized by the International

Covenant on Economic, Social and Cultural Rights, which calls for a state to ensure progressive realization of economic, social and cultural rights, "to the maximum of its available resources."

The inherent problems of Humana's indicators are compounded by the way *Engendering Development* transforms them into population-weighted regional averages. Such averages are dominated by the grades assigned to the biggest countries in a region and obscure how each state is discharging its duties to ensure there is no discrimination against women

An alternative approach to investigating women's enjoyment of rights

An alternative approach is to investigate changes in the enjoyment of specific rights, using published statistics for specific countries; and if possible for specific groups of men and women, such as poor people, or indigenous people. Unfortunately, available international data sets charting relevant changes over time are rarely disaggregated in ways that would permit that. Here we look at women's enjoyment of rights specified in Articles 23–26 of the Universal Declaration of Human Rights, in the period of the 1980s and 1990s, years when the neo-liberal policy regime has been dominant. We look at data on outcomes rather than on laws, reflecting the fact it is the substantive enjoyment of rights that we are interested in. The major sources of data used are a UNIFEM report (UNIFEM 2000) on progress in fulfilling the Beijing Platform for Action agreed at the Fourth World Conference on Women in Beijing, 1995; and a *Social Watch* report (Bissio (ed.) 1999) issued by an international network of NGOs which is monitoring progress towards the fulfillment of commitments made by governments at the World Summit on Social Development in 1995. We look not only at gender gaps, but also at the absolute levels of realization of key rights for women, commenting where possible on the claims made in *Engendering Development* about the impact of structural adjustment measures.

Article 23 of the Declaration of Human Rights deals with employment rights. It begins by stating that "Everyone has the right to work, to free choice of employment." (Reflecting the prevailing gender relations of the mid twentieth century, it does not recognize unpaid care work as work.) It is clear that women's participation in the labor force has increased in most parts of the world in the 1980s and 1990s (UN 1999: 8). But of course, this was happening in many countries in the 1950s, 1960s and 1970s before the major turn to neo-liberal polices. However, there is evidence that the trend was strengthened in countries that introduced structural adjustment programmes (Çagatay and Özler 1995). In particular, there have been dramatic increases in those countries which have reoriented their manufacturing industries to the world market; and the service sector has increasingly absorbed large numbers of women. In a very wide range of countries, women's share of paid employment in industry and services increased in the period from 1985 to 1997 (UNIFEM 2000: 73–5). The exception is Eastern Europe, where the transition from central planning to

[handwritten: informalization]

market-based allocation of resources has been accompanied in many countries by falls in female participation rates, though this may partly reflect an "informal-ization" of women's work and reduced visibility of women in labor force statistics (ibid.: 73).

[handwritten margin note: Art. 23 Human Rights]

Women's increased participation in the labor force does not necessarily mean that women enjoy the various rights specified in Article 23, such as "just and favorable conditions of work," "protection against unemployment," "the right to equal pay for equal work," "the right to just and favorable remuneration . . . supplemented by . . . social protection," and the "right to form and join trade unions." The lack of all of these rights in many export-oriented factories has been well documented (UN 1999).

[handwritten margin note: problem]

In industry and services, women on average typically only earned about 78 percent of what men earned in the late 1990s (UNIFEM 2000: 92). There is some evidence that the gap has narrowed in a number of countries during the 1980s and 1990s. Data from the ILO suggest the gap has fallen in 22 countries, of which 17 are developing countries (ibid.: 94). Of these, none are in Africa and 11 are in Latin America. Studies listed in the report on *Engendering Development* (World Bank 2001: Appendix 3) suggest a fall in the gap in two countries in Africa and eight countries in Latin America. However, these two publications do not always agree on the countries in which this has happened. For instance, the UNIFEM report has the gender gap widening in Chile and Venezuela, while the World Bank report indicates that it has narrowed. The UNIFEM report cautions that data on the gender wage gap in developing countries is likely to reflect mainly the earnings of those in full-time "formal" employment, as much informal employment is not captured by statistical surveys in many countries. It reports that studies by the international network, Women in Informal Employment Globalizing and Organizing, suggest that the gender wage gap is likely to be higher in informal employment. The evidence does not seem sufficiently robust for the weight placed on it by *Engendering Development*, which claims that it is an important piece of evidence that structural adjustment has not had an adverse effect on gender equality in Latin America and Africa. In so far as the gap has been narrowing, it is more likely to reflect mainly the experience of better-educated and better-off women than that of poor women. It is important to point out that rapid economic growth is not necessarily associated with a lower gender wage gap. In East and South East Asia, the countries with the fastest growth have had the biggest gender wage gaps (Seguino 2000).

Many jobs have been reorganized to make them more "flexible," but "flexibility" has turned out to mean a weakening of labor standards rather than a better balance between work and life (Standing 1999). There has been "feminization" of employment not only in terms of increases in women's overall share of paid employment but also in the sense that the labor market conditions of men have deteriorated and become more like the precarious labor market conditions that have typically characterized many "women's jobs." There has been a decline in the proportion of jobs that have security of employment, rights

[handwritten note at bottom: Other publications are proving WB wrong w/ statistics.]

against unfair dismissal, pension rights, health insurance rights, maternity rights. There has been rapid growth in "informal employment" that lacks social protection. It is estimated that well over half of the urban jobs in Africa and Asia are informal, and a quarter in Latin America and the Caribbean. The share is higher for new jobs, with as many as 83 per cent of new jobs in Latin America and 93 per cent in Africa being informal (Charmes 1998). Women's share of informal employment is typically higher than their share of formal employment.

Women's increased participation in the labor market does mean that barriers which formerly excluded women from paid employment are crumbling, and that women's right to paid work is increasingly being recognized. However, one must be cautious in interpreting this as evidence that women have "free choice of employment." The choices that poor women make are constrained by the pressures of poverty. Case studies document the way that neo-liberal policies have forced poor women in poor countries to accept whatever paid work they could get, despite deteriorating pay and conditions, in order to feed and clothe their families in the context of rising prices and falling male employment (Gonzalez de la Rocha 2000; Moser 1996).

Moreover, as well as women gaining employment, many women have lost employment, through displacement by cheaper imports (as a result of trade liberalization), or recession, or financial crisis (UN 1999; Lim 2000; Kucera and Milberg 2000), and governments have often given priority to the problems of unemployed men. For instance, in the case of South Korea, after the Asian financial crisis in 1997, the government promoted a campaign to "Get Your Husband Energized," calling on women to combat depression and lethargy among unemployed men. There was no reciprocal call for husbands to "energize" unemployed wives (Tauli-Korpuz 1998). In the case of Indonesia, after the 1997 financial crisis, employment creation programs were introduced, but whereas they created jobs for 2.6 per cent of male workers, jobs were created for only 1.7 per cent of female workers (Frankenberg *et al.* 1999).

Article 24 of the Declaration states that "Everyone has the right to rest and leisure, including reasonable limitation of working hours and periodic holidays with pay." The impact of neo-liberal policies on women's enjoyment of free time has been a major area of concern to feminists. Very long hours of work and enforced overtime have been documented in many export-oriented factories in developing countries. Moreover there is reason to expect that the time that has to be spent in poor families on unpaid work caring for family members will have to be increased to compensate for cutbacks in expenditure on public services. This will be intensified by strategies to reduce expenditure as prices of food and other basic goods rise as a result of cutbacks in subsidies and devaluation of the currency. Shopping around and buying unprocessed food both take up more time. Unless men and boys increase their participation in unpaid care work in poor families, the time that poor women and girls have for rest and leisure is likely to fall. This is hard to document since the collection of time use data is in its early stages in most developing countries. Case studies in a range of countries have documented the time pressures that poor women in poor countries face and the way in which neo-liberal policies intensify those pressures (Floro 1995; Moser 1992; Elson 1995; Zohir 1998). The squeeze on the time of adult women may mean that demands on daughters' time intensifies – with adverse implications for their schooling (see Moser 1992 and Senapaty 1997). There is no sign of these pressures leading to men playing a substantially greater role in unpaid care work in households.

The right to an adequate standard of living is addressed by Article 25, which makes specific reference to health, food, clothing, housing, medical care and social services. It also specifies that everyone has a right to social security in the event of "unemployment, sickness, disability, widowhood, old age or other lack of livelihood"; and states that "motherhood and childhood are entitled to special care and assistance." Let us first consider some evidence on the numbers of people living below the poverty line in the late 1980s/early 1990s. The World Bank produces statistics on the number of people living on less than one US dollar a day (defined as living in "extreme poverty"). In 1987 there were 1227 million people in this position; by 1993 the number had increased to 1314 million (Bissio (ed.) 1999: 43). Of course, population as a whole has been growing at the same time. Overall, the proportion of people living in extreme poverty fell only slightly over this period, from 30.1 per cent to 29.4 per cent. In three regions the proportion rose: in Latin America and the Caribbean from 22.0 to 23.5 per cent; in sub-Saharan Africa, from 38.5 per cent to 39.1 per cent; in Europe and Central Asia from 0.6 per cent to 3.5 per cent (ibid.: 43). During this period the proportion living in extreme poverty in Asia declined somewhat, but this changed in the late 1990s, as financial crises hit living standards: "progress slowed temporarily in some Asian countries in the late 1990s, and ground to a halt or reversed in others" (IMF/OECD/UN/WB 2000: 6).

There are no comprehensive statistics on what proportion of these poor people are women and girls, making it hard to come to conclusions on the degree to which there has been a feminization of poverty. There has been a growth in the proportion of households which are female-headed, but the evidence is mixed on whether these households are disproportionately poor. There are ways of measuring the degree to which women and girls are over-represented among poor people, using data from household surveys, but neither the World Bank nor national statistical offices have attached any priority to producing such measures (for further discussion see UNIFEM 2000: 95–6).

Access to health services is another important dimension of the right to an adequate standard of living. There is widespread agreement that health workers with midwifery skills are key to reducing maternal mortality. Data by region on the proportion of births attended by skilled health personnel in 1988 and 1998 shows little progress in Latin America and the Caribbean (from 70 to 77 per cent) and in Asia (excluding India and China) (from 29 to 32 per cent). In the Middle East and North Africa progress was more substantial (from 48 to 61 per cent) but in sub-Saharan Africa, the proportion fell (from 50 to 46 per cent) (IMF/OECD/UN/WB 2000: 14). Country-level data covering all regions suggests that in about just over one-third of 132 countries in the world, there was a reduction in the proportion of births attended by skilled health personnel from around 1990 to around 1996 (calculated from Bissio (ed.) 1999: 31–2). There has also been a fall in access to health care in general in the same period in a wide range of countries. In 20 developing countries out of 43 for which data is available, the proportion of the population with access to health services fell (calculated from ibid.: 29). Such a fall is likely to imply more burdens for poor women, as they have the main responsibility for maintaining the health of other family members.

Problems in maintaining family health are compounded when safe drinking water is unavailable. In 15 out of 62 developing countries for which data is available, the proportion of the population with access to safe drinking water fell in the period from around 1990 to 1995 (ibid.: 38). Poor nutrition compounds health problems. Data from the Food and Agriculture Organization suggests that national-level food availability fell in 67 of 159 countries in the same period (calculated from ibid.: 26–7). Child malnutrition has also increased in a third of 60 developing countries for which data is available for the period 1990–1996 (calculated ibid.: 28). When the price of food or health care rises, girls may be more at risk than boys of having their needs unmet. As *Engendering Development* puts it, "the demand for investment in women and girls tends to be more sensitive to changes in prices (or costs) than demand for investment in men and boys" (World Bank 2001: 165).

Many people have suffered loss of livelihood in circumstances beyond their control and have not enjoyed any social security, in contravention of Articles 22 and 25 of the Declaration. In many parts of sub-Saharan Africa, women farmers have been particularly hard hit by privatization of land, as western-style private property regimes have been introduced at the expense of non-market systems of land tenure. "By conferring formal ownership on land and water, privatization has in general strengthened the control of already powerful groups over these resources to the detriment of small-scale farmers, particularly women's rights and access to resources" (UN 1999: 40). In South East Asia many women lost their jobs as a result of the financial crises of 1997 but measures to help workers regain a livelihood were directed mainly to men (Frankenberg *et al.* 1999; Tauli-Korpuz 1998).

Article 26 refers to the right to education. The enjoyment of this right is best measured in terms of educational outcomes. However, cross-country data on short-run changes in the number of boys and girls, men and women with particular types of skills and qualifications is scarce, so here we look at enrolment rates. During the period 1980–94 the gap between girls' enrolments and boys' enrolment at primary level did indeed narrow in developing countries, but in sub-Saharan Africa this was a result of a fall in the enrolment of both boys and girls, with boys' enrolment falling farther (Colclough *et al.* 2000: 8). This evidence of equalizing down in primary education in sub-Saharan Africa calls into question the validity of the conclusions of *Engendering Development* on gender and structural adjustment. As discussed above, one of the pieces of evidence invoked to justify the conclusion that on balance females' absolute status and *education*

gender equality improved during structural adjustment was that girls' schooling rose relative to boys between 1985 and 1990 in sub-Saharan Africa and Latin America and the Caribbean. In sub-Saharan Africa, according to UNESCO data, the gross primary enrolment rate for girls was 68 in 1980 and 66 in 1990, while that for boys was 87 and 79 respectively (ibid.: 8). The gap indeed narrowed – but not in a way that was consistent with the realization of the right to education of either boys or girls. It is essential to look at absolute levels of enrolment of girls as well as at the gender gap if we want to evaluate how far girls have enjoyed the right to education in the neo-liberal era.

Engendering Development does provide some analysis for sub-Saharan Africa which looks at both gender gaps and absolute levels of primary and secondary enrolment, comparing so-called "adjusting" and "non-adjusting" countries, defined by whether the country ever took a structural adjustment loan from the World Bank. It claims that the trends are similar in both groups of countries, on the basis of population-weighted trends, implying that "adjustment" has had no particularly adverse impact. However, there are two important limitations to this analysis. The first is that some countries introduce neo-liberal policies without taking structural adjustment loans: pressure from private investors can be just as potent as from the IMF and World Bank. The second is that use of population-weighted averages obscures the accountability of governments for the realization of rights. The outcome for the "adjusters" group in sub-Saharan Africa is dominated by what happens in Nigeria, which has by far the biggest population in that group.

Evaluating the environment for the realization of women's rights

Article 28 of the Universal Declaration of Human Rights also suggests we need to go beyond an examination of individual rights to examine whether an enabling environment for the realization of rights is being constructed. Article 22 reinforces that point, stating that:

> Everyone, as a member of society, has the right to social security and is entitled to the realization, through national effort and international co-operation and in accordance with the organization and resources of each State, of the economic, social and cultural rights indispensable for his dignity and the free development of his personality.

The most recent UN *World Survey on the Role of Women in Development* (UN 1999: 46–54) argues that neo-liberal economic policies have transformed the public policy environment in ways that are detrimental to women. Three aspects of this are singled out for comment: a deflationary bias in macroeconomic policies; an increase in economic instability; a reduction in the ability of the state to raise resources for redistribution and social protection (i.e. social security). Deflationary bias refers to the way in which governments are constrained by pressures from financial markets to cut spending and maintain low interest rates, keeping employment and output growth below their potential. This pressure constrains policy in any country with liberalized capital markets, irrespective of whether it is in receipt of stabilization and structural adjustment loans from the IMF and World Bank. Evidence from across the regions is cited in the World Survey showing that low growth has more negative effects on women's "formal" employment than on men's. Increased volatility in capital flows has resulted in "booms" followed by financial crises in East Asia, Eastern Europe and Latin America. Women have typically borne the brunt of managing household adjustment to these crises and of cushioning their societies against the disintegrative impact of these financial shocks (Singh and Zammit 2000; Lim 2000; Floro and Dymski 2000; Elson 2002).

Governments have been constrained in their ability to provide social protection because of trade liberalization, which reduces import and export taxes; and pressure from mobile capital to reduce corporate and capital gains and income taxes. To keep budget deficits within reasonable bounds, public expenditure has had to be reduced and public services have deteriorated. There has been a "commodification bias" in which it has been assumed that provision by the private sector is inherently better than provision by the public sector for many goods and services (Elson and Çagatay 2000). Neo-liberal policies have increased the need for social security against market risks and at the same time reduced the capacity of states to finance this. As a result there has been a retreat from the objective of providing universal forms of social security to the objective of providing only narrowly targeted "social safety nets."

It may be objected that for poor women in poor countries nothing much has changed, since they have never enjoyed the benefits of good public services, stable employment and universal social security. Moreover the systems of social protection which did exist were frequently biased in favor of men, who were assumed to be the "breadwinners." Women were assumed to be "dependants" of men, and accessed benefits through husbands or other male relatives (UN 1999; Elson and Çagatay 2000). However, the changing direction of public policy means that poor women in poor countries have been deprived of even the prospect of the progressive realization of a non-discriminatory system of decent jobs and public services and broad-based social security systems. That is no longer the object of public policy in most countries. Neo-liberal economic thinking suggests that this goal is no longer attainable because of resource constraints. While there are indeed real resource constraints on the full achievement of such objectives, the impact of these is much exaggerated. Successive UNDP *Human Development Reports* have shown how much more could be done within the constraints of existing resources. It is the constraints on the raising and spending of public money which are the immediate barriers, but these are socially constructed constraints. More over, they are constraints that have been intensified by neo-liberal policies, in the name of free enterprise, efficiency, and growth (Elson 2004).

Conclusions

The World Bank has begun to engage with gender equality issues, but it does so in ways that do not challenge the neo-liberal paradigm. This chapter has discussed limitations of the treatment of women's rights in *Engendering Development* and proposed an alternative evaluation which presents a far less rosy picture of what has happened to women's economic and social rights in the context of the neo-liberal policy regime. The evidence reviewed above suggests that there has been regress, rather than progress, in the realization of women's economic and social rights in many countries, even though in some countries progress has been made.

Bibliography

Bissio, R. (ed.) (1999) *Social Watch*, Montevideo: Instituto del Tercer Mundo.

Bunch, Charlotte (1990) "Women's Rights as Human Rights: Towards a Revision of Human Rights," *Human Rights Quarterly*, 12(4): 486–98.

Çagatay, N. and Özler, S. (1995) "Feminization of the Labor Force: The Effects of Long Term Development and Structural Adjustment," *World Development*, 23(11): 1883–94.

Charmes, J. (1998) "Informal Sector, Poverty and Gender: A Review of Empirical Evidence," background paper for World Bank, *World Development Report 2000*, Washington, DC.

Colclough, C., P. Rose and M. Tembon (2000) "Gender Inequalities in Primary Schooling: The Roles of Poverty and Adverse Cultural Practice," *International Journal of Educational Development*, 20: 5–27.

Cook, Rebecca (ed.) (1994) *Human Rights of Women, National and International Perspectives*, Philadelphia, PA: University of Pennsylvania Press.

Elson, D. (1995) "Household Responses to Stablisation and Structural Adjustment: Male Bias at the Micro Level," in D. Elson (ed.), *Male Bias in the Development Process*, second edition, Manchester: Manchester University Press.

Elson, D. (2002) "International Financial Architecture: A View From the Kitchen," *Femina Politica*, 11(1): 26–37.

Elson, D. (2004) "Engendering Government Budgets in the Context of Globalization(s)," *International Feminist Journal of Politics*, 6(4): 623–42.

Elson, D. and N. Çagatay (2000) "The Social Content of Macroeconomic Policies," *World Development*, 28(7): 1347–64.

Elson, D. and J. Gideon (2004) "Organizing for Women's Economic and Social Rights: How Useful Is the International Covenant on Economic, Social and Cultural Rights?" *Journal of International Gender Studies*, 8(1 and 2): 133–52.

Floro, M.S. (1995) "Economic Restructuring, Gender and the Allocation of Time," *World Development*, 23(11): 1913–29.

Floro, M.S. and G. Dymski (2000) "Financial Crisis, Gender, and Power: An Analytical Framework," *World Development*, 28(7): 1269–83.

Fraser, A. (1999) "Becoming Human: The Origins and Development of Women's Human Rights," *Human Rights Quarterly*, 21(4): 853–906.

Frankenberg, E., D. Thomas and K. Beegle (1999) "The Real Costs of Indonesia's Economic Crisis: Preliminary Findings from the Indonesia Family Life Surveys," Labor and Population Program Working Paper Series 99–04, RAND.

González de la Rocha, M. (2000) *Private Adjustments: Household Responses to the Erosion of Work*, New York: UNDP.

Humana, C. (1986) *World Human Rights Guide*, second edition, London: Hodder and Stoughton.

—— (1992) *World Human Rights Guide*, third edition, New York: Oxford University Press.

International Monetary Fund/Organization for Economic Co-operation and Development/United Nations/World Bank Group (2000) *A Better World for All: Progress Towards the International Development Goals*, New York, Paris and Washington, DC: International Monetary Fund.

Kucera, D. and W. Milberg (2000) "Gender Segregation and Gender Bias in Manufacturing Trade Expansion: Revisiting the 'Wood Asymmetry'," *World Development*, 28(7): 1191–210.

Landsberg-Lewis, I. (ed.) (1998) *Bringing Equality Home: Implementing the Convention on the Elimination of All Forms of Discrimination Against Women*, New York: UNIFEM.

Lim, J.Y. (2000) "The Effects of the East Asian Crisis on the Employment of Women and Men: The Philippine Case," *World Development*, 28(7): 1285–306.

Moser, C. (1992) "Adjustment From Below: Low-Income Women, Time and the Triple Role in Guayaquil, Ecuador," in H. Afshar and C. Dennis (eds), *Women and Adjustment Policies in the Third World*, London: Macmillan.

—— (1996) *Confronting Crisis. A Comparative Study of Household Responses to Poverty and Vulnerability in Four Poor Urban Communities*, Environmentally Sustainable Development Studies and Monographs Series No. 8, Washington, DC: World Bank.

Peterson, S.V. and L. Parisi (1998) "Are Women Human? It's Not an Academic Question," in T. Evans (ed.), *Human Rights Fifty Years On. A Reappraisal*, Manchester and New York: Manchester University Press.

Shuler, M. (ed.) (1995) *From Basic Needs to Basic Rights*, Washington, DC: Women, Law and Development International.

Seguino, S. (2000) "Gender Inequality and Economic Growth: A Cross-Country Analysis," *World Development*, 28(7): 1211–30.

Senapaty, M. (1997) "Gender Implications of Economic Reforms in the Education Sector in India: The Case of Haryana and Madhya Pradesh," unpublished PhD thesis, University of Manchester.

Singh, A. and Zammit, A. (2000) "International Capital Flows: Identifying the Gender Dimension," *World Development*, 28(7): 1249–68.

Standing, G. (1999) "Global Feminization Through Flexible Labor: A Theme Revisited," *World Development*, 27(3): 583–602.

Tauli-Korpuz, V. (1998) "Asia Pacific Women Grapple with Financial Crisis and Globalization," *Third World Resurgence*, 94 (June).

UNIFEM (2000) *Progress of the World's Women 2000*, New York: UNIFEM.

United Nations (1999) *1999 World Survey on the Role of Women in Development: Globalization, Gender and Work*, New York: United Nations.

World Bank (2001) *Engendering Development*, New York: Oxford University Press.

Zohir, S.C. (1998) "Gender Implications of Industrial Reforms and Adjustment in the Manufacturing Sector in Bangladesh," unpublished PhD thesis, University of Manchester.

Index